RAVEN
WALKS AROUND THE
WORLD

THOM HENLEY

RAVEN

WALKS AROUND THE

WORLD

LIFE OF A WANDERING ACTIVIST

HARBOUR
PUBLISHING

Harbour Publishing Co. Ltd.
P.O. Box 219, Madeira Park, BC, V0N 2H0
www.harbourpublishing.com

Edited by Rebecca Hendry
Index by Eustacia Kwok
Dustjacket design by Anna Comfort O'Keeffe
Text design by Mary White
Maps by Roger Handling
Photos are from the author's collection unless otherwise credited
Printed and bound in Canada
Printed on paper certified by the Forest Stewardship Council

Harbour Publishing acknowledges the support of the Canada Council for the Arts, which last year invested $153 million to bring the arts to Canadians throughout the country. We also gratefully acknowledge financial support from the Government of Canada and from the Province of British Columbia through the BC Arts Council and the Book Publishing Tax Credit.

Library and Archives Canada Cataloguing in Publication

Henley, Thom, 1948–, author
      Raven walks around the world : life of a wandering activist / Thom Henley.
Issued in print and electronic formats.
ISBN 978-1-55017-807-4 (hardcover).—ISBN 978-1-55017-808-1 (HTML)
      1. Henley, Thom, 1948- —Travel. 2. Voyages around the world.
I. Title.
G465.H46 2017   910.4'1   C2017-904657-8
                                                            C2017-904658-6

This book is dedicated to my parents,
who never discouraged my wanderings,
and to my Haida family and friends
who took me into their hearts and homes.

Haw'aa Haada Laas
(Thank you good people)

Contents

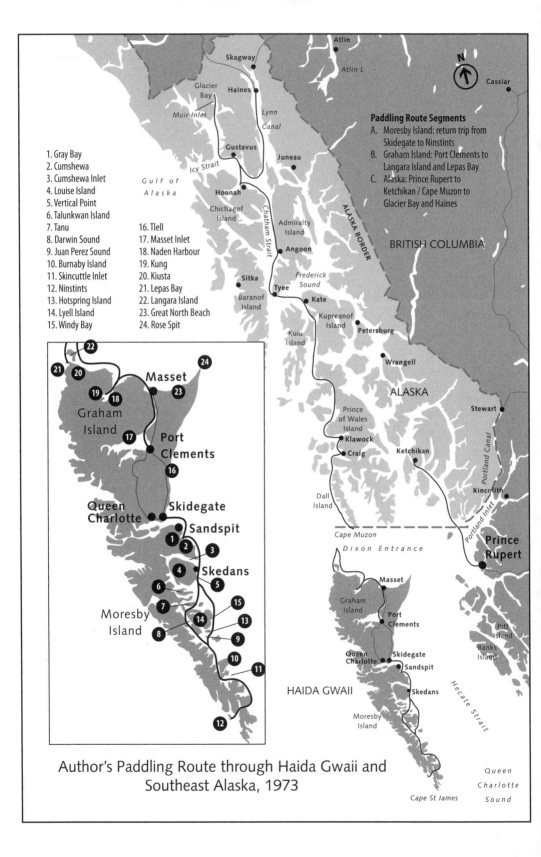

1. Gray Bay
2. Cumshewa
3. Cumshewa Inlet
4. Louise Island
5. Vertical Point
6. Talunkwan Island
7. Tanu
8. Darwin Sound
9. Juan Perez Sound
10. Burnaby Island
11. Skincuttle Inlet
12. Ninstints
13. Hotspring Island
14. Lyell Island
15. Windy Bay
16. Tlell
17. Masset Inlet
18. Naden Harbour
19. Kung
20. Kiusta
21. Lepas Bay
22. Langara Island
23. Great North Beach
24. Rose Spit

Paddling Route Segments
A. Moresby Island: return trip from Skidegate to Ninstints
B. Graham Island: Port Clements to Langara Island and Lepas Bay
C. Alaska: Prince Rupert to Ketchikan / Cape Muzon to Glacier Bay and Haines

Author's Paddling Route through Haida Gwaii and Southeast Alaska, 1973

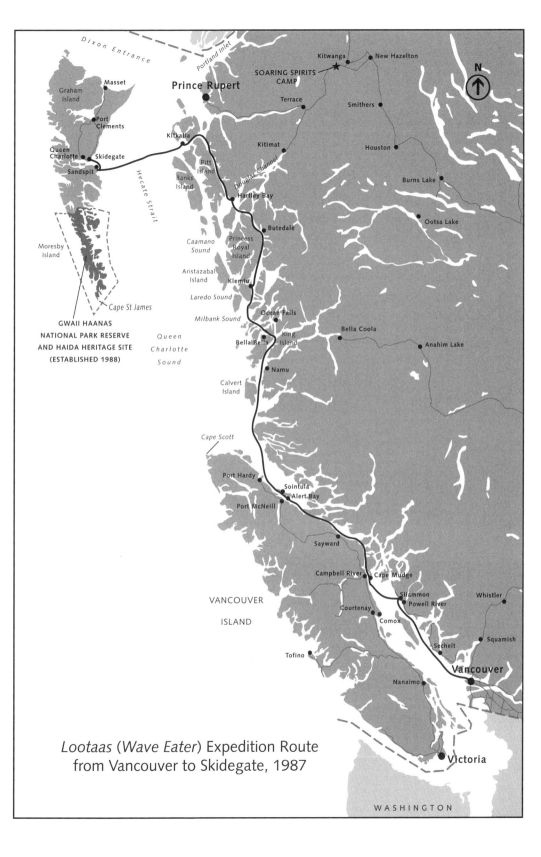

Lootaas (*Wave Eater*) Expedition Route
from Vancouver to Skidegate, 1987

CHAPTER I

Cloud Busting

had never heard of Haida Gwaii until the night I first went there at age twenty-three, but in my childhood dreams there always was such a magical place—lost in the Pacific, green and misty and more than a little mysterious. Call it geographical convergence, serendipity or mere coincidence, but somehow that first encounter touched a subconscious wellspring of my earliest memories. Why was it, I wondered, that my childhood crayon drawings never depicted the place of my birth, the cornfields, woodlots and big red barns of the flat Michigan countryside? They depicted instead deep blue seas, towering snow-capped mountains, waves crashing on rocky headlands and tall conifer forests. Haida Gwaii was a world apart from the landscape I grew up in, and it wasn't even part of the country of my birth, but somehow my unexpected arrival there felt like coming home, truly coming home, for the first time.

It was a long journey to get there, in both the physical and psychological sense. In May of 1970, I left Michigan State University in my third year and decided to hitchhike to Alaska to go back-packing in Mt. McKinley National Park. It was meant to be a summer sojourn from my studies in cultural anthropology and psychology, but it turned into a long-term exile and a radically new direction in my life.

As a student, I had been active in the antiwar movement and had made the conscientious decision to deliberately give up my student deferment status, get reclassified 1-A and refuse induction should the draft board call me to serve in Vietnam. It was an impassioned more than a reasoned decision, as I had never carefully considered the consequences. In my mind, the real draft dodgers were university kids privileged enough to get student deferments while less fortunate Afro-American, Chicano and Indigenous Americans went in their place.

It took weeks to hitchhike the thousands of kilometres from Lansing, Michigan, to Anchorage, Alaska. A great youthful Klondike spirit was burning in my soul as I rode the dusty Alaska Highway in the back of pickup trucks and marvelled at the eternal summer daylight in this Land of the Midnight Sun. With each passing kilometre the land seemed more and more sublime. I watched wolves darting across the road in the dust of the pickup, bull moose with mouths full of water lilies standing chest deep in idyllic little lakes, and sunsets merging seamlessly into sunrises. This was the epic landscape I'd always dreamed of, immortalized in my mind through Jack London novels and the poetry of Robert Service, whose books I had read repeatedly, curled up in a couch in a home too small to contain my spirit and wanderlust. For the first time I felt fully alive, fulfilling both dreams and destiny, at least until I reached Anchorage—a great anticlimax if ever there was one. Looking up and down the busy, car-congested streets with their 1950s faceless buildings, I felt I was back where I'd started—another Lansing plopped down ignobly in the Great Land.

As if to confirm that first negative impression, my first night in Anchorage I was robbed of everything I had. The brand-new Kelty backpack, tent and sleeping bag I had worked so hard to acquire in Michigan were stolen at a youth hostel, along with the gear of everyone else staying there that night. It was an inside job. A few days later I spotted some of my equipment in the window of a Fourth

Avenue pawnshop brazenly displaying a sign: "Hock it to me!" The Anchorage police would do nothing to help me reclaim my gear, but as it turned out, it was the most fortunate misfortune ever to befall me.

Still angry and depressed from being ripped off, I was moping around the Anchorage railway station when an old "sourdough" challenged me.

"Why the long face, fella? Looks like you got a dark cloud hanging over ya." He showed no sympathy for my pitiful tale. "Hell, you don't need all that fancy camping stuff," he scolded. "Take this army surplus blanket—I can get me another one at the shelter." The blanket was dirty, tattered and crawling with enough critters to keep a taxonomist busy for days, but I didn't want to offend the homeless old coot so I took it.

"Now git yer ass on that freight car there." He pointed down the tracks. "And don't hop off 'til ya see McKinley. It's the biggest mountain in North America," he hollered after me when I was some distance down the tracks. "Ya sure as hell can't miss it!"

I sure as hell did.

At that point in my life I wasn't much of a freight-train hopper, and my jumping-off point turned out to be the tiny interior community of Talkeetna. Denali (the Great One), as I was told the Athabaskan Indigenous peoples had long ago named what later became Mt. McKinley, was clearly visible from Talkeetna, but Mt. McKinley National Park was still a long way off.

A man with a broad grin, a limp leg and a gaggle of adoring dogs spotted me on the single dirt road that ran the three-block length of this log cabin frontier town. "Need a job?" he said warmly without bothering to ask my name or anything else about me.

"Sure," I responded.

"Fine, then. I need someone to clear the brush beside my hangar over there." He pointed to a dense thicket of young poplar trees beside a rusty red airplane hangar. "There's food, and a dry place to roll out your blanket inside, if you like," he offered kindly, obviously recognizing my need.

I soon discovered it was the legendary Don Sheldon, a celebrated bush pilot who first mapped the Alaska Range and had survived a half-dozen bush plane crashes after being shot down in World War II. He was one of the nicest people I could hope to meet given my circumstances.

The hangar was full of mountaineering equipment and freeze-dried food left over from McKinley expeditions—these would be my rations. The contents and instructions were usually written in German or Japanese, so every meal was a genuine surprise.

While clearing the brush for Sheldon's new hangar site I somehow became his right-hand man, pumping gas for his planes, packing gear and grub for his expedition drops, and occasionally flying up with him to base camp to deliver supplies. He loved to airdrop gallons of hard ice cream on top of McKinley climbers struggling with the continent's coldest and loftiest heights. He loved to tease me too. "Look, ptarmigan tracks in the snow," he was fond of saying while circling the

"Look Thom, ptarmigan tracks," legendary bush pilot Don Sheldon was fond of saying to me from absurdly high elevations above the Alaska Range as we'd fly in supplies to climbers on Mount McKinley. The "bad-ass bush pilot," who had survived multiple plane crashes and mapped the Alaska Range, befriended me in Talkeetna and employed me as his right-hand man in the summer of 1970.
GREY VILLET PHOTO, THE LIFE PICTURE COLLECTION, GETTY IMAGES

plane from an absurdly high vantage point. A quick drop and a ski landing on a snowfield would always prove his point.

Sheldon kept trying to get me to go up for a weekend at his tiny one-room hut on the Ruth Amphitheater—one of the largest and highest glacial fields in the Alaska Range. Some Talkeetna folks cautioned me, however, telling of the time he forgot a guest and left him stranded in that hut for nearly a month without much food. "He's a bit absent-minded, you know," they'd say, sitting around the communal dinner table at Talkeetna's iconic Roadhouse Inn, kicking back coffee that would make your hair stand straight after the best homemade dinner in Alaska.

One week I shared the hangar with a Japanese man, seven years my senior, named Naomi Uemura, who never let on that he was Japan's greatest hero. We'd fish for grayling together at the confluence of the Chulitna, Susitna and Talkeetna Rivers where the great sweep of the Alaska Range was stunningly visible, at least during the rare times the clouds parted. Naomi always seemed more intent on watching the clouds veiling and unveiling the continent's highest summits than watching his fishing lure. He had such a sincere honesty, unassuming nature and genuine interest in what I was doing that it never occurred to me the guy could be famous.

One day finally dawned cloudless. Denali (Mt. McKinley) was clear from its base to its 6,190-metre (20,310-foot) majestic summit, and both Sheldon and my Japanese friend flew off so early I was still in my sleeping bag in the hangar. I hope Naomi's not going for the Ruth Amphitheater offer, I thought as I rubbed the sleep from my eyes. Ten days later on August 26, 1970, I read the banner headlines in the *Anchorage Daily Times*: "McKinley Climbed Solo!" There was the grinning picture

Naomi Uimara took this self-portrait atop Mt. McKinley. He was the first person to reach the top alone. WIKIPEDIA PHOTO

of Naomi taking a self-portrait with a timer on the highest summit on the North American continent—a summit he reached in half the normal climbing time with an ultralight pack and his indomitable spirit. It was the first solo conquest but not Naomi's first record-breaking achievement. I learned later that he was the first to reach the North Pole solo and the first to raft solo the length of the Amazon. Tragically, Naomi returned to Alaska fourteen years later to attempt the first winter ascent of Denali, but he disappeared and perished in a storm while descending the summit on February 13, 1984. His words always served as an inspiration to me: "In all the splendor of solitude ... it is a test of myself, and one thing I loathe is to have to test myself in front of other people."

While my hangar buddy was glowing in the publicity of the first solo climb of Denali, little did I know the long arm of the law was starting to reach out for me from Michigan. In the meantime, the state of Alaska had opened land for settlement along the railway, and I joined other back-to-the-landers rushing to stake and claim a five-acre parcel—for free!

Nineteen kilometres up the tracks north of Talkeetna, I found an old abandoned trapper's cabin that I restored to habitable condition while I searched for the perfect homestead site. In late September I was cutting my winter supply of firewood when the passing train hurled the bag of mail for our little community out the door of the baggage car. It landed close enough for me to walk to it. A letter from my parents marked "Urgent" told me that my summer of love was over: the Michigan Draft Board had sent me an unanswered Notice of Induction while I had been travelling. "The FBI know you're in Alaska. Get out!" my parents warned. The FBI had questioned some friends and two of my younger brothers as to my whereabouts after my departure from Michigan, but it wasn't until my aunt Ruth inadvertently gave information about my cabin in Talkeetna to an informant posing as a friend that my life underground began.

I packed and headed south just one step ahead of my pursuers. My nearest neighbour and friend Steve Rorick, who lived just over a kilometre south on the tracks, was taken in for questioning by the

I'm on the left, sitting beside my mom (Agnes), older brother (Mike) and dad (Victor) in our Lake Michigan summer cottage. I posed for this photo shortly before hitchhiking to Alaska for a backpacking trip in the summer of 1970. It turned out to be an unexpected one-way journey for life.

police. They thought he was Thom Henley, and it took him some time to convince them otherwise.

It was, for me, a rather shocking transition to go from being an honours student, Boy Scout, altar boy, Junior Rotarian and Ford Foundation Science Award recipient to suddenly becoming a felon wanted on two criminal charges: refusing induction and interstate flight to avoid prosecution. Although my parents, both World War II veterans, did not initially support me in my antiwar stance, they weren't about to betray me.

More than a little dumbstruck by my sudden predicament, I caught a train south to Anchorage and found myself sharing a coffee with a wino on the city's notorious Fourth Avenue. He had been hitting on me for some spare change for booze, but I agreed only to the coffee. The seriousness of my dilemma had not fully sunk in, and I started mumbling over coffee about my problems with the law when a large dirty hand, stinking with whisky and salvaged cigarette stubs, reached across the table and covered my mouth. "You shut the hell up, boy," he whispered as he looked around the room to see if anyone had overheard. "You don't even know who the hell you're talking to." If the old geezer had grabbed and shaken me and thrown me into the frigid waters of Cook Inlet, he couldn't have shocked me more. It was a profoundly personal awakening. I was no longer the "good boy" society had laboured for two decades to mould—I was suddenly an enemy of the state, a felon, traitor and fugitive. I had to get out.

My homeless and alcoholic acquaintance proved to be a shrewd strategist and, fortunately for me, chose to be my partner in crime instead of putting himself back in the booze through possible reward money from turning me in. He was a former Merchant Marine, before the juice got the better of him, and he knew a thing or two about marine law.

"The *Wickersham*'s leaving tomorrow evening," he said. "You need to get on it." The MV *Wickersham* was a vessel of the Alaska Marine Highway System, which normally plied the inside protected waters between Bellingham, Washington, and the town of Haines on Alaska's panhandle.

"How's that gonna help me?" I asked.

"The damn boat's built in Norway," the old wino shouted as if I were deaf.

"So what?" I responded with equal belligerence.

My accomplice put his coffee down, pulled one of the cigarette stubs from his tattered shirt pocket, lit it and proceeded to explain the Jones Act. Designed to protect US shipbuilding, this act makes it illegal for a foreign-built vessel to travel from one US port to another without a stop in a foreign country. "If you can get aboard," he said with the air of a seaman who knew his ropes, "they can't legally take you off in the USA. The ship must stop in Vancouver."

I didn't have enough of the required money to allow legal entry into Canada, but that didn't deter my strategist. "Take whatever money you got and convert it to traveller's cheques tomorrow morning," he told me. "Go back to the bank before closing time, tell them you've lost them, and have them replaced ... you'll have double the show money you have now." It was good advice again. The next morning I headed to the bank.

I phoned in reservations for the sailing and showed up just before the MV *Wickersham* set sail. This was her first-time-ever feasibility run across the open waters of the Gulf of Alaska, and procedures were anything but fine-tuned. "Where's your ticket?" the purser demanded as I tried to board at the last minute.

"Didn't have time to purchase it before the office closed," I lied while flashing my ID in a phony show of credibility.

"Go to the chief purser's desk right away and pay for your ticket and your stateroom," he said as they pulled up the passenger gangway. Of course, I didn't do what he wanted. I couldn't afford having my name on any passenger list for police checks. I was a fugitive now; I had a licence to lie.

I stowed away inside a lifeboat with a snug cover. It wasn't exactly first class, with an old army surplus blanket for bedding and a jar of crunchy peanut butter for food, but at least I was spared the nausea of a ship full of seasick passengers puking in their cabins. All the way out Cook Inlet from Anchorage, I kept hearing on the public address system: "Will passenger Thomas Patrick Henley please report to the chief steward's office." By the time we hit the open Gulf of Alaska and a good October gale, the crew didn't give a damn anymore about who was on board and who wasn't. By the time we reached Vancouver, the staff was so weary of mopping vomit that they paid no attention to who was departing. Canada Customs and Immigration were considerably more alert.

"You're not on the passenger list," they challenged me as I attempted to disembark.

"Must be a typo error." I shrugged innocently.

"How long do you intend to stay in Canada? How much money are you carrying?" they asked firmly.

"Only a day or two to see the sights," I answered respectfully, flashing a wad of phony traveller's cheques. I was in.

A hippie at the dockside recognized a kindred spirit getting off the *Wickersham* and commented in passing, "Lay low, man. It's pretty heavy here." I had no idea what he was talking about. This was Canada, I was safe—or so I thought.

I headed for nearby Stanley Park, which I'd noticed as the ship passed closely by on its way to berth. The maples were in their autumn array, and their red and gold colours, reminding me of Michigan, beckoned to me. I was strolling along a park path with my backpack on, lost deep in thought about what to do next, when a policeman on horseback trotted alongside and forced me off the trail.

"I'm gonna bust you for possession of a weapon," the officer said sternly.

"What weapon?" I asked in astonishment. I looked in the direction of the officer's steely gaze and realized he was referring to the skinning knife attached to my belt. "Oh, that's just my bush knife," I answered, trying naively to be friendly. "I just came down from Alaska, and everyone up there wears them." I smiled and started to put the knife inside my backpack.

"Now I guess I'll bust you for a concealed weapon," the cop growled. It was obvious I was dealing with an attitude here more than an issue, so I disposed of the knife in a park litter bin.

"Look, smartass," the cop responded in a venomous tone. "We've had our hands tied long enough, but now we're gonna start winning." With that cheery thought he rode off, and I searched for a phone booth.

I was told in Alaska that Vancouver had a free hostel set up for American draft dodgers, deserters and conscientious objectors. I counted myself in the third category, as I'd stopped dodging the draft when I deliberately gave up my safe student deferment status at MSU, and I had never enlisted, so deserting was never an option. I did not consider any one of these titles more honourable than the others; I just happened to be a Vietnam War objector, along with more of my generation than the US government was ever willing to admit.

The person who answered the phone at the hostel said they could give me floor space in the basement to roll out my blanket as the house was crammed full, but they also sounded the same seemingly paranoid warning: "It's pretty heavy around here, man." It wasn't until I spotted a newspaper at a bus stop newsstand that I had any idea what was going on. "War Measures Act Declared" read the banner headline in bold five-inch font. Prime Minister Pierre Elliott Trudeau, a one-time strong civil libertarian, had imposed martial law on the entire country to deal with the kidnapping of a British diplomat and the murder of a French cabinet minister by the Quebec separatist group Front de Libération du Québec (FLQ).

Vancouver's right-wing Mayor Tom Campbell was using the unprecedented and unrestricted powers to run hippies and draft dodgers out of town. Welcome to Canada, I thought; I now have the same rights as any Canadian citizen—none! I had come here for freedom, but arrived on the day Canada became a police state. The War Measures Act has been invoked only three times in Canadian history: World War I, World War II and the day I arrived as a refugee.

The Vancouver hostel for war objectors was no picnic—two RCMP squad cars were parked out front keeping a twenty-four-hour-a-day watch on the place. As luck would have it, the guy who ran the place had a French Canadian girlfriend, and that made her an FLQ suspect. Anyone arriving or departing from the house was also suspect and was followed. This was certainly not what I had come to Canada for, and it influenced my direction: I would not apply for asylum in a country under martial law—what would be the point?

I needed a quiet place to sort out my life over the winter, I decided. I would then return to Alaska in the spring under an alias identity. "Head out to the west coast of Vancouver Island, man," I was advised by one of the Canadian volunteers running the hostel. "Lots of 'heads' are living on the beach south of Wickaninnish; it's cool, man. No one will hassle you there." It was good advice; empty space has always provided Canada's greatest freedom.

Even though the summer of love was well over in the States, Florencia Bay on the west coast of Vancouver Island was still hippie heaven. I was told the summer crowd there had been enormous, with everyone living right on the beach in makeshift driftwood shacks. The few hardy souls determined to winter over had built more substantial squatter shacks well above the highest winter storm line, nestled in the dense salal and Douglas firs. I found myself drawn to the far northern edge of the beach where, with the experience and knowledge gained by helping neighbours in Alaska build their cabins, I erected a small log cabin on a two-metre bench. It was a mere three-by-four-metre single room made of beach logs, split-cedar shakes for roofing, clear plastic for windows, driftwood planks for floor and furnishings, and half of a fifty-gallon drum washed up on the beach for a rustic wood stove. It was spartan, but it was home. Everyone on the beach had animal or plant names, and I was dubbed Huckleberry for the red huckleberry patch beside my house. I was happy with the nickname as it allowed me time to work out a suitable alias when I returned north.

It was an unforgettable winter, with great west coast gales whipping the sea into such wild fury that metre-deep foam often blanketed the beach like snow. We got snow too, plenty of it, though it never lasted long. Mostly we were hit by hurricane-force winds, and the few hardy winter residents would hunker down and batten their hippie hut hatches while huge thousand-year-old cedar trees toppled in the forest. I'd never felt so small and vulnerable before in my life. But I also felt free, unbelievably so, and unencumbered by social expectations. There was a richness of spirit here in the kindred souls inhabiting the bay, where community clambakes were held and amazing music jams stretched through the surf-crashing night into the wee hours of the morning.

I didn't know it at the time, but this was also an important education for me. I grew intimately knowledgeable about the Pacific coast, not as an academic exercise, but as a survival imperative. I had a few guide books, but I also learned by trial and error. I discovered that a raw mussel on a hook cast from a headland on a handline made of stinging nettle fibre at the right stage of the tide was sure to land a Tommy cod or other rockfish. I learned where and how to dig for razor clams, horse clams, butter clams, geoducks and cockles; where to gather abalone, chitons, limpets and urchins. I grew up a Midwestern kid on hamburger, potatoes and cornflakes, but now I was stalking the wild onion, sea asparagus, miner's lettuce, stinging nettle, seaside plantain, chocolate lily and even savouring seaweed. They say that only a fool could starve to death on such a coast, but fools have done it. I was determined not to be one of them.

A wild cat I named Josephine moved in with me that winter and delivered a litter of kittens in my lap. I was amazed at her level of trust. Because I couldn't afford cat food, I'd gather and steam mussels for her each day. Occasionally she'd suffer a case of paralytic shellfish poisoning. A stiff cat on the floor was my canary-in-the-coal-mine sign to lay off the mussels for a while. Josephine always recovered, of course, and she'd curl up in my lap to purr herself to sleep with no apparent hard feelings.

Because I could not legally work in Canada and could not risk deportation, I had to be careful to obtain needed funds quietly and discreetly. I collected Japanese glass fishing floats that had crossed the Pacific on the Kuroshio Current and been cast high up on the beach by winter storms. Selling them to souvenir shops in the nearby towns of Ucluelet and Tofino could earn me a few bucks. Once every few weeks I would hike the nineteen kilometres from Florencia Bay to Ucluelet collecting beer and pop bottles that had been cast into the ditches by weekend revellers. The deposit refunds never amounted to much, but I could usually outfit myself with a few staples like brown rice, rolled oats, raisins, brown sugar and whole-wheat flour to supplement my wild food diet. When the roadside foraging was especially good I'd treat myself to a pint of ale in the local pub with some salt and vinegar potato chips. These seem like such simple pleasures in retrospect, but mine was a very basic—but joyous—life. I was living on less than $300 a year, an average person's cigarette budget at the time, but feeling rich beyond measure. It was one of the greatest lessons in my life, as it taught me to never fear poverty.

In the late spring of 1971, Alaska beckoned me back once more. Throngs of migratory birds were flocking north along the Pacific Flyway and I heard the same inexplicable calling. I said goodbye to my cabin, to my new-found friends and to Josephine (yes, the cat was still kicking). She'd do better on a summer diet of wild mice than a winter of mussels, anyway. About the only thing I took with me, besides wonderful memories, was the nickname Huckleberry, which would resurface years later even though I didn't use it on my own.

My new identity in Alaska would be Thomas A. (for Arctic) Wolf. When I arrived back under my new alias, I took what little savings I had from my beer-bottle collecting and opened a bank account in Anchorage. My pitiful finances didn't really require a bank account; I was merely after the colour-photo bank card the branch issued. With this simple piece of phony ID, I was able to secure an Alaska driver's licence and eventually a Social Security card so that I could legally work as Thomas Arctic Wolf. Alaska has always offered fugitive Americans the best perks for first-time criminals.

Some time later the FBI got wise to the Thomas Wolf identity, and I did a fast name change again to that of a friend who looked similar enough for me to use duplicate ID. I will not reveal that full name to protect my accomplice, but I can admit to having to learn to respond to the name Dale while never responding to Thom.

Life in Alaska was a joy. I returned to the trapper's cabin beside the railway tracks north of Talkeetna, where a small community of back-to-the-landers had been growing. This whistle stop in the wilderness eventually became known on Alaska maps as Chase, and I often wondered how many of the residents there were also on the run. I met wonderful and bizarre characters, people like Dirty Dave, a crazy, burly Chicano biker from Los Angeles who roared up the tracks on his Harley one day. All week long, Dirty Dave would throw his leftovers and table scraps into a big stew pot, then invite all the neighbours over on Saturday for Dirty Dave's Stew Night. The gruel was always heavily laced with cayenne pepper to suit the Chicano palate and presumably mask the colour and odour, as well as kill the critters crawling in it. Disgusting as it was, you didn't dare refuse the invitation and risk insulting the host—he was armed and dangerous. "Mighty good, Dirty Dave," we'd compliment the chef as we gagged back another bite.

Robert Durr and family lived on the back lake, a four-kilometre hike in from the tracks. He was a psychology professor from some Ivy League school back East who had followed Dr. Timothy Leary's advice to "tune in, turn on and drop out." His wife made the transition well from cocktail parties and caviar to boiling moose meat over a smoky fire, but they didn't reject all the refinements of their former lifestyle—halfway along the bush trail to the Durr complex you could always count on hearing classical music echoing with loon calls across the pristine lake.

Denny Dougherty and his partner Edie were two of my closest Talkeetna neighbours and friends. Denny was a star athlete in school and a Vietnam vet who built a five-storey A-frame log cabin on the edge of a little lake. It was an impressive structure but impossible to heat in the winter, and Denny was forever cutting firewood just to keep his water buckets in the kitchen from freezing. He had a larger goal in life—to someday be the first to ascend Nix Olympus—the highest mountain in our solar system, located on Mars. Edie was the more grounded of the two. She had been a fashion model in LA who gave it all up to mush dogs with Denny in Alaska rather than strut her stuff on the catwalks.

There were other characters too numerous to mention here. The history of Alaska and the history of Haida Gwaii, as I would later learn, have been shaped by eccentric characters. I felt fortunate to be among them and to continue my formal schooling with those living on the edge.

Summers in interior Alaska in the early 1970s were fleeting; the snow wasn't fully gone until June, and it was back on the ground in late October. But there was a timeless quality to the season brought on by the perpetual daylight. I can recall drifting lazily down Arctic rivers in my kayak, watching the low-angled sun set the sky ablaze for hours as it slowly crawled across the horizon to begin a new day's sunrise. With all this light, flowers and other vegetation didn't just grow here, they exploded; sometimes a single cabbage required a wheelbarrow to transport it from the garden to the root cellar at the end of August.

Winters in Alaska were pure magic. The snow fell deep in the upper Susitna Valley, where North America's highest mountains trap the Gulf of Alaska's moist air moving up Cook Inlet. On many mornings, I had to dig two to three metres up from my cabin doorway to find ground level at the rooftop and step outside to discover a world transformed with dwarf trees. Just the highest tops of the black spruce trees still stood above the snow line. The small log cabin was well insulated by the deep snow, requiring little wood to keep it warm and cozy. The problem was daylight: it was such a fleeting midday phenomenon on the southern horizon that at times I slept right through it into the next night.

They call the Alaska Railway the Moose Gooser because the engine cars waste so many moose that use the tracks as the only snow-free corridor along the Susitna River. The "cowcatcher" pushes along the dead moose on the front of the engine car until the carcass

A friend took this photo of my dog, Moosejaw, and me in front of the old trapper's cabin I was living in located nineteen kilometres up the Alaska railway tracks from Talkeetna. The snowfall is always deep in the upper Susitna Valley where the moist air from the Gulf of Alaska is trapped by North America's highest mountains. STEVE RORICK PHOTO

The Alaska Railway ran along the Susitna River close to my cabin and was also known as the Moose Gooser. In the winter months the railway tracks provided a snow-free animal corridor. The engine car's "cowcatcher" delivered a steady supply of frozen moose carcasses, which at first I fed only to my dog, Moosejaw, but eventually I ate such meat myself. DMFOSS PHOTO, THINKSTOCK

reaches an elevated trestle, where it gets dumped to the side. There was just such a trestle located near my cabin, and I took advantage of the frozen carcasses to feed my dog, Moosejaw. I was a vegetarian at the time, riding the Moose Gooser to and from Anchorage once a month, where I would stock up on grains, nuts and veggie burgers shipped up from California. When the ecological and moral absurdity of what I was doing finally struck me, I started feeding myself, as well as my dog, from frozen, train-killed moose carcasses. Talk about a radical dietary change; I didn't use the outhouse for days.

With cabin fever setting in, I once joined neighbours Denny Dougherty and Steve Rorick on an extended winter pack trip. The −45° Celsius temperatures made this one of the most harrowing experiences of my life. The darkness proved a great challenge. December is altogether the wrong month for winter expeditions. From the time the tent was dropped, the dog team harnessed and the sled loaded and secured, we had only an hour or so of twilight to

Soon after I set off on a week-long winter pack trip with Alaska bush neighbours Denny Dougherty and Steve Rorick and our combined sled dogs, we came to realize that the long December darkness was absolutely the wrong time for such an adventure.

travel in before total darkness set in and we had to set up camp again and sit out another twenty-two hours. Lighting a fire was a do-or-die predicament, for once the thick mitts came off, one strike of a match was all the time nature allowed before the fingers went too stiff to strike a second one.

In the end, it was winter darkness, not the cold, that drove me out of Alaska. I'm a bird; I need to fly where there's light.

In the summer of 1972, I worked the herring spawn fishery in Prince William Sound and saved enough money to purchase a seventeen-foot collapsible Klepper kayak. It was the perfect craft to give me the freedom to explore some of the Yukon and Alaska's wildest places: the great river systems of the Yukon and Mackenzie, the Porcupine, the Stewart, the Hess, the Ogilvie and Peel. I also built up a bit of a grubstake from firefighting and working the potato harvest in Alaska's Matanuska Valley. I could now afford a six-month trip "outside," as Alaskans refer to the rest of the world.

While kayaking alone for months in the Haida Gwaii and Southeast Alaska wilderness, I relied on a camera timer to get a picture of myself coming ashore in my Klepper kayak.

It was already November and bitterly cold when I started hitchhiking south from Fairbanks with my impractical cargo—a large backpack and the collapsible kayak broken down into two big travel bags. Mine was no idle endeavour. I was setting off to kayak the headwaters of the Amazon from Pucallpa to Iquitos, Peru. Standing along the barren highway with tears freezing to my cheeks, I began to wonder if some of Denny Dougherty's "climbing mountains on Mars" madness hadn't rubbed off on me. This would be an eleven-thousand-kilometre hitchhiking journey, and only pickup trucks or empty hauling vans could possibly accommodate my load. Dreams die hard and tropical sun beckoned. I pressed on.

After days of being stranded at Haines Junction in the Yukon, unable to get a ride south down the Alaska Highway, I opted for a lift to the seaside community of Haines and stowed away on the ferry to Ketchikan. An island set in the wilderness with no bridges or roads connecting out of town, Ketchikan is not exactly a hitchhiker's paradise either. Stranded on the dock, I was pondering my predicament when a burly logger walked up to me. "Want some work?" he asked bluntly, with no introductions.

"Sure, why not," I answered. Before I could ask him exactly what work he had in mind, I was boarded on a Cessna float plane at dockside with all my gear and flown out to Gildersleeve Logging Camp on Prince of Wales Island.

"Here's yer hard hat, caulk boots and yer bill," a no-nonsense foreman said when I landed. "You owe us $85 for the flight," he added when he saw me staring in disbelief at the billing. "Now get to work." I'd been shanghaied!

It was late November, the first snow had fallen and loggers were walking out in droves to avoid the dangerous conditions, heading instead to warmer pastures—hooker parlours in Seattle. I was to be a "choker man"—the lowest-level job in the camp. Wrapping freezing-cold steel cable around logs buried under a foot of snow was not the tropical holiday I'd had in mind when I left Fairbanks. To make matters worse, the "rigging slinger" was a madman who was consistently blowing the whistle to the "yarder" to start hauling the logs before I was in the clear. The yarder couldn't see below the steep hill we were working on, so all he had to go on was the rigging slinger's whistle and singularly sick sense of humour. If it was time for me to die at age twenty-two, then I wanted it to be kayaking whitewater at the headwaters of the Amazon or lost in the Andes, not crushed in an Alaskan clear-cut by a log destined to become toilet paper.

I loathed the logging camp. It was a prison with dollars supplanting guards, providing pizza, pie and pin-ups as perks until payday. Driving in the smoke-filled "crummy" in the first light of dawn, I would look out at the tortured landscape and back at the tortured souls swearing their way to the work site. Rather than gag on cigarette smoke in the crummy where the crew ate their lunches and cussed out every living critter on God's green earth, I would work my way through the logging slash and take my lunch in the peace of the forest, the only piece we had left. "Hell, he's probably down there eating huckleberries," the crew would joke to one another, and before long they nicknamed me Huckleberry. It was weird to get the same nickname from both ends of the spectrum—hippies and rednecks, but then those stereotype labels are just titles too.

December 10 was my last day of work. "What the hell do you mean, you're not working today?" the foreman growled when he came to find me after I hadn't responded to the wake-up call.

"Sorry," I said. "I never work on my birthday."

"Like hell you don't," he raged. "You work, or you're fired!"

I have my principles. So I was fired. I had completed twenty-three successful revolutions around the sun, and that alone was cause for celebration. Having been born on the exact hour, day and year that all the countries of the world gathered to sign the Universal Declaration of Human Rights in Paris, I wasn't about to compromise on my right to have the day off. As luck would have it, I had made just enough money by December 10 to pay the company back for my air transport to and from their camp, as well as to buy a ferry ticket from Ketchikan to Seattle. I was Amazon-bound again.

The journey south was anything but easy. I can vividly recall the hitchhiking ordeals, like struggling to move my three large packs through downtown LA while trying to locate an on-ramp to an expressway. I could carry only two bags half a block at a time before returning for the third bag, all the time keeping all bags in sight lest they be stolen.

Mexico and Guatemala proved even more challenging. By the time I reached the border of Honduras I was so sick and dehydrated from amoebic dysentery that I became unconscious on the roadside. I regained consciousness a few days later in an old woman's adobe hut, and I recollect vigil lights burning all around me, fresh flowers, copal incense wafting its sweet perfume into the air of the mud-walled room and a statue of the Immaculate Heart of Mary looking down on me. A gathering of the devout were reciting the rosary in their native tongue over my lifeless body and the scene had the air of a wake. Like Tom Sawyer witnessing his own funeral, I was sure I had died, was on my way to heaven and witnessing my death in spirit form. Recovering Catholics never quite shed the illusions.

Good health has never been one of my strong points. I'd had polio when I was seven, spinal meningitis at age fourteen and an acute appendicitis attack a few years later, so the odds of even making it into my twenties were squarely against me. This was the fourth big strike, and I should have struck out long ago. Little did I know that plague, cholera, typhoid, three bouts of malaria, dengue and tick fever would still stalk me in later years. If there is any lesson to be learned surviving deadly illness, it is to never take life for granted … to cherish each day as a miracle, a gift. That's why I don't work on my birthday.

El Salvador proved to be my nemesis and turnaround point. It had taken me six months to get that far, my health was poor, and the Amazon still seemed as distant as ever. So with no real feeling of failure, I started the long journey back north, little aware of the changes that lay ahead.

I was travelling through the Sonora Desert of Mexico, just a few days south of the Texas border, when I was dropped off by my ride in an unusually rough-looking cow town. My driver had cautioned me about the dangers of this region: *"Muy peligroso, señor—muchos banditos aquí!"* I promptly headed out of the dangerous bandit town to spend a somewhat safer night along a quiet desert road. It was growing dark and I had hiked far, but I could still hear the drunken revelry and occasional gunshot from the cantinas even when the town was becoming little more than lantern light on the horizon.

Exhausted, I left the roadway and searched the surrounding desert for a place to set out my bedroll under the spectacular star-studded sky. The ground was strewn with rocks, boulders and prickly pear cactus pads, so it took some time to find a clear space to bed down. At long last I discovered a soft patch of earth, just the right size, beside a large saguaro cactus. Must be a bedding site for wild burros, I reasoned as I stretched out a horsehair rope around the perimeter of my sleeping area to deter prowling rattlesnakes. The rope was a gift from a Yaqui Indian elder I'd met a few days earlier. "A rattler will never cross the scent of a horse," he assured me. The old man befriended me because he could see that, like him,

I enjoyed sleeping alone out in the desert. It struck me that he might be a mystic or shaman of some sort.

I was asleep almost from the moment I lay on my back with my head below the trunk and beautiful branching arms of the saguaro. I may have slept only a few minutes or an hour, I'll never know, before I awoke frozen in terror. Sweat was pouring from every pore of my body, my jaw was locked open and my eyes stared skyward in an unblinking gaze. I was sure my heart would seize up too. I'd never known such total terror in my life because I had no way of understanding the source. I lay there awake all night, unable to move a muscle, wet my parched tongue or scarcely blink my desert-dust dry eyes, but grasping fully the meaning of horror.

The stars slowly worked their arced path across the black velvet sky, and a large desert owl, not too distant, hooted throughout the night. Only with the first light of dawn was I able to close my parched mouth and painfully dry eyes. It was not until the first ray of sun slowly worked its way down the cactus and touched my face that I found I could move my neck. As I did so, I turned and saw that the woody base of the saguaro had been carved flat with a knife and inscribed with the name and date of a burial. Whoever's grave I'd spent the night lying atop had an insanely powerful spirit, and I started to see things differently after that.

The rest of my return journey north was uneventful by comparison. I did spend a memorable week with a Navajo family in their Monument Valley hogan, a traditional Navajo hut of logs and earth, where I was inspired by their octagonal log architecture and closeness to the earth, but for the most part I was just wed to the road. I had grown so weary of lugging the damned kayak around for six months that when I got to British Columbia I decided to start paddling back to Alaska. I thumbed a ride to Prince Rupert, deciding that would be a safe and suitable location from which to work my way back through the Inside Passage waters.

It was raining in Prince Rupert. It almost always rains in Rupert, that soft but seemingly endless drip that descends in a fine mist for days. The sky was leaden and my energy low by the time

I'd dragged all my gear and grub down to the dockside. Like the old Otis Redding song, I found myself, quite literally, "sittin' on the dock of the bay, watching the tide roll away" when a Mama Cass-type character came strolling down the plank way. She was dressed in light cotton, a full-length floral printed dress, and she flowed down the dock like she was not of this earth. Ignoring me altogether, she stopped at the end of the pier and stood there staring at the ominous western sky. After about fifteen to twenty minutes of this strangely frozen pose, I couldn't help but ask her if she was okay. I had once worked backstage at a Jefferson Airplane rock concert at Michigan State University where blotter acid was handed out freely to all stagehands, so I knew the stone-dead look of an overdose. No, she wasn't tripping, she assured me, just "cloud busting." She carried on with her self-appointed task while I remained respectfully silent.

"What are you here for?" she asked after a while, without looking away from a brightening spot in the sky.

"Setting off to kayak home to Alaska," I responded.

"Cool," she said, "but aren't you going to kayak across to the Queen Charlotte Islands first?"

"Where's that?"

"Out there where I'm busting that hole in the sky."

Sure enough, a patch of blue was opening in the west. I grew excited. "How do you get there?" I asked.

"Paddle, if you want," she said, "but it's a long way out and Hecate Strait kicks up pretty fast. There's a freighter that takes a few passengers. It's leaving from the pier here this evening."

"Thanks for the tip, sister," I said and set off to inquire about ticketing.

"The name's Stormy," she called after me.

I stopped dead in my tracks. "You mean like Stormy in Ken Kesey's gang?" I was stunned. Was this one of Ken Kesey's bus-riding beatniks, one of the infamous "Merry Pranksters" immortalized in Tom Wolfe's book *The Electric Kool-Aid Acid Test*? But she didn't answer. Stormy was too busy admiring her handiwork, the clouds parting like great curtains of satin in the west. I went to book passage for the opening.

CHAPTER II

The Eagle's Gift

I wanted to leave Haida Gwaii from the moment I arrived. The Northland Navigation freighter pulled into the Masset dock near midnight and disembarked its half-dozen passengers amid a crowd of curious onlookers. The twice-weekly arrival appeared to be the biggest event in town, but the mood was surprisingly sombre given how few of those gathered at the dockside were actually sober.

I strolled up the pier past a series of faceless aluminum-sided buildings that lined the length of Main Street, an absurdly wide boulevard void of any shade trees, shrubs or flowers. The town, from this vantage point, bore no resemblance whatsoever to the fabled Misty Isles I'd been envisioning during my passage. The road ended abruptly—as if ordered to "halt!"—at a Canadian Forces military base, CFS Masset. I stopped under a lamppost to dig through my wallet in hopes of finding enough money to book passage back to the mainland on the return sailing. I was short; I would have to paddle.

Resigned to my misfortune, I returned down Main Street and tried to view the village from a more positive angle. The military makeover was sadly apparent, but a few turn-of-the-century wood-frame houses and some well-kept gardens were nestled in here and there among the hideous to hint of the charms of an earlier era.

I didn't know it at the time, but Masset was once destined to be a hub of the Pacific Northwest. In the heady days before World War I, British railroad magnate Charles Hays conceived of a plan to make Prince Rupert Canada's principal Pacific port and the terminus of his Grand Trunk Pacific Railway. Vancouver would have been little more than a backwater, while Masset was expected to become an agricultural breadbasket to feed Prince Rupert's great metropolis, envisioned at fifty thousand. The vast lowland bog from Masset to Tlell was parcelled out for settlement and some hardy pioneers dug drainage ditches by hand to try farming the muskeg. It never worked, and Hays's dream died a sudden death too when the visionary went down on the *Titanic* in 1912. My own spirits, this June night sixty years later, had sunk almost as low.

I was dog-tired after disembarking the ship, but I still had the kayak bags to deal with. I stashed them beside a road embankment near the BC Hydro office and made a hasty bed of cedar boughs under a grove of trees beside Masset Inlet. It was not a good sleep, with Saturday-night revellers racing by along the road above me and the tide rising up to my feet, so I awoke at first light to end the ordeal. Camouflaging the two kayak bags as best I could under logs and rocks, I shouldered my backpack and set off north along the road. I wanted to find a beach where I could camp for a few days while I sorted out my next move. Several kilometres later I walked into Haida Village, a long series of Indian Affairs dwellings fronting the road along Masset Inlet. A Haida man in his thirties was the only sign of life on the road this early Sunday morning. He staggered up to me, pulled out a folding knife and with glazed eyes and an unsteady bearing, introduced himself with the words: "I should slit your throat, you stinkin' white man." He was the first Islander to speak to me since I'd arrived, and I took this to be my official welcome.

I remained calm and left my acquaintance staring drunkenly into the void where I encountered him, working my way presumably out of harm's way to the beach just beyond the cemetery of the village. Here, finally, was food for the spirit. A majestic sweep of sand and gravel beach stretched more than 160 kilometres along the shores of

Dixon Entrance and Hecate Strait. Breakers rolled endlessly down the long reach of shoreline, roaring like bowling balls down some infinite corridor. The air was heady with oxygen and the rich aromas of salt, seaweed, seabird droppings and the occasionally fishy burp from some offshore sea lion. Across the deep cobalt blue of Dixon Entrance, the southernmost islands of Southeast Alaska shimmered in the sun. This was the Queen Charlotte Islands (QCI) I had been hoping for, and I felt a great weight lifting from me, as if someone had come along to shoulder the bags of my kayak and gear. For six months and almost 10,000 kilometres of hitching, that kayak had hung around my neck like an albatross; now I would finally get it on the water where it belonged.

I was feeling much more positive about the Islands now, and as if to bolster my spirits even more, the following afternoon the man who had threatened me was all smiles as I walked back through the village. It was as if he had been awaiting my return, though he seemed to recall nothing of our first encounter. He pointed to a doorway where an old Haida woman was looking at me. "She's been expecting you to join her for lunch," the man said pleasantly.

"What?" I asked in utter astonishment. "Yesterday morning you wanted to slit my throat and now ..." He acted as if he hadn't heard me and went on his way. The old woman beckoned me inside.

A traditional Haida feast had been set out by the woman's grandchildren. There was barbecued salmon, fried halibut, razor clam fritters, steamed Dungeness crab, herring spawn on kelp, dried oolichan and oolichan grease, octopus, abalone, seal meat, wild berries, boiled potatoes and bannock. I'd never seen a spread like this in my life. You couldn't order this in any restaurant in the world, and even if you could, few could afford it.

The woman's name was Eliza Abrahams. She was the oldest living Haida, and according to accounts I heard later, she was the most traditional. Eliza spoke little English but was bright and fluent in her own tongue. The two of us dined together and laughed and enjoyed each other's company even though there was little common language between us. After we ate, far too much, she had her family

Always immersed in her culture, Eliza Abrahams is seen here weaving a cedar bark hat in 1976. Three years earlier, she was the first person on Haida Gwaii to befriend me, welcome me into her home and serve me a lavish Haida lunch. Had it not been for the generosity and hospitality of this oldest and most traditional Haida Nonnie I might have left Haida Gwaii a few days after my arrival. ULLI STELTZER, 1976, HAIDA GWAII MUSEUM AT KAY'LLNAGAAY, SKIDEGATE, BC, CANADA

go into her dresser drawers to bring out all of her button blankets and family heirloom regalia to set on my lap. "What's happening here?" I finally felt compelled to ask one of Eliza's attendants, even though I ran the risk of appearing rude.

"She's been waiting a long time to see you," came the bewildering answer.

I had never really believed in destiny. At least, my lifelong liberal education had taught me not to. I always wanted to think that I made my own choices in life; for better or worse, I did what I truly wanted. If I wasn't exactly always in control of a situation, neither was I merely subject to the whims of fate. I believed this. I wanted to believe this. I needed to believe this. But my little lunch with Eliza made me start to question it all.

The pace quickened now; I was embarking on a journey that would mould me and hold me in its spell for decades to come. I returned to the place I had stashed my collapsible kayak, retrieved the two big bags and started hitchhiking south. Before long I was offered a ride from Masset along the seventy-mile length of the Islands' only highway to Queen Charlotte City, a misnomer if ever there was one. This small settlement of only a few hundred souls, spread out along the north shore of Skidegate Inlet, had become the preferred gathering place for alternative-lifestyle youth arriving from the mainland. It was Canada's Ellis Island; all it needed now was an upright eagle or raven statue bearing a torch: "Send me your dispossessed, your stoned and your penniless." For $65 you could buy a home site on "Hippie Hill" from John Wood, in all probability the world's only real estate developer who never charged a penny more for the land than he had paid for it. Or you could join other refugees from the North American middle-class suburban dream and squat on Haida land—or Crown land; it depended on how you looked at it. In either case, the issue was rarely raised in the early '70s.

Ron Suza and Pete Townson were two of the handful of "heads" who chose to settle on remote Burnaby Island at the southern end of the Queen Charlotte Archipelago. They hadn't been there long, however, before their cabin burned down and they found themselves back in Queen Charlotte City, the night I arrived, performing at their own benefit concert. It was a great event with a wealth of local talent, a throbbing sense of community spirit and enough cannabis smoke in the dark dance hall to stone you on entry.

Somehow in the dark and the din I made a new friend, Glenn Naylor, a British bloke who had the best of both worlds—a log cabin along Burnaby Narrows and a house on Hippie Hill. He too was a kayaker and was planning to paddle back to his cabin on Burnaby Island in the next few days. "Why don't you join me?" he offered. "You can crash at my place on the Hill until we go." Great good fortune was smiling at last.

It was a beautiful night up on the Hill, as the hippie homeowners called it, and I rolled out my sleeping bag on Glenn's porch to drink in the sweet summer air. By 2:00 a.m., the musicians had moved from the community hall to a house on the far side of the Hill where a great musical jam was ensuing. The sounds sweeping over the land were in many respects typical of the era: the rich unplugged sound of acoustic guitars, the wail of harmonicas, the flutter of flute and the steady rhythm of conga drums. Only the drumming stood out as something out of the ordinary. The rhythm was drawn from some-where deeper than the stoned groove everyone else was jamming to. It seemed to come from the land itself. The trees, the rocks, the cedar-plank floor I slept on—all reverberated that pulse. Although I did not get a glimpse through the trees of the musicians that night, I felt connected in spirit to that "talking drum."

"Who was on the conga last night?" I casually asked Glenn over breakfast porridge.

"Oh, that must have been Gary Edenshaw," he answered; "He's a Haida from Skidegate." Ten years later, long after my life and Gary's had become inextricably linked, the Haida elders deliberated long and hard to honour him with a new Haida name. His uncle Percy Williams had bestowed upon him the name Ghindigin, the "Questioning One," but somehow he'd outgrown that. The new name that better suited him, the elders decided at length, was Guujaaw, Haida for "drum." I could have told them that.

It was 8:00 a.m., June 21, 1973, when Glenn Naylor and I launched our kayaks from the beach in Skidegate Village, the Haida community just five kilometres east of Queen Charlotte City. I recall the time exactly not because it felt like some historic moment, but because it was the first time in eight months I wasn't bearing the weight of the kayak ... it was bearing mine. I felt wondrously weightless and free as we rode the ebb tide out Skidegate Inlet and felt the great swells of Hecate Strait. We had just enough clearance to glide over the long sandy spit that reaches out from the northeast tip of Moresby Island and gives this second-largest island in the archipelago the name of its only permanent community: Sandspit.

We were bucking tide now. This region has the greatest tidal fluctuation on the Canadian Pacific coast, and it wasn't worth the effort to push on against it. Of course, it pales in comparison to the Bay of Fundy's reported fifty-foot fluctuation in the Atlantic, but an eighteen-foot rise and drop in the water level every six hours is nothing to toy with either. We sat out the flood tide at Gray Bay.

It was late evening before the currents were running in our favour again, but there was still plenty of daylight to travel. This was, after all, the longest day of the year, and in this northern latitude, there would be light until 11:00 p.m. We managed to reach Cumshewa Rocks by sunset; it was an offshore seabird island with hundreds of nesting gulls. The tide was very low so Glenn and I gathered gooseneck barnacles and a few gull eggs for our dinner. When goosenecks are steamed, the shell and outer sheath of the barnacle slips off and a tasty morsel of meat melts in the mouth. Gooseneck barnacles have a rich flavour, a bit like crab, to which they are related. They are so delectable it's surprising they've never worked their way onto epicurean menus.

I was told the Haida name Cumshewa means "rich at the mouth of the inlet," and we certainly felt as rich as kings dining with the gulls on the most dainty of delicacies that night while the sun set over the long, glassy, smooth reach of Cumshewa Inlet. It was the perfect summer solstice party.

We slept out the few hours of darkness under the stars on barren rock, washed smooth from eons of pounding waves. Hundreds of gulls sounded our alarm clock at first light; there was to be no sleeping in unless we wanted to be whitewashed in gull droppings. Glenn headed south to a logging camp on Thurston Harbour, where he wanted to check on his mail, while I detoured up Cumshewa Inlet to view one of the old abandoned Haida village sites I had seen on my nautical chart. We agreed to meet that night at a place on the chart named Vertical Point.

Cumshewa absorbed me that morning like a deep dream. It was otherworldly stepping into the moss-hushed forest of that ancient village site. Shafts of sunlight pierced the morning mist and softly illuminated the remains of century-old totems. Great heraldic beasts with large ovoid eyes and broad, raised eyebrows stared in bewilderment as if forever frozen in the surprise of their own demise. Cumshewa, like many Haida villages, had been decimated and abandoned following a devastating smallpox epidemic in 1862–63. In one horrible summer nearly three-quarters of the Haida population succumbed to the deadly disease. The real tragedy is that it could have been averted.

American gold-rushers flocking from San Francisco to Victoria, British Columbia from around 1858 brought with them the horrible scourge. Vaccine for smallpox was available at that time, and all white settlers and their Chinese servants in Victoria were immunized. There was no recorded attempt to vaccinate the large Indigenous population residing in Victoria or anywhere else along the coast.

When one looks at the history of Indian wars, relocations, ethnocide and genocide against the First Peoples in North America, it is difficult to excuse this as an oversight. An even more sinister scenario is documented in Tom Swanky's academic book *The True Story of Canada's War of Extermination on the Pacific*. According to the author, Victoria's famous Dr. John Helmcken, while pretending to vaccinate the Indigenous peoples, was actually inoculating them with smallpox at the urging of Governor Sir James Douglas.

A cargo cult had developed around the European trading centres along the Northwest Coast and in the 1860s, a century after first contact, the principal trade centre was Victoria. In addition to the Songhees Village of the Coast Salish peoples located in Victoria Harbour, Kwakiutl and Haida encampments were set up for trade near what is now Victoria's cruise ship terminal. It was not uncommon for Northwest Coast Indigenous nations to hold rights to land through marriage, peace agreement or some other arrangement in the midst of another Indigenous nation's traditional territory. Such was the situation for the Haida settlement located near the entrance to Victoria Harbour in the fateful year 1862.

It may be our feeble attempt to fathom the unfathomable, but very often the great tragedies that befall humanity are reduced to simple tales. We are told that the great fire that burned down Chicago started when Mrs. O'Leary's cow kicked over a lantern during milking, and that the maiden voyage sinking of the *Titanic* was God's punishment for the ship having been christened the "unsinkable." So too, the smallpox scourge that decimated the North Pacific coast nations has been reduced to a mere tale.

According to the "official" story, Sir James Douglas ordered the Haida settlement to be cleared out of Victoria, at gunpoint if necessary, to "protect" them from the spread of smallpox. The Haida, for centuries, had been considered the lords of the coast and refused to allow themselves to be humiliated through such a disgraceful departure. Mustering their courage, the Haida regrouped their canoes offshore and returned in war formation to face the cannons. It was a display of pride more than any other, but it became a cornerstone of the smallpox tale. The Haida stayed just long enough to contract the deadly illness, so the story goes, and as they paddled up the coast they stopped at every village to boast of their daring deed and in so doing spread the smallpox. Cumshewa was one of the villages the death canoes stopped at.

A great sadness hung over Cumshewa at the time of my visit; it was as if the world had closed in on itself. Human skulls, still working their way to the surface from burial mounds blanketed under thick moss, told of the magnitude and swiftness of the disaster that befell this once thriving community so "rich at the mouth of the inlet."

I fell asleep in the sun on a mossy promontory of land where there was evidence of otters frolicking and cracking open crabs. It would be wrong to say that I fell into a deep dream; it was more a trance, an altered state, an almost out-of-body experience in which the village came fully alive again. Children laughed and squealed with delight as they bounded barefoot over the gravel beach to help haul in halibut from returning fishing parties. Women strung strands of kelp with herring roe attached to dry in the sun atop cedar drying racks. Smoke curled from each of the sixteen longhouses and count- less smokehouses so that the air was permeated with the rich aromas of alder-smoked clams and spring salmon, boiling crab and other foods fresh from the sea. Somewhere down the beach the sound of wood being slowly chipped away told of a canoe being fashioned from a great cedar log. Nearby, a master carver was putting the finishing touches on a huge ceremonial pole to proudly proclaim the lineage of his family for all the world to see.

It was late morning before I paddled away from the ghost village and crossed Cumshewa Inlet to Louise Island. Huge beds of bull kelp, stretching far offshore, indicated that I was running with the tide. Sea lions, cormorants and pigeon guillemots bobbed in the tide rips running strong off Skedans Point. Something felt totally different, yet strangely familiar, as I paddled through the breaking tide rips. I was used to river running where the current is swift but waves are stationary, or lake travel where the waves are moving through stationary water. Now I had to cope with both conditions simultaneously. The sea here could go from calm to raging tide rips in a matter of minutes and one had to be alert, to live and learn, or risk not living long.

A perfect peninsula juts out from the eastern shores of Louise Island and embraces two superb landing beaches. This stunning setting was the site of one of the greatest strongholds and most cele-brated Haida villages. Those born at Koona, also known as Skedans, were truly masters of their universe, at least until the epidemic hit. Now, like neighbouring Cumshewa village to the north and Tanu to the south, Koona is but a hollow, brittle shell of its former glory. Most of its monuments in cedar today grace the museum lobbies of the world, while a few forgotten grizzly and eagle mortuary poles lean dangerously or recline on the ground sprouting flowers for their own funerals.

What made the tragedy that befell Skedans especially poignant this June day in 1973 was to witness the sacred resting place of its one-time inhabitants being desecrated through logging. An alumi-num-sided trailer had been skidded up the beach and into the village site from a barge, and a bulldozer was being used to haul logs down from the hillside. It was a small gyppo operation run by a married couple and a few hired hands, but the impact on the site was massive. How could a major archaeological site be treated in this way, I wondered. Wouldn't the Haida believe their ancestral spirits would be outraged? The answer to both of my questions came some days later.

If there was a silver lining in the dark cloud that hung over the Skedans site that day, it was the warmth and genuine hospitality of the couple that held the logging concession. They invited me in for dinner and sent me on my way with fresh homemade bread, still hot from the oven. But paddling south to my rendezvous with Glenn at Vertical Point, I was saddened to see in the distance the massive clear-cut scars and associated landslides on Talunkwan Island. Little could I have known what a rallying point this mangled island would become in my future endeavours.

We found ourselves stormbound on Vertical Point the next morning. A roaring southeaster had turned Hecate Strait into a fury of white froth and mountainous waves. Glenn and I hunkered down and battened the hatches in a small cabin built on the Point by Benita Sanders, an acclaimed artist residing in Queen Charlotte City. Pots of wild mint tea and a few select books from Benita's little library helped ease the slow passage of the day.

Though the wind had abated the following morning, the seas were anything but calm. Glenn felt confident that the worst of the storm was over and that we should push on. A certain lady friend he was anxious to see again at his Burnaby Narrows cabin may well have been clouding his judgment. We paddled out of the protected little cove fronting Benita's cabin and were engulfed by the sea.

The swells were enormous, but at least they weren't breaking. Only on the crests of the waves could Glenn and I see each other, though we were never more than fifty metres apart in our separate kayaks. Dropping back into the wave trough after topping each crest was like being consumed, swallowed up by the sea. Huge walls of steel-grey water obscured any hint of land. It was as if the leaden sky itself had fallen and sunk into the sea, still writhing in the depths from the wrath of the storm. Humbling as the experience was, it was also exhilarating.

Entering the sheltered, calm waters of Klue Passage and the serenity of Tanu Island after the harrowing high seas was to know the true meaning of salvation. Could there be a more serene setting in the world than the moss-hushed silence of Tanu? Tanu in Haida translates to "where the eel grass grows," and this ancient village site not only supported an amazing diversity of marine life, it once rivalled any culture in the world for artistic expression. Pole carvers from Tanu were sought after up and down the coast for their brilliant designs and masterful carvings. One Tanu pole is the subject of a painting by Emily Carr titled *Weeping Woman of Tanu* (1928) and depicts the tale of Frog Woman shedding tears that turned into frogs after the brutal burning of her children. Today, the pole has been cut into sections and is displayed in the glass rotunda of the Royal BC Museum, but the spirit of what the master carver captured is still very much a part of Tanu.

I spent hours wandering among the massive longhouse ruins being reclaimed by the forest. A few superbly crafted corner posts still stood, but the roofs of the longhouses had long ago collapsed. Beams smothered in a dozen species of moss spanned the ground pits, some of which were twenty-five metres across. It must have been a Herculean endeavour to construct one of these massive multiple family dwellings. I knew from my anthropology courses that eight or more nuclear families of the same clan all lived under the same roof, and forty to fifty people would have resided in the largest of these houses. Living within the clan house brought with it a strict social code based on rank. The clan chief resided along the back wall farthest from the entranceway, which was often a carved tunnel-like passage through the bottom carved figure of the house's frontal pole. Only one person at a time could enter through this portal and they had to bend over to do so. This allowed the house to be easily defended, even by women and children, as intruders could be clubbed in the back of the head one at a time as they entered. It is said the Haida positioned their slaves closest to the entranceway to further foil attack. The cry of a stabbed slave at night was all the security alarm system a household needed. Then again, if the slave was from a neighbouring tribe and recognized common language in the attackers, he might become a liability more than an asset.

Everyone cooked on a central hearth in the middle and lowest level of the two- to three-tiered floor and found some semblance of privacy along the upper sleeping levels where bent cedar storage boxes and blankets divided the room into private quarters. The Haida longhouse was seen as a living being as well as a container of souls; it had skin (the planks forming the walls) and bones (the rafters and central supports). The heart was the central hearth and a mouth for exhalation was symbolized by the smoke hole. Two distinctive styles to Haida longhouses distinguished them from all others on the Northwest Coast—the two-beamed and the classic six-beamed. These houses displayed great architectural ingenuity designed to meet specific and demanding environmental conditions. Perched atop excavated house pits, the Haida longhouse was

amazingly roomy inside while keeping a low profile outside, a necessary condition for the gale-force winds and the occasional tsunamis
they were subjected to. To protect against frequent violent earthquakes the Haida, like the Japanese, designed their homes to have
no inflexible parts. Every piece of the structure had free movement
within the grooves and notches that held it all together. A house
could also be easily dismantled and moved to another location, yet
another way of coping with changing food supply or security needs.
To better cope with enemy raids and warfare, the houses were often
so close together that one could not easily walk between them. This
fortress effect required defence only on the farthest flanks to prevent
war parties arriving by canoes from sneaking behind.

We left the ruins of Tanu to slowly work their way back into
the earth and paddled into the most spectacular coastal wilderness I
had ever seen. All the way down Darwin Sound and into Juan Perez
Sound I couldn't help but marvel at the astonishing density of eagle
nests, the profusion of seabirds, falcons and marine mammals, and
the stunning biodiversity of the tidal zone. The forest itself was the
greatest feature, a wonderfully untouched ecosystem with age classes
of trees ranging from a few months to several thousand years old.
The ancient cedars, with their multiple dead tops bleached a lustrous
silver grey, spoke of the antiquity of these post-ice age forests. Like
the greying hairs of an old wise one, they spoke to the need for reverence and respect, something noticeably lacking in Northwest Coast
forestry practices.

It took nearly a week to reach Burnaby Narrows and the small
community of back-to-the-landers who resided there. Glenn's dove-
tail-notched log cabin stood boldly on a high gravel bench just above
all but the highest of tides. Only a few times a year did he have to
move all of his belongings and himself to the upper loft while the tide
inundated the house, he told me.

It is the rush of tides between Juan Perez Sound in the north
and Skincuttle Inlet in the south that has always made Burnaby
Narrows a choice place to live. As the tide ebbs, the Narrows
present one of the richest and most spectacular life zones on the

Pacific coast when thousands of miniature geysers squirt skyward as butter clams, little necks, geoducks, horse clams and cockles expel water from their siphons. At low tide the seabed becomes a kaleidoscope of colour with bat stars in every hue of the rainbow, sun stars in lavender and red, bright-red blood stars, and ochre, orange and purple pisaster starfish. Along the shoreline of the Narrows one can see evidence of thousands of years of Haida occupation represented by deep shell middens. The only trace of the village that once occupied this important site are these shell disposal sites and a small grove of crabapple trees growing in a clearing not far from Glenn's cabin.

A great party was thrown at the cabin for our arrival and it was there I met Axel Waldhouse, an Eastern European immigrant to Canada who wanted to join me on my kayak journey south to Ninstints, a village on remote S'Gang Gwaay Llanagaay (Red Cod Island). It is the most intact ancient village on the entire Northwest Coast and I very much wanted to go there.

It was a wild and somewhat harrowing experience to paddle around the southern end of the Queen Charlotte Archipelago several days later and out to the exposed west coast with the highest recorded winds and wave action in all of Canada. Every feature of the landscape here reflected the fury of this coast: the wild, wind-sculptured trees, the flotsam and jetsam hurled deep into the forest and the splash zone of the rocky shore, void of vegetation ten to twenty metres above the tidal level. What people would have chosen this small, storm-lashed fortress for their home, we wondered as we paddled the huge Pacific swells toward the isolated island.

Axel and I were less than a kilometre from the island and lost in our own thoughts when something huge surfaced behind us as we paddled. A great black island of flesh rose from the depths, exhaled with a blast of air that showered us in a fine mist, and then rolled forward with one, two, three ... far too many dorsal fins! For weeks I had hoped to get a glimpse of an orca, a minke, a fin, humpback or grey whale, but what was this? Scannah, the legendary five-finned killer whale, was a monster of myth, or so I'd been told.

Still unnerved and a bit spooked by the encounter we'd had offshore, Axel and I arrived on the deserted island. The haunting eyes of a dozen mortuary poles lining the beach stared at us unblinking as we hauled the double kayak up an ancient canoe launch cleared of large rocks. Those eyes continued to follow us in an eerie gaze as we moved reverently about the site.

Ninstints in 1973 was awe-inspiring. It was like coming upon Angkor Wat in Cambodia or Tikal in Guatemala before the archaeologists arrived to cut back the jungles. Unlike museum display poles with their chemically treated wood in climate-controlled confines, nature made it beautifully clear these poles belonged here. The trees that embraced them, the roots that split them and the stunning arrangements of ferns, flowers, salal and moss that adorned them— all made it apparent that the forest was reclaiming a part of itself.

Ninstints boasts the world's largest display of totem poles in their original setting, and although the site hadn't yet been declared a UNESCO World Heritage Cultural Site, it seemed just a matter of time before it would become known to the world. What makes this fortress island such a world-class attraction is not the poles but the wilderness in which they are set. A visitor can look out in any direction and see the same unspoiled scenes the inhabitants of the island saw for thousands of years—a setting hauntingly alive and still echoing with the spirits and drum songs of those who lived here more than a century ago. The legendary Haida transformations from human to animal form and back again seemed not only plausible here, they appeared to occur before our eyes.

If there is any sense of conventional reality on Haida Gwaii, it is blurred at the best of times. The merciless moisture and relentless fog of the west coast creeps in so often from the surrounding seas to obscure the headlands and highlands that the landscape itself becomes a phantom, an ever-changing figment of the imagination. If we in our cynical, scientific age can find power and spirit afoot here, one can only imagine the effects it had on the Haida, a people who did not deny or cast aspersions on the supernatural. To them, the great supernatural beasts and transformed forces that rule these isles are real, like Kostan, the giant crab that can crush a fifty-foot Haida freight canoe with a single claw, or Goghits, humans that revert to a state of primal wild being and hide in haunting forests of towering trees.

One evening while Axel was slowly cooking supper over an open fire, I hiked across the island to view the sunset on the wild west side. It was a savage scene. Wind-tortured trees gripped bare rock headlands where waves, built up over the world's largest ocean, exploded like bombs and roared their defiance at an island that had the audacity to interrupt their passage. Eagles cried in the dying light of day as they circled cliffs covered in eerie lichen that glowed blood red as if the setting sun had suddenly dissolved and been cast like wet watercolours across the granite faces. Racing against darkness to return to camp, I was surprised to see Axel approaching me on the trail. He must have been worried, I thought, and I called out to him, "Hi Axel, I'm fine. I was just ..." He was no longer there; a raven cried and flew off into the forest canopy. I raced back to camp to find Axel asleep beside the fire.

It was in this weirdly affected state that Axel and I left Red Cod Island and began the long journey back to Burnaby Narrows. There we parted ways. I was kayaking on my own now and would be for months to come. I crossed Juan Perez Sound to Hotspring Island, a paradise on earth if there ever was one. I lingered a few extra days to soak in the soothing geothermal springs set in natural rock grottos overlooking the spectacular islands and distant mountains that rimmed the sound. I was totally alone, but there was life everywhere: soaring eagles, barking seals, a gaggle of squawking gulls. Clever ravens cracked and opened clams by repeatedly dropping them from great heights onto the rocky shore and hyper little humming-birds buzz-bombed the pool I soaked in as they darted from flower to flower, sipping the sweet nectars of red columbine and multi-hued foxglove flourishing early in the season thanks to the geothermal warmth. Every so often one needs moments of pure bliss.

Rather than return north through the protected waters of Darwin Sound, as Glenn and I had done on our southbound journey,

I decided to paddle the more exposed east coast around Lyell Island. When the tide turned against me at midday I pulled into shore to wait out the ebb at a place marked on my chart as Windy Bay. Nothing was particularly outstanding about this bay compared to countless others I had stopped to explore along the way—at least, not until I set foot in the forest.

Here was the temperate rainforest of fairy tales, an enchanting garden of massive moss-draped trees: western red cedars, yellow cypress, Sitka spruce and western hemlock with bases three to six metres in diameter. Fifty metres overhead, the crowns of these conifers formed a cathedral dome where shafts of sunlight penetrated the mist and the sea breeze sent a perpetual rain of needles shimmering to the ground. There was little, if any, understorey here; instead, a deep, luxurious mantle of moss in subtle shades of green carpeted the ground and a few fallen forest giants. Windy Creek flowed through this valley like a living artery; its crystal-clear waters babbled and flowed over clean spawning gravels and formed back eddies behind fallen trees where several species of salmon fry found shelter. Eagles perched in trees overhead eagerly awaited the return of the

Standing beside a massive western red cedar at Windy Bay in 1973, I was awed by the majesty and antiquity of South Moresby's temperate rainforests. RICHARD KRIEGER PHOTO

Windy Creek flows through the moss-smothered forests of Lyell Island like a living artery.

salmon migration, and black bear trails, already centuries old before I walked them, meandered along the stream bank.

I found myself mesmerized, listening in reverence to the calls of the varied thrush and Pacific wren as if they were a Gregorian chant in a great cathedral. It was hours before I returned to the beach and began gathering firewood to cook some bannock for dinner. I still had another hour or two before the tide would flood again and I could resume my journey north.

I had combed the entire length of the beach for firewood and was in the process of flipping the last of the bannock in the pan when an eagle landed in a tree behind me and started calling relentlessly for its mate. I scanned the skies for some time in vain, but soon discovered that lying on the beach less than ten metres from my fire site was a dead eagle. I was overwhelmed. The eagle's body still felt warm so it couldn't have been dead for long. I wondered how I could have missed this transpiring in the time I was on the beach.

I took the eagle carcass in my hands and was astonished at the size of the wingspan. Knowing that the Queen Charlotte Islands' museum was nearing completion in Skidegate and realizing that I was just a few days' paddle from returning there, I decided to try saving the carcass so it could be used as a stuffed museum specimen. It would be a shame, I reasoned, to kill an eagle for this purpose when this one was so perfectly intact.

I made a small offering to the eagle's spirit, then carefully cut open and disembowelled the body cavity and restuffed it with damp moss. I had learned to keep fish fresh for some time with this same procedure in Alaska, so I felt confident the carcass would not spoil before I reached Skidegate.

The eagle's mate was still crying from the treetop when I loaded up the carcass in the stern of my kayak and paddled out of the bay. The sea was flat calm without a breath of wind that evening, and I offered up a prayer to the eagle's spirit to give my kayak the wings of an eagle. A fresh, steady breeze came up out of the southeast and I figured I could make Vertical Point before dark if I made use of my sail. A white bedsheet I had used for bedding throughout my Central American sojourn was now doubling as a square-rigged sail whenever the winds were favourable. I had drawn a stylized Haida eagle head on the sheet with a waterproof felt pen some weeks earlier, so it seemed fitting that moment to hoist sail.

Ten nautical miles away and out of sight to me, Percy Williams, the chief councillor of Skidegate, had set anchor for the night on the north side of Vertical Point. Wanting to stretch his legs after a long day of salmon trolling, he rowed ashore in his skiff and hiked across the narrow neck of land to hunt for deer. Scanning the beach unsuccessfully, he found himself gazing out to sea. He wasn't looking for anything in particular; it was just a built-in Haida instinct that had helped his ancestors survive more than twelve thousand years on a coast where war parties arrived by sea.

What Percy had seen that evening completely baffled him, as he later recounted to me. It was not a war party, but a great eagle flying low over the water, its wings wet and glistening in the sun, and it was coming straight toward him. Although he had been a seaman all his life, Percy had never before seen a kayak, and the wing-like movement of the paddle blades catching the last rays of the setting sun and the large white, sheet sail depicting the head of an eagle had totally mystified him.

The sun had already set before I made my landing on the beach and began hauling my gear up above the high-tide line to make camp for the night. There in the twilight, amid the silver-grey beach logs, I was surprised to see a Haida man with a sweater as weathered and hair as grey as the old cedar log upon which he sat. People behave oddly when they've been out of the social loop for a while, so instead of the customary courteous hello, I said nothing. But I immediately thought, I want to show this man my eagle. I took the carcass from the kayak stern and carried it up the beach, holding it out with both arms proudly.

The old man stood, startled, and took a few steps back, all the while watching me intently. "Why do you bring me this eagle?" he said cautiously.

"Because there aren't many left," I responded without thinking.

For me, growing up in Michigan where DDT poisoning and habitat loss had decimated the North American bald eagle population, the statement was true. For Percy Williams, growing up in Skidegate where eagles on the beach are as common as pigeons in a city park, my statement was bewildering. Neither of us said anything further for some time, until finally we sat on a beach log and casually started talking about my journey and how extraordinary I found the Haida Islands. I expressed deep concern about the clear-cut logging I saw working its way progressively south and I lamented what was happening at Skedans. Skedans, it turned out, was the ancestral village of Percy's mother, and as Haida trace their clan lineage matrilineally, it was his village as well. The logging concession had been sold, he told me, because Skidegate needed funds to build a new basketball court and community recreation facility for their youth. "We'll never do that to a village site again," Percy said, though he never let on that he was both a hereditary and elected chief of Skidegate. For me, our impromptu encounter was a moment in time soon forgotten; for Percy it proved profound, and would influence the course of Haida history.

The eagle carcass never did make it to the Queen Charlotte Islands' museum. The museum society didn't want it: Ottawa was supplying all their bird specimens fully stuffed and mounted. The Windy Bay eagle found its way to a storage freezer in Victoria's Royal BC Museum, only to be returned to Haida Gwaii seven years later as part of the regalia donated to the Haida Gwaii Rediscovery Camp. I had never shared the eagle story with anyone so I was dumbfounded when Peter Prince, an independent filmmaker from Victoria (who now lives on Salt Spring Island),

ReDiscovery: The Eagle's Gift film promotion featured Gerald Amos wearing Rediscovery regalia made from the same eagle carcass I had found at Windy Bay in 1973. RICHARD KRIEGER PHOTO

produced an award-winning documentary on Rediscovery that he titled *ReDiscovery: The Eagle's Gift*. The promotional poster featured Gerald Amos, a Haida participant on Rediscovery, wearing the wings and body feathers of that same Windy Bay eagle.

It was then that I came to the realization that I was merely a player on the Haida Gwaii stage; the best I could do was bear witness to my own unaccountable involvement.

CHAPTER III

Drawing the Line

At one time or another we all adhere to boundaries, borders and lines in our lives. They help us establish our territories, define our relationships, set sight on our goals, or just bring some semblance of order to a world that all too often appears chaotic. Somehow, though, it's not adhering to pre-existing boundaries but creating new ones, or defying established ones, that define us most. Heroes and fools, geniuses and social misfits know what it's like to do so. A person's actions can create a boundary just as their other actions can challenge and break a boundary down. My involvement with South Moresby and Rediscovery would soon put me at both ends of that spectrum, though it would confound me how I got there.

Arriving back in Skidegate in July 1973 after my kayak trip through South Moresby left me in a bit of a quandary and had me asking myself, "What exactly am I doing on the Queen Charlotte Islands?" I decided to press on back to my cabin in Alaska, my original goal when Stormy had detoured me with her cloud-busting trick back in Prince Rupert. I needn't return to the mainland to do so, I reasoned; I could paddle back to Alaska across Dixon Entrance. If the Haida could make this sixty-kilometre crossing in their dugout canoes, surely I could do the same in my kayak, I thought with all the self-assurance and blissful ignorance of a twenty-three-year-old convinced of his immortality.

Rather than deal with the long, shelterless northeast shores of Graham Island, the largest of the 150 Haida Isles, and treacherous Rose Spit, I decided to head north through Masset Inlet from Port Clements, a small logging-based community in the heart of Graham Island. According to Haida legend, this passage was made possible by Taaw, the younger brother of a larger hill by the same name. These hills, it is said, once resided side by side in the centre of Graham Island until the two brothers had a dispute over who was eating too much of the food. One night the younger Taaw left his sibling in a rage and stomped out across the bogs in the dark. His aimless wanderings carved out what is now Masset Inlet, an unusual body of water that extends from a wide bay near Port Clements fifty kilometres down a long, narrow channel to Old Massett at the mouth of the inlet. When Taaw reached the shores of Dixon Entrance he continued wandering east along the beach until he came to the mouth of the Hiellen River. Taaw looked out over the twenty kilometres of glistening white sand that forms the Great North Beach and knew he'd found his new home. Here was food in abundance: razor clams, cockles, weathervane scallops and Dungeness crabs that washed in on the big storm tides and piled up like windrows along the beach.

From the top of Taaw (Tow Hill) today, one can look out from this ancient volcanic basalt plug and view Masset Inlet to the west and Rose Spit to the east. Naikoon, "the nose," was the name the Haida gave this great sandspit that extends out into Dixon Entrance and marks the boundary with Hecate Strait. East coast erosion from the prevailing southeast winds is depositing sand at the tip of Rose Spit so fast that the land is growing two to three kilometres ahead of the colonizing vegetation.

The Great North Beach is noted for another reason—it is the sacred site of Haida creation. It was here, legend tells us, that a bored but ever curious Raven heard sounds emanating from a cockleshell on the beach. Prying open the strange bivalve, Raven inadvertently released the first humans—the Haida.

I was thankful to Taaw for the passage he had created as I raced out of Masset Inlet in my kayak on the strong ebb tide that midsummer morning. It seemed amusing that an early European explorer had once sailed to the head of this inlet thinking he had found the fabled passage to the Orient.

I stopped briefly at Yan, a lovely ancient village site opposite Old Massett at the mouth of Masset Inlet, and then proceeded out into the open waters of Dixon Entrance. I could see that a storm was beginning to brew but foolishly pressed on toward Langara Island. A pod of feeding killer whales surfaced from directly below me, giving me quite a start. The sea grew dark and threatening; steep breaking waves compounded the huge swells rolling in off the open Pacific and the wind built to gale force. There were no boats in sight and no apparent landing beaches; only kayak-crunching waves exploding on fortress-like rocky headlands. I needed to find shelter, fast. The orcas appeared again, nearer to shore, and one of them breached in a spectacular display, which couldn't help but catch my eye even amid the storm. It was a good thing I looked, for directly behind the breaching whale I spotted a narrow opening into a small bight. Riding the breaking swell, I shot through the passage into a perfectly calm harbour where a dozen salmon trawlers were tied up at a floating dock. The place was called Seven Mile and it was a harbour day, with the entire fleet sitting out the storm. All eyes turned on me in astonishment as I paddled my seventeen-foot canvas kayak in out of the storm. "It's a good thing the Lord looks after fools," was the only comment I elicited from a fleet of fishermen looking down on their first kayak sighting in these waters.

The next day dawned bright and cheery, and if the sea wasn't exactly calm, neither was it life-threatening. I set out at dawn and paddled westward along with the trawlers. Virago Sound acts like a great funnel, drawing boats into Naden Harbour, another important Haida heritage site. Sitting on the western point of land that constricts the passage to Naden Harbour is the strategically positioned but serene setting of Kung. The ancient village site of Kung gave me the feeling of coming in out of the storm; it probably gave its ancient inhabitants the same sense of security.

The following day I pressed westward and camped at Pillar Bay, where a stunning conglomerate of rock pillar stands proud of the water a hundred metres offshore at high tide. Some say a shaman's bones rest atop the thirty-five-metre pillar. It would certainly take superhuman powers to place a corpse or the bones of the deceased there.

Working my way up the east coast of Langara Island, I kept a close eye on the weather and the southernmost of the Alaskan islands, barely visible across the sixty-kilometre expanse of Dixon Entrance. A lighthouse stood on Langara Point and another across the entrance at Cape Muzon, Prince of Wales Island, Alaska. My plan, which seems absurd in retrospect, was to depart Langara Point at first light, paddle all day and through the night using both light stations as beacons to guide me in the dark. I had calculated that I could paddle thirty kilometres a day, meaning I should be able to reach Alaskan shores by dawn the next morning. What I had not accounted for was fog that, more often than not, obscures both light beacons, currents running east and west through the passage—which can pull a kayak completely off course—and the prevailing southeasterly wind. The wind in particular would prove my nemesis.

The Haida, I learned later, never set off for Alaska from Langara Island, but from Tow Hill on North Beach so that if the prevailing wind, a southeaster, came up, they still had a chance of reaching Dall Island in Alaska before being blown out into the open Pacific. My route would likely have put me in Korea.

I felt a bit anxious about my uncertain adventure when I pushed off from a beach on Langara in my kayak, but I was well rested and well stocked with bannock, dried fruit, nuts and adequate fresh water. The swells rolling in off the Pacific were on average two to three metres, but the surface waters were calm, at least until midday. Langara Island was growing distant behind me when the wind came up on the turn of the tide. The eastwardly flooding tide now encountered strong resistance from the southeast wind and the seas built up alarmingly fast. Learmonth Bank, a submerged shoal that would be a substantial-sized island if sea levels dropped a few metres, was directly on my course and the tide was ripping dangerously over it. With the wind stiffening, I had to make a decision as if my life depended upon it—and it did! After a blast of wind and a breaking wave spun my kayak around, I got the message. Years later, Haida elders would tell me that 180-degree kayak spin had nothing to do with weather. "You were sent back to us," they insisted.

It was well after dark when I found myself wearily trying to work my way through huge breakers rolling over the reefs on the west side of Langara Island. At least I was in the lee of the southeasterly storm, and I could smell the reassuring aroma of land. The flood tide drew me into Parry Passage, where I searched the dark shores in vain for somewhere to land my craft. It was well past midnight when a glowing white beach of crushed clamshells appeared like a ghostly apparition in the dark and I was finally able to pull ashore. I had been cramped in the kayak for eighteen hours, using a bailer for a toilet and drawing my strength from adrenalin more than food. Now my body wanted to collapse, and it did. Too exhausted to pitch my tent, I cuddled up in a dry spot under an old cedar log lying under a grove of young spruce trees. All night long I wrestled with demonic dreams, sea monsters in wild waves and wrens singing for lost souls beneath weathered totem poles.

It was nearly noon before I awoke the next day and wiped the sleep from my eyes, only to wonder if I wasn't still dreaming. The huge ovoid eyes, flared nostrils and thick lips of a Haida totem pole stared back at me from my place of slumber. Later, I would learn I had inadvertently landed at Yaku, another abandoned Haida village site, and had unknowingly slept under a collapsed totem pole.

I was famished and almost instinctively headed for the tidal zone for food. Thousands of tiny clam geysers spouting from the tidal flats suggested at least one good reason why this village was located here. I was so absorbed in digging for butter clams and littlenecks that I failed to notice a dozen kids sneaking up behind me. Suddenly I was surrounded by the twenty-four muddy gumboots and wet sneakers of a gaggle of Haida teenagers. "What are you doing?" they asked as they looked down at me.

"Digging clams," I answered matter-of-factly. "What are you guys up to?"

"Watching you," came the cheeky but very Haida reply.

The Haida youth were all from Old Massett and were working on an archaeological dig at nearby Kiusta Village, another ancient Haida habitation site. One of the boys, Lawrence Jones, in the spirit of Haida hospitality, invited me over to their camp for lunch. I jumped at the invitation; the clams could wait. It was a simple meal of soup and salmon sandwiches, but it seemed like a feast to my famished body. I was so delighted to be safe and in the company of people again that I offered to wash all of the camp dishes. This made me instantly popular with the kids on chore duty and provided a casual opportunity to visit with Nick and Trisha Gessler, the archaeologists overseeing the excavation.

When Nick learned that I had studied anthropology at Michigan State University, he told me they were short staffed and could employ me temporarily while I awaited calmer weather to make the crossing to Alaska. In retrospect, I think he was merely trying to save my life from another foolish attempt at crossing Dixon Entrance. I accepted the generous offer, moved my kayak and camp to Kiusta, and started working on the dig. Kiusta had been the site of the earliest contact with Europeans and the first foreign trade on Haida Gwaii; it offered great promise of significant archaeological finds and insights into that era.

Nearly every day after work hours, Nick and Trisha would encourage me to hike the Kiusta trail that led to a beach on the west coast. I had seen and camped on so many beautiful beaches from Alaska to Honduras over the past eight months that I was in no rush to do so. It was more than a week before I followed their advice.

The kilometre-long trail through pristine rainforest was enchanting, but Lepas Bay itself was more breathtaking than any bay I had ever beheld. A crescent-moon-shaped bay of fine ivory sand framed two lovely offshore islands, one a grassy seabird colony, the other cloaked in old-growth forest. A creek divided the beach and bordered a great rocky outcrop that cut off the northwestern edge of the bay at high tide. For some inexplicable reason I found myself drawn in that more difficult direction.

After climbing the cliffs above the crashing waves, I headed to the far western end of the bay. Dramatic sea stacks adorned in bonsai-like conifers, lush salal, ferns, red columbine, bluebells and yellow cinquefoils rose from the white sands as bold and beautiful as the fabled Hanging Gardens of Babylon. The waters on this end of the bay reflected the jade green of the surrounding forest with sky blue in the shallows gradually deepening to the dark cobalt of the open sea. Eagles nested on the westernmost point, deer grazed peacefully in a meadow of beach grass and a family of otters frolicked over the rocks. All my childhood drawings suddenly came alive in this place. I was home.

A strange compulsion had come over me; I had to do something here. I wasn't quite sure what it was, but hours later when I returned to Kiusta I found myself as bewildered as the Gesslers with my words: "I don't think I'm going to work on the archaeological dig anymore, but could I please borrow a hammer, a saw and a handful of nails? I'm going to build a log cabin on Lepas Bay."

Towering above the beach, this is one of several dramatic sea stacks at Lepas Bay, a place I came to love like no other.

Several weeks later, when the octagonal cabin made of beach logs was already three rounds of logs high, the utter absurdity of what I was doing finally sank in. I already had a cabin in Alaska. Why was I building another one in a country where I couldn't legally live or work to support myself? I was discussing this dilemma

Bringing an end to three months of solitude, a friend unexpectedly arrived on Lepas Bay and shot this photo of me in 1973 erecting the final round of logs on the Navajo hogan–styled roof of my cabin.

with the Project Kiusta youth around their dinner fire one evening in late August when Clarence, the Tsimshian skipper of a salmon packer named the *Ogden*, dropped by the camp to say goodbye. "I'm making the last run of the season to Prince Rupert," he announced. "Anyone need a ride?"

Before I was fully aware of the move I was making I had my kayak disassembled and stowed back into the two storage bags, my tent dropped, and all my gear aboard the departing *Ogden*. The entire Project Kiusta team gave me a rousing send-off from the shore where countless guests had been welcomed and seen off for thousands of years. I sat out on the open deck watching the shores of Haida Gwaii fade away in the dark. I was finally returning to my home and friends in Alaska after a nine-month odyssey. I had come to the Queen Charlotte Islands on a whim and I was leaving on a whim; this was just another stopover on a grander journey. So why was I fighting back tears all the way to Prince Rupert?

A few days later, kayaking west of Ketchikan, Alaska, I really began to think I'd made the wrong move. A storm came up so suddenly that I had to make an emergency landing on a barren rock island with an automated light beacon. I swamped the kayak in a breaking wave near shore, and while I struggled to save my craft and myself, the storm devoured my tent, sleeping bag and most of my food provisions. I had to spend the most miserable night of my life cold, wet and hungry, seeking refuge from the wind behind the only shelter this island had to offer—a steel sign that read, "US Government Property. Trespassers Will Be Prosecuted." I wished I'd stayed on Haida Gwaii.

When the storm abated nearly thirty hours later, I limped back to Ketchikan in my damaged kayak and set out to re-equip myself with a second-hand tent, sleeping bag, a cooking pot and some grub, all purchased with the small earnings I'd made working at Project Kiusta. In Ketchikan, quite by accident I bumped into a logger I'd met at the Gildersleeve Logging Camp back in December. He had bought a boat and was working as a salmon trawler now, and he offered to drop me off at Cape Muzon. Nearly a month after my aborted attempt to cross Dixon Entrance, I found myself at the beachhead I was striving toward.

The paddle up the west coast of Prince of Wales Island was marred only by the clear-cut scars on the slopes, some of which I'd contributed to in El Capitan Pass. I could see and feel the presence of Haida and Tlingit peoples in this region everywhere, from the intertidal zones where I discovered a beautifully carved stone net weight to the shell middens along shore where the wives of loggers were sometimes seen passing their idle hours by digging (illegally) for glass beads and other artifacts at old village sites. There were living communities too, like Hydaburg, where I enjoyed the local restaurant's specialty, a Hydaburger, and the Tlingit village of Kate on Kuiu Island, where no one spoke a word to me for two days until it was time for my departure. What I mistook for the rude cold shoulder turned out to be cultural protocol. Strangers had to be observed carefully, often for several days, before being approached in greeting.

One of the most harrowing days of my Southeast Alaska adventure was crossing Frederick Sound, a thirty-kilometre expanse of open water connecting three major inside water passageways where tidal currents ran strong and winds could whip up the waters in minutes. As on my ill-fated attempt at crossing Dixon Entrance, I required a long period of good weather to complete the fifteen-hour crossing of Frederick Sound. This sound also had cross-currents compounding kayak navigation difficulties, so once again I set off at dawn and once again I encountered rough weather midway across. My destination that day was Admiralty Island. Tlingit elders back in Kate had cautioned me again and again, "Whatever you do, don't camp at Tyee." Tyee is the name for the southern end of Admiralty Island where three rivers converge to meet the sea. It was late August, prime salmon-spawning season, and huge brown bears were converging here to put on winter fat. Admiralty Island boasts the world's highest concentrations of Alaska brown bears; they outnumber people living on the island three to one. The Tlingit's name for the island is Kutznahoo (Fortress of the Bears), and one requires but a single encounter with these eight- to twelve-hundred-pound carnivores to understand the local reverence.

It was nearly dark before I reached the shores of Admiralty; the tide was ebbing south down Chatham Strait and I didn't have enough strength left in my arms to buck the current. Against my better judgment, and the more than ample warning from others, I found myself landing on the beach of my worst nightmare, Tyee. Half a dozen brown bears were fishing for salmon in the shallow channels spreading out across the broad, muddy tidal flat. I had to haul my kayak and all my gear through ankle-deep mud to get above the tide line, all the while trying to not attract the attention of or provoke the extremely territorial bears. I was utterly exhausted and long past any boost adrenalin could give, having battled threatening seas all day. An old abandoned trapper's cabin perched on the edge of the forest became my all-consuming goal. If I could make it inside I'd be safe, I reassured myself. A huge bruin caught my movement and started to follow me across the tidal flats at a slow but determined pace. I rushed for the cabin, threw my gear inside and bolted the door. I was famished and exhausted and just about to pull out some trail mix and spread my bedroll when I heard clawing and biting on the wooden door. I must have passed out, because I awoke the next morning beside my backpack fully dressed and wearing muddy gumboots. Fear, exhaustion, or both, had taken their toll.

Paddling the west coast of Admiralty over the next week was exhilarating and more than a little unnerving. The snow-capped mountains of Baranof and Chichagof Islands across Chatham Strait glistened in the sun, but they also created williwaws—strong blasts of wind that rebounded off the high mountainsides and struck the strait with a vengeance. Tidal currents were especially pronounced and it just wasn't worth the effort to buck tide. Pulling ashore to wait out the tidal change or to make camp for the night usually involved a brown bear encounter. You feel very small indeed when both of your feet fit easily into an Alaska brown bear footprint on the beach where you pull ashore, or when one of these beasts rises up from its grazing in tall shore grass and lets you know with teeth-chomping certainty that it was there first.

Angoon, the only community on Admiralty Island, is an ancient Tlingit site and a delightful living community today. I enjoyed many hours during a rest layover there listening to the elders' tales over bannock and Labrador tea.

I happened upon another opportunity for income when I arrived by kayak in Hoonah, a small Tlingit village on the north end of Chichagof Island where I was offered a job aboard a salmon packer operating in Icy Strait. My job was simple: to weigh and determine the species of salmon being sold to the packer boat, then to poke ice into the body cavities as I packed the fish into ice bins, belly side up, in the ship's hold. It was not a bad job; the pay was good and the scenery in Icy Strait was sublime with humpback whales breaching, eagles circling the fleet and sea otters bobbing in the kelp beds. Still, I longed to continue my journey.

It was already mid-September when I finished the packer job and set off again in my kayak for Glacier Bay. Not long after departing Hoonah, I stopped to wait out the tide on a small island at the entrance of Icy Strait that was overgrown in berry bushes.

While working my way inland through the thick salal, munching ripe berries by the mouthful, I suddenly came face to face with Kushtaka, the legendary Tlingit Land Otter Man who can transform himself from animal to human and back again. I remembered having seen a photo of him in a book somewhere. The Haida recognize this same animal/spirit being, whom they call Slugu, and it is always an uncertain encounter. I was completely taken aback to suddenly come upon this lifelike face carved in stone and standing at my height in the bushes. It was a mortuary carving on a gravesite island, I came to realize, and quickly departed the isle.

I camped on the south side of Icy Strait the night before the long crossing to guarantee an early start. Shortly after I pushed off from the small beach a heavy fog rolled in, and I spent the entire day trying to navigate the strait without a compass. It was evening before I spotted land again and, as luck would have it, a perfect little landing beach appeared before me through the parting fog. I was thrilled. I had made it safely across the strait—or so I thought. Something was strangely familiar about this beach, and my morning footprints in the sand, crossed over by land otter tracks, confirmed it. I had paddled all day through the dense fog in a huge circle and arrived right back where I'd set off twelve hours earlier. Somewhere there was a lesson in that, or Kushtaka just has a mischievous streak.

When I eventually did cross over and enter Glacier Bay, it proved to be one of the most powerful experiences I'd ever had. I met a young man named George Dyson with a homemade baidarka—an Aleutian-style kayak. He had travelled up from Vancouver to Juneau on a barge and paddled the short distance from there to Glacier Bay. He was looking for a paddling partner to travel to the head of the bay, but I preferred my own craft. We travelled our crafts together up into the bay for several days before he returned to Bartlett Cove and Vancouver. I pressed on to Muir Inlet to view the primal landscape left by one of the world's fastest-receding glaciers.

To journey from the mouth of Glacier Bay to the base of its thirty-two tidewater glaciers is to journey ten thousand years back in time. One proceeds150 kilometres from climax (old-growth) hemlock rainforest to spruce and scrub willow brush, which gives way to colonizing plants like dryas, lichens, and ultimately barren rock and ice. Muir Inlet in 1973 was opening up at the rate of 1.2 kilometres per year. One could stand on land that had been buried under 1.5 kilometres of ice since the last ice age, and be the first to do so. It was an awe-inspiring experience to work the kayak through the countless icebergs to the very front of the Muir Glacier and watch tons of ice cascading off the face with a tumultuous roar. Then all would become calm again; the waters would glass over and mirror snow-capped mountains and glacier-blue bergs where seals lounged in the sun and dragonflies darted back and forth before resting with outstretched wings on the blue bow of my kayak.

It was already early October before I left Glacier Bay and worked my way up Lynn Canal to Haines, Alaska, and highway connections back to the interior. Thousands of bald eagles were now gathering in the gold cottonwood trees lining the Chilkat River, awaiting the chum salmon return near the ancient village of Klukwan. It seemed much longer than ten months since I'd hitchhiked this road in the other direction. When I finally did reach Talkeetna in the Alaska interior and hiked up the railway tracks to my old trapper's cabin home, I had nearly a year's worth of mail piled up on my table, courtesy of my neighbours.

One of the many letters waiting for my return was from a high school girlfriend who had learned that I was kayaking for months along the Canadian coast. She informed me of a Canadian amnesty program designed to legalize US war objectors, draft dodgers and deserters. Anyone who had been in the country more than a few months could come forward and be granted landed immigrant status with no repercussions. I no longer needed to hide my identity, and I could work in Canada.

Haida Gwaii beckoned, but instead I found myself on the road again, hitchhiking to Whitehorse, Yukon Territory. I went straight to the Canada Customs and Immigration office and explained my situation. "Am I eligible under this program?" I asked.

"You certainly are," a friendly officer replied. "But tell me, how did you get by so long in Canada without being able to work?"

It was too long a story to tell. "I'll write a book someday," I replied jokingly.

While waiting for my landed immigrant papers, I was granted a work permit and got a construction job in Whitehorse doing all-night steel work for cement foundations at a new housing development. There was something about wiring steel rods together at thirty to fifty below zero in the dark of a Yukon night that told me this was not my life's calling. It did, however, earn me the best grubstake I'd had in years, and I was able to return to Haida Gwaii early the following spring to pursue my real dream of returning to Lepas Bay to finish my cabin.

It was April 1974 when I arrived back on Haida Gwaii. After outfitting myself with tools and a few staple food items—flour, rolled oats, rice, milk powder and brown sugar—I set off by kayak for Lepas Bay.

I had written to the Massett Band Council requesting permission to cross Kiusta Indian Reserve to complete building my cabin. I could just as easily have requested a recreation lease on Crown land from the provincial government in Victoria, but I failed to see where the province had any jurisdiction. There had been no treaty, purchase or conquest of Haida lands by any state, so title clearly resided with the Indigenous inhabitants. The response letter from the Massett Band Council was heartwarming: "Thank you for the respect you have shown the people of Haida Village. Permission is granted to cross Kiusta Reserve for the purpose you have stated. We wish you happiness and success in your endeavours on Lepas Bay."

I didn't realize at the time that I was embarking on a three-month hermitage; I just had this compulsion to go back. Loneliness is an odd beast, and had I given it much thought it might have deterred me from going. But I can honestly say that it never became a part of my reality in the more than three months I saw no other humans. I found myself talking to the trees, the eagles, the rock spires and the ravens. I spoke not to their physical manifestations but to the spirit of these beings. Spirit was everywhere, and each day of my solitude it became more and more apparent that the boundaries we set to distinguish humans from animals, the animate from the inanimate, and the living from the dead are but feathery figments of our imaginations. If there was a fundamental academic lesson for me in Solitude 101, it was the simple truth that loneliness has nothing to do with being alone. The loneliest experience of my life was standing with ten thousand revellers in Manhattan's Times Square on New Year's Eve. My three months alone on the west coast of Haida Gwaii never once brought on feelings of such emptiness.

Lepas Bay likely takes its English name from the Lepas barnacle, a species of gooseneck barnacle that attaches to logs cast afloat for long periods in the open ocean, then washes ashore on storm tides to provide food for eagles, seagulls and scavenging bears. The Haida name for the bay, T'aalan Stl'ang, means "long sandy beach," but a much older name for the bay, Tidaalang Stl'ang ("medicine man lying down bay") appears to be in reference to Newcombe Hill (Tidalang Kun), a huge volcanic plug that borders the southern end of the bay. None of these names capture the majesty of the place.

I loved this bay like no other, and I frequently caught myself singing its praises in song. Walking on the beach, slap-happy barefoot in the breaking waves, I bellowed like an opera singer. It was good to be alone. For years my high school music teachers had told me to shut up in choir practice. "You're tone deaf," they'd snap, eventually shaming me into silencing myself. Now there was all this bottled-up song inside me that wanted to come out. If it was my destiny not to sing like a lark but croak like a toad, then I was going to do it with all my might; the west coast waves would hear me, and they wouldn't judge.

Completing my beachcombed log cabin was a joyful undertaking. Each round of logs went up slowly, but each log had a story to tell. I had no chainsaw, only a small Swede saw with a flimsy blade that had to be sharpened after every cut. Sand in the driftwood wore down the metal teeth faster than the teeth of an old cuss chewing too much tobacco. It might take me an hour or more to complete a cut, but in that time I could pause to watch the flight of a falcon or the frantic flutter of a Pacific wren darting among the logs in search of insects, or just drink in the sea's sweet scents wafting in on the waves.

Simple as it was, there was a universal nature to this house. The octagonal design and domed roof were modelled after the Navajo hogan I'd stayed in at Monument Valley, New Mexico, a year earlier. A slab of red African gumwood, which washed in on the waves, provided a beautiful coffee table and bookshelves that contrasted nicely with the silver-grey planks from a ship's hold cover that I used for flooring. Japanese inscriptions were carved on the planks I used for my door, and bamboo, which had drifted across the Pacific from Asia on the powerful Japan Current, provided attractive eavestroughs and window lattice that added a touch of charm to my clear plastic windows. Everything seemed to arrive on the beach just as I needed it. The day I finished building a half loft in the cabin for sleeping, I went beachcombing for wood to make a ladder. There, washed in on the tide directly in front of the cabin site, was a teakwood and rope

That's me in 1974, kicking back in gumboots on my Lepas Bay cabin cot that's covered in a Oaxaca blanket I'd used for a bedroll during my Central American sojourn. Other furnishings included a beachcombed deck chair tossed off a yacht somewhere in the wild Pacific. RICHARD KRIEGER PHOTO

ladder from a Chinese junk. Remarkably, it had just the right number of rungs to reach the loft.

I interspersed days I worked on the cabin with days set aside for exploring, food gathering, kayaking, or catching up on laundry and a good book. One thing I noted was how acute and animal-like my senses had become. I was never really afraid, but the slightest movement, sound or smell instantly caught my attention. My balance seemed extraordinary; I don't recall ever slipping once in all the times I packed heavy logs on my shoulders over slippery wet rocks and unstable piles of driftwood.

When I did finally see another human after nearly a hundred days of solitude, my initial response was to flee into the forest like a startled deer. The upright creature walking toward me on the beach turned out to be a friend from Victoria. Conversation was difficult at first, but when I did start talking I scarcely shut up for days. I also found myself slipping, tripping and failing to notice subtle sounds and movements around me. It was only then that I realized what a numbing effect society has on our basic senses; it dulls the acuteness of our vision, hampers our hearing, and allows us the luxury of losing our balance every now and then. Subconsciously, we rely on others to help us should we blunder; we expect someone to see what we might overlook, hear what we might miss and smell what we might not pay attention to. Solitary bush life, on the other hand, forgives few mistakes; without being paranoid, your animal instincts become acute.

Living on the west coast of Haida Gwaii is a humbling experience; it puts your very existence in perspective. I had been told by Haida elders that listening to the pounding surf too long as waves thunder in from the largest ocean in the world can drive a person mad. A certain level of madness or defiance might be necessary to even live in such a place. There is a small bay just past Hippa Island to the south of my cabin on Lepas Bay that the Haida called Gusgalang Gawga, which translates roughly as "mooning the wind." Defiance is one thing, but a west coaster must never get too cheeky. Storm waves can toss ten-thousand-pound logs deep into the forest on a high tide, capable of crushing my little Hobbit House like an eggshell, and then there was the ever-present threat of a tsunami.

I was also told by Haida elders that if the surf suddenly went quiet during the night due to a quick drop in the tide, I was to grab a torch and run up a high hill behind my cabin. Ancient Haida legends tell tsunami tales of entire generations of people wiped out by walls of water rising from the deep Pacific.

By July 1, I had plenty of neighbours again. Project Kiusta was back in full swing with the archaeologists and Haida summer students, and the salmon trolling fleet was back for the season. Only ten weeks later all returned to quiet again. I had to make a decision: either paddle back to Masset in early October or be cut off from society for another six to eight months while the autumn and winter gales raged. It was easy for me to see why some people become hermits even if they have no particular issue with society. My period of solitude had been the single most powerful learning experience of my life, but I knew that if I wanted to continue to grow, I needed society again. I closed my cabin for the winter by hanging a piece of carved driftwood on the wall that I inscribed with the words of Lord Byron: "There is a pleasure in the pathless woods, / There is a rapture on the lonely shore, / There is society where none intrudes, / By the deep Sea with music in its roar: / I love not Man the less, but Nature more, / From these our interviews."

It was mid-October when I paddled my kayak back to Masset and headed down the Island highway to Tlell. Murray Dawson, whose grandfather owned the Green House beside the Tlell River bridge, had offered to share the space with a number of people in need: Trudy Trueheart, Sparkle Plenty, Apple Rosie, Muskeg and others. Somehow a Huckleberry seemed to fit right in, and I was invited to share the space. We were all bedding down on the open-air porch one beautiful autumn evening, enjoying the wonderful orchestration of frogs, when a young Haida man arrived. It turned out to be Gary Edenshaw, otherwise known as Ghindigin, the man playing the congos when I had stayed at Glenn's house on the Hill. He had been hitchhiking from Masset to Skidegate, and the Tlell River was as far

The Green House beside the Tlell River is where Ghindigin and I drew the line on the map by lamplight in October 1974 to designate and launch the South Moresby Wilderness Proposal.

as his ride took him before traffic south ceased for the night. There was still some space on the porch, so we offered him a blanket and invited him to stay the night. It must have been between 2:00 and 3:00 a.m. when I heard a deep voice from the far end of the porch ask matter-of-factly, "Anyone awake?"

"Yeah, I am," I said softly, not wanting to wake the others.

"Oh yeah, what are you thinking?" came the inquisitive response from Ghindigin, "the Questioning One."

I explained how I had been dreaming about my kayak trip the year before through the South Moresby wilderness, how I longed to go back there and how it pained me to think that it wouldn't be the same with the logging starting up on Burnaby Island. Ghindigin was instantly and intently interested. We took our discussion inside, lit an oil lamp, pulled out a map of the southern half of the Haida archipelago and looked at the lines. Tree Farm Licence #24, held by ITT-Rayonier, had three cut blocks remaining to be logged in the South Moresby region: Blocks 3, 4 and 5.

"How far has the logging gone?" Ghindigin asked.

I drew a line south of Talunkwan Island along the border of Blocks 2 and 3, extended it out into the Pacific in the west and Hecate Strait in the east, and brought the lines back together again south of Cape St. James, the southernmost tip of the archipelago. "Proposed South Moresby Wilderness Area," we printed boldly on the map. Every resident of the Green House who woke that morning was asked to sign a petition calling for South Moresby to be saved. The Islands Protection Committee was born.

It seems astonishing in retrospect that a line so casually drawn would appear on government maps almost from that day forward and galvanize a national debate over land-use issues that would surpass any other in Canadian history. It seems even more extraordinary that this same line on the map survived three government-appointed planning teams, over more than a decade, that were never allowed to consider an option of total protection for the land encompassed by those borders. The most remarkable thing of all is that the line we drew by lamplight beside the Tlell River in the autumn of 1974 is today the exact boundary that distinguishes the Gwaii Haanas National Park Reserve and Haida Heritage Site from the rest of the world.

Raven works in mysterious ways.

CHAPTER IV

Against the Wind

If there was method to our madness in thinking we could save South Moresby, it was unknown to any of us. For more than a decade the players cast on both sides of this eco-drama would perform their designated roles as if scripted by a master playwright. The lead characters were, for the most part, just that—characters, an eclectic group of eccentrics with so little knowledge of or regard for the political process that they completely befuddled it. Raven, the legendary Haida trickster, seemed to be at work once again, opening a clamshell of unlikely heroes and antagonists and creating stranger-than-fiction situations.

Shortly after drawing the line for the battlefield, Ghindigin told me an important meeting was coming up in Skidegate to discuss the logging plans for Burnaby Island. The Skidegate Band Council was to be briefed by the Ministry of Forests, ITT-Rayonier (the tree farm licence holder at that time), federal Fisheries Department and BC's Fish and Wildlife Branch. Ghin said he would ask his uncle Percy Williams if we might be able to attend and present our proposal. A few days later Ghin dropped by the Green House in Tlell to confirm that we could attend, but as observers only. He had shown his uncle our proposal on the map. "You're asking for too much," the revered uncle told his nephew.

"No, Uncle," the Questioning One respectfully replied. "It's not enough."

A journalist was visiting the Islands at the time and, for lack of any other interesting scoop, somehow was directed to the Islands Protection Committee at the Green House. When he learned of our proposal and upcoming meeting, he told us to prepare ourselves with some hard-hitting reporter-style questions should there be an opportunity for public input. It proved excellent advice.

The small meeting room upstairs in the old Skidegate Community Hall was jammed when Ghin and I arrived at 8:00 the night of the meeting. We took our humble places in the back of the room beside a few local onlookers. Percy Williams opened the meeting by thanking all the officials for attending, then proceeded to tell a story. He had been deer hunting one evening a year earlier at Vertical Point when he saw a giant eagle approaching him from far out at sea, an eagle that appeared to be coming directly toward him. The chief councillor was more than halfway through the story before I recognized myself as the central character. My God, I thought, this is the same man I met on the beach. I hadn't even recognized him. Percy completed the story and fell silent for a moment, then added, "I've come to see our beautiful Islands differently since the day that eagle was brought to me. Maybe there isn't so much left." He paused to look back at me in the far corner of the room. "That eagle messenger is here tonight and I would like for him to speak," he said. All eyes turned in the direction of Percy's gaze, and suddenly Ghin and I realized the meeting was ours.

The officials had come to do a snow job on a community that was all too dependent on logging. No one was expecting even mild opposition to the logging plans, much less some hard questioning. "What type of environmental impact assessments of the logging plans have been carried out by the two branches of government, considering that this area holds many unique features of national and international significance?" we asked. "What guarantee can the tree farm licence (TFL) owner, ITT-Rayonier, or the concession holder, Beban Logging, offer to ensure that landslides resulting from logging, which have devastated the slopes of Talunkwan Island, won't also occur on the equally steep slopes of Burnaby Island? What public input will be allowed in the decision-making over such a vast tract of public land?" we asked. Every branch of government and the forest industry appeared dumbfounded by the questions; they were publicly embarrassed and deserved to be. Viola Wood, a much-respected senior citizen of Queen Charlotte City and writer for the Islands' newspaper *The Observer*, was seated at the back beside us. She rose and publicly proclaimed: "I want to be a member of the Islands Protection Committee. How can I join?"

What started out as a concern for Ghin and me would slowly build into a powerful force that would ultimately involve millions. Some of the people first conscripted to the cause were unlikely supporters, like Dan Bowditch, the Queen Charlotte Islands director for BC Hydro.

The Islands Protection Committee (IPC) hadn't even been legally constituted as a society when it took on a cause far removed from South Moresby. The residents of Tlell had been lobbying the government for years to get hydroelectric power to the small farming and recreational cottage settlements on Graham Island's east coast. One day, residents of the Green House awoke to see the lovely grove of trees along Beitush Road, which runs along the south bank of the Tlell River, being cut down for a hydro line. The charm and intimacy of the little dirt road would be forever lost. A protest blockade in front of the BC Hydro equipment brought IPC members face to face with the director of BC Hydro, a young, clean-cut graduate in engineering from the University of British Columbia. Dan Bowditch knew how to smooth ruffled feathers. Risking the wrath of Tlell property owners who would benefit from the power, he ordered a stop to the work until he had permission from head office to install a buried line. The IPC blockade gave Mr. Bowditch the leverage he needed to apply for the extra allocation in funds. It proved a win-win situation for all parties involved, and Dan and his wife Ursula became prominent and much-respected members of the Islands' fledgling environmental group. Years later when the IPC had become the Islands Protection Society (IPS), and environmental leaders from across Canada gathered on Haida Gwaii to co-ordinate strategies, they would be astonished to be picked up at the airport by a BC Hydro vehicle and transported to their billets at the home of the BC Hydro director. "How did you guys arrange this?" they'd ask in astonishment. "BC Hydro is the biggest enemy where we come from!"

There were other long-term supporters of the IPS who held respectable positions in society: schoolteachers like Vic Bell, Marilyn Miller, Jane Nelson, Bob Dalgleish, David Sufrin and Tom Schneider; social worker Judy Kerr, artist John Broadhead, professional photographer Jack Litrell, performing artist Lark Clark, BC Hydro employee Wilfred Penker, Village of Masset council member Margo Hearne, researcher Lynn Pinkerton, legal aid adviser Eloise Jones and QCI director of health and human resources Vicki Sexsmith. But for the most part our rank and file were a ragtag group. The fact that the IPS was not taken seriously allowed for its success; the provincial and federal agencies, the logging companies and woodworkers' unions completely underestimated the power of a small but determined group of people and the force of public opinion. Perhaps nowhere was this disdain more apparent than in the hallowed halls of the Victoria legislative building.

One of the first undertakings of the Islands Protection Committee was to gather the names of five hundred adult Islands residents to call for a moratorium on logging and mining in the proposed South Moresby Wilderness area until "complete environmental impact assessments" had been conducted. It seemed like a reasonable enough request, and it didn't take us long to gather the signatures. I asked Viola Wood and Trudy Carson, two lifelong New Democratic Party supporters, to accompany me in presenting the petitions to the NDP premier, Dave Barrett. Viola had her hair styled especially for the occasion and Trudy put on her best dress and borrowed a suit from her brother for me to wear. We arrived in Victoria respectfully dressed for the occasion, only to be completely brushed off. We would be allowed to present our petition not to the premier, but to our MLA, Graham Lee, who happened to be the minister of highways at the time. Our honourable representative met us in a T-shirt with his feet on his desk, chomping a big Cuban cigar. He had all the arrogance of someone not destined to hold office for long. "Oh sure, I'd like to put a big fence around BC and protect all of it," he said. "But you know that's not practical," he added condescendingly. "As for petitions—" He nodded his head in the direction of the wastebasket. "Well, they don't carry much weight around here." Before we left we were told that if we played our cards right we could end up holding a high office someday. "That's where decisions are made," our honourable MLA added as we departed.

Trudy and Viola were outraged and wanted to burn their NDP cards on the legislature lawn. I wasn't discouraged; I had expected as much.

Years later, when John Broadhead and I were trying to get the South Moresby message across to the new Social Credit premier, Bill Bennett, we were called in from the hallways of the Parliament Buildings by none other than Graham Lee, still the MLA for our riding, but now sitting in opposition.

"You're wasting your breath on this government," he grumbled, as if his government had ever listened to us. "You know, boys," he went on, lecturing in his most partisan and patronizing tone while chomping his cigar, "there are two kinds of people in this world—"

John cut him off. "Yes, Graham," he said, "there are those who think there are two kinds of people in this world, and those who know better."

The honourable Mr. Lee's jaw dropped and the ash fell from the tip of his cigar as we departed his hallowed chamber.

During the terms of three different governments—those of Dave Barrett, Bill Bennett and Bill Vander Zalm—we never once had an opportunity to meet with the premier of British Columbia to discuss the South Moresby cause. This became the largest environmental issue in the province and eventually in Canadian history, but only one other elected official in high office, Sam Bawlf (minister of recreation and conservation), could spare us a few minutes of his time in the nearly thirteen years we campaigned to save the area.

The closest we ever came to meeting the premier was very early in the campaign when the Green House gang invited Dave Barrett for tea. Elections were in the air and his government was touring the Islands to lend Barrett's personal weight to safeguarding the seat of this NDP stronghold. A beautiful handmade invitation signed "the Plenty Family" asked the premier and his entourage to stop by the Green House for tea on his Islands highway route. It was a sparkling, crisp autumn day, and the Green House porch was arrayed in branches of fiery leaves, green moss and amanita mushroom floral arrangements. The Plenty Family—Sparkle, Trueheart, Apple Rosie and others—had prepared homemade muffins and a lovely tea with rosehip and mint. At 3:30 p.m. the premier's entourage pulled up to the side gate entrance, surveyed the scene for a few minutes, then drove on to Masset with no apology or explanation. It was our second disappointment of the day; earlier we'd received a notice from the owner to vacate the premises within thirty days.

But the Plentys still had plenty to celebrate that day: there was the enchantment of the riverside, the magic of flute music and the pleasure of having nearly pulled off a good caper. We drafted and posted a letter to the premier that evening: "Dear Mr. Barrett, we were so sorry that you could not join us for the tea this lovely autumn day by the Tlell riverside. We'd invite you again next year, but you won't be premier, and we won't be here."

Everything came to pass.

There were other bizarre escapades in those early years, some of which grabbed national attention, like the "Berserk Dentist and the Golden Humbug." Robert Orr, DDS, was the only dentist on the Islands at that time and he became a supporter of the South Moresby cause. His support included everything from volunteering time and money to dentistry; more than one South Moresby campaigner got free fillings from the good dentist. But Dr. Orr had looked into too many young mouths full of rotting teeth in recent months, and he was growing infuriated with the two-tiered structure of government services. Why, he wondered, did RCMP get gold fillings at taxpayers' expense when government funding paid only for teeth extraction for Indigenous people?

A week before Halloween, Robert Orr dropped by the new IPS holdout in Delkatla. With the eviction from the Green House in Tlell, I'd been taken in by Ghin's extended family at a house in Delkatla, just across the boat harbour from New Masset. "I might just go berserk tomorrow," Dr. Orr said to Ghin and me, half-jokingly. "If you see me start to lose it at the Co-op store, call the police," he added.

The next day he came by and asked me to go shopping with him. He seemed calm enough as we entered Delmas Co-op on Main Street, but when he saw two complete aisles in this five-aisle store devoted exclusively to Halloween candy, he went bonkers. Racing down the aisle, he swept the candy clear off the shelves and onto the floor, all the while screaming at the top of his lungs: "It's poison! It's *poison!*"

Bewildered mothers clutched their children and whispered in their ears, "He says candy's poison." The butcher grabbed a large cleaver, jumped over the poultry counter and went in hot pursuit of the dentist gone bonkers. After I saw an entire cardboard display of candy come crashing down near the checkout counter, I went for the pay phone to call the police. Someone had already beaten me to the task. While the dentist-gone-berserk was being hauled out of the store in handcuffs, I knew this was a story and decided to phone CBC News. "Sorry to bother you, but the only dentist for five thousand Islands residents has just been arrested by the RCMP for trashing a Halloween candy counter." Reporters were burning the lines into police headquarters even before the doctor had been fully booked. Barbara Frum on CBC's *As It Happens* show went nationwide with the story. "Doctor Orr, how did it feel?" she asked in her hallmark style.

"It felt great!" the berserk dentist replied.

For weeks, letters and telegrams poured in from across the country and around the world: "Bravo, an act of sanity!" cheered the

European Dental Association. Robert Orr had become an overnight celebrity, and he took every opportunity to make his case known about the inequity of government dental services.

But the RCMP felt "had," and they wanted their man. Robert Orr, DDS, was formally charged with "damaging confectionery." When the much-anticipated court day arrived, Masset's small judicial chamber was packed with people and the press. The RCMP sternly dumped out the evidence before the judge: bag after torn plastic bag of candy. Carey Linde, the defence lawyer, rose and asked for the charges against his client to be dropped as erroneous.

"Your Honour," he implored, "my client has been charged with damaging confectionery, not damaging plastic bags. Unless the Crown can present evidence of damaged confectionery, I ask that these charges be dropped." The police were steaming mad; another clearly guilty criminal was about to get off the hook because of a shrewd lawyer. A poker-faced officer rose to the bench and began inspecting one by one the jellybeans, the Jum-Jills, the candy corn and gumdrops. The courtroom held its collective breath for a piece of hard evidence. Finally, the RCMP officer rose proudly from his task, held a square, striped rock candy between two fingers and proclaimed with bombastic self-satisfaction, "Your Honour, the Golden Humbug has a chip out of it!"

The courtroom exploded in laughter. Had the defence lawyer not been reeling with uncontrollable giggles himself, he might have approached the bench to note that Golden Humbugs more often than not were chipped during shipping and store handling; there was no way of proving his client had caused the damage. Instead, the Mounties once again got their man. Robert Orr, DDS, was found guilty, ordered to pay a fine and released on condition that he never trash a candy counter again. The "Berserk Dentist Defence Fund," a spontaneous collection from courtroom witnesses who were more than happy to pay the cover charge for a top comedy act, paid the fine.

On a more serious note, bucking the system does have its consequences, even in a liberal, democratic country like Canada. Our completely legal and by-the-books campaign to save South Moresby brought on some almost immediate repercussions—the type of harassment that should be an embarrassment in a truly free society.

In the early spring of 1975, I was still staying with Ghin and his family in Delkatla, awaiting calm seas to paddle back to Lepas Bay for the summer. I had received a large food order of staples from a wholesaler in Vancouver for my summer provisions—big bags of flour, cornmeal, rolled oats, dried fruit, nuts and a tub of peanut butter—and I was temporarily storing them on the covered front porch of the house. One afternoon I returned to the house to find my food bags cut open and the household in disarray from an RCMP raid. There was no search warrant, and when the Edenshaw family asked what was going on, the police said they were "looking for guns." It struck me as blatant act of vandalism and a strangely unwarranted attack on a group of pacifists pursuing the legal process to protect a natural area of national significance.

Years later, in the full heat of the Moresby campaign, the principal players suddenly found themselves personally subjected to a full federal audit. Revenue Canada had absolutely no reason to suspect anything was inappropriate, but it did tie up South Moresby strategists for months while we compiled daily expense records for three- to five-year periods. In the end, the government owed each of us back pay for excess taxes.

It was Ghindigin, more than anyone, who understood the full nature of our undertaking. "This is war, Huck!" he said to me once. Most supporters of the South Moresby cause had little invested in the struggle other than a love of nature and a desire to protect it. Ghindigin, on the other hand, saw the campaign to save Haida Gwaii as nothing less than an issue of Haida survival. Although he came from a ten- to twelve-thousand-year-old culture with a reputation for being merciless in armed combat, Gary Edenshaw was every bit the peaceful warrior who wore his convictions as his armour and his powers of persuasion as his only weapons. He knew the pen was mightier than the sword, especially in an age when high-tech weapons and nuclear arsenals made armed combat largely ludicrous. He never wavered from his conviction that the power of public opinion could eventually win out over the mightiest stockpile of weapons, the powers accorded to the wealthy, or the most stubborn and intransigent branch of government. But just as Ghindigin was a pacifist of sorts, he did not shrink from confrontation either. In the summer of 1978 he went toe to toe with the commanding officer of the Canadian Forces in Masset, challenging military authority on their march through the village—and he stopped them.

CFS Masset was, more often than not, a contentious issue. The radar base was first installed during World War II but greatly expanded during the later days of the Cold War. A huge radar dish positioned on North Beach was said to be capable of monitoring nuclear subs throughout the North Pacific. Base operations were top secret, and not even the wives of CFS Masset personnel were allowed to know the true nature of their husbands' assignments.

When the new, expanded base was put down on top of the Village of Masset in 1972 it was to be a federal experiment in integrating civilian and military communities. Masset realized the benefits of an expanded tax base, an increase in jobs, consumers and a larger electorate with more clout in Victoria and Ottawa. But the base's drawbacks were more serious. CFS personnel tended to shop only at their exclusive CFS store, remaining largely isolationist in their social interactions in spite of the fact that a local man served as commanding officer, and they had the numbers to control the local vote on all issues. The Masset military base not only made this small village on Canada's most remote western shores ground zero for a global nuclear exchange, it also seemed to many Haida a federal ploy that further disempowered them. Ghindigin likened the circle complex of base housing to the covered wagons circling to ward off attacking Indians in the Old West.

Such were the tensions in the air that summer of 1978 when the Village of Masset council, largely elected by the base, decided to bestow an old medieval honour on CFS Masset: The Freedom of the Village. Commanding Officer Peter Stewart-Burton, a local man with a mix of Haida and Caucasian blood from a very respected family, was about to be transferred to a new post, so it was reasoned there would be no better opportunity to turn over the key to the city and forever wed Masset with the base than at that time. Mayor Nick Grosse was to preside over the ceremony and grant the CFS perpetual rights to march through the village with bayonets fixed.

Ghindigin and others were furious that no Haida had been consulted. They made placards bearing the words "Who Asked Us?" and "Really Gross Nick" as they confronted and blockaded the entire base regiment that was approaching the reviewing stand in front of the village office. The Esquimalt military band, flown in from Victoria for the occasion, went suddenly silent as Ghindigin and Commanding Officer Stewart-Burton came literally nose to nose in front of the reviewing stand. "I order you to step aside and let my men pass," the commanding officer barked for the entire crowd to hear.

"You don't order me to do anything," Ghin responded with equal authority. There was a long moment of hushed silence. The commanding officer appeared completely confounded by a person not obeying his direct orders. If Masset was to be the test case for bringing together civilian and military communities in Canada, you couldn't have asked for a more symbolic moment.

"Go home, Edenshaw!" a few rattled base wives bellowed from the sidelines. While the irony may have been lost on them, other Haida, who were not part of or necessarily in support of the protest, couldn't help but think, "Go home, Edenshaw, indeed!"

People stationed on Haida homeland were defiling one of the most respected family names, handed down by countless generations of Haida. What had started as a simple protest was bringing up all the old animosities with racial overtones and the possibility of real violence. No one seemed to know what to do. Fortunately, both Ghindigin and Peter Stewart-Burton were level-headed men with enough Haida blood between them to know that "making your name good" is the bottom line in any engagement. Ghin agreed to let the CFS regiment pass if they removed the bayonets from their rifles and never again fixed them in the streets of Masset. Peter Stewart-Burton gave the order to his men and the bayonets came off. A cheer went up from the base wives as their husbands marched past and a cheer went up from the Haida protestors as well. Everyone enjoyed the free hot dogs and pop together, but there would be no "freedom" of this village.

I, and everyone present, had borne witness to one of the most dramatic moments in modern Haida history. The act of total defiance in the face of power would sink deep into the consciousness of every Haida observer that day. It would be years before such a posture would be called for again, but

Guujaaw, looking every bit the warrior in the early years of the campaign to save South Moresby.
RICHARD KRIEGER PHOTO

when it was, Ghindigin, the Questioning One, would be known as Guujaaw, the Drum, and he would not stand so alone.

Ghindigin was by no means the first Haida to make a stand for the land, even if he was a decade ahead of most on the South Moresby issue. There had been a long and proud tradition of Haida spokesmen and women, great orators who had left eloquent and compelling testimonies in defence of Haida rights, since the time of European contact. Chief Gaala of Old Massett had carried that tradition forward with great authority until his untimely death, as did Lavina Lightbown, an outspoken Haida activist. Philip Gladstone, chief councillor of Skidegate, supported the South Moresby cause right from the start at the All Islands Symposium we arranged to get public input and a broader base of support for the cause. Nathan Young from Skidegate legally challenged the logging of South Moresby as an infringement on his trapline. Willard Wilson, the Skidegate Band Council administrator, was behind the Moresby cause every step of the way, and Miles "Buddy" Richardson, who would become the first president of the council of the Haida Nation after completing college, told Guujaaw, "We're going to be there. We're going to be there. Just keep on."

But it was Percy Williams, the chief councillor of Skidegate and hereditary chief of Skedans, who gave the South Moresby proposal the biggest boost when he asked that Burnaby Island not be logged. Rather than risk a confrontation with a pro-logging community, the TFL holder agreed to defer the logging of Burnaby Island for five years until they finished logging Lyell Island. Rayonier still fully intended to log Burnaby, but this unexpected change of plans gave the South Moresby proposal a fighting chance. Lyell Island was near the northern border of the proposed protected area, while Burnaby was situated at the very heart of it. If Burnaby was logged, no case could have been made for South Moresby as a large, intact wilderness area.

The spectacular Burnaby Narrows, with one of the world's most prolific shellfish beds, possessed intertidal starfish of amazing diversity and colour. It was proposed to be a log dump and sorting ground. Instead of the dazzling beauty of the site that is now featured on Canadian calendars and greets visitors from around the world in a huge illuminated wall mural at Vancouver International Airport, the Narrows would have been buried several metres deep in rotting bark and debris. Today, Parks Canada, Fisheries and Oceans Canada, and the BC Ministry of Jobs, Tourism and Skills Training all boast of the world-class beauty of Burnaby Narrows, but none of them supported the effort to save it. It is to the everlasting credit of Percy Williams and the Skidegate Band Council, not to any federal or provincial protectors of public interest, that the Narrows still shine.

Three things made the Islands Protection Society unique in its time. Its creation marked the first registered environmental group in Islands' history. It was decades ahead of other groups in Canada calling for a large protected wilderness area on the Pacific coast, and it effectively combined the voices of Indigenous and non-Indigenous people in a land-use issue for the first time in Canadian history. A simple, and somewhat unlikely, friendship between Ghindigin and me became the basis on which much of this was built. Had that friendship eroded or dissolved in any way in the early years of the Moresby struggle, it is doubtful the outcome would have been the same. When new supporters were enrolled in the cause, they began their education in Haida protocol and Islands ways with Ghindigin. Ghin knew how to challenge people to show their real colours. If they harboured racial prejudice in their hearts he brought it to the surface—fast. Ghin had a strange way of endearing people to him and recruiting supporters to the Moresby cause, but somehow his style worked. One instrumental supporter was Dr. Bristol Foster, former director of the Royal BC Museum and founding director of the BC Ecological Reserves program. Dr. Foster was trying to land a party of naturalists on S'Gang Gwaay Llanagaay (Anthony Island) when he and his party were met by a barrage of rocks. "Ghin was hurling rocks at my tour group and telling us all to go away," Bristol recalls, laughing. "We'll give you one of our women in exchange for peaceful entry," Bristol offered jokingly. Peace was reached and no one was disappointed.

I too was challenged, not by Ghin, but by a close friend of his, Freddy Yeltatzie. Thinking back on this, the test may have come from Ghindigin himself. Freddy Yeltatzie was a mountain of a Haida man who had spent the better part of his adult life pumping iron behind bars. He was a living legend in BC's correctional institutions; some say he once pried open the bars of a prison cell with his bare hands. Freddy, a lifelong friend of Ghin's, was paroled just about the time we started the Moresby campaign. He must have resented Ghin working closely with a "Yatz-Haida," a white man, because shortly after we casually met I received a serious challenge. "Freddy thinks you're an American spy sent here by the CIA," Ghin said to me one day. "He says you've got twenty-four hours to get off the Islands." I didn't respond at first. This was some kind of a test, I thought, and the Haida hate weakness. "So what should I tell him?" Ghin asked at length.

"Tell him he's got twelve hours to come and apologize," I announced foolishly but defiantly. I was a dead man.

"Whoa!" Ghin said, surprised but chuckling. "He's a pretty big Haida, Huck!"

"I don't care," I said. "That's just how I feel about it." Instead of getting me pried apart like the prison bars, my headstrong but admittedly stupid stand somehow proved the right thing to do. So what was this all about, I wondered—some kind of Ghindigin joke, another strange coincidence, or just the Misty Isles and their mysterious ways? Freddy and I never discussed the incident, but became friendly acquaintances and eventually brothers when his mother, Mary Swanson, adopted me into his family some years later.

Ghin wasn't the only one setting challenges in those early years. The Islands Protection Society issued a manifesto of its own—*About Time for an Island* was our first publication—a bold, precedent-setting challenge to the status quo of resource extraction on Haida Gwaii. It raised hackles, but also drew in more supporters. Cartoon work in the magazine by Bob Dalgleish helped Islanders find humour in the serious issues we raised and reflected well the light-hearted spirit of the magazine's creators. One particular cartoon took aim at Parks Canada's plans to "create the illusion of wilderness" in South Moresby much like the leave strips that hide the logging scars in Pacific Rim National Park.

Our second publication, *All Alone Stone*, named after a small island in the heart of the South Moresby wilderness, had a much more sophisticated look, thanks largely to John Broadhead (locally known as JB), a professional artist who wholeheartedly joined the cause. Bob Dalgleish, feeling increasingly hard-pressed to do all the artwork I requested of him, suggested I meet JB, who he said was a much more accomplished artist than himself. JB was tying trout fishing flies with the colours and flags of various nations and listening to classical jazz when I first met him at his Masset home and studio. "I want to see if trout have any national preferences," he explained to me, only half joking. This guy needs a cause, I thought. I showed him the rough layout for our next IPS publication and asked if he could suggest any ways to make it better. "That wouldn't be too hard to imagine," John said in his typically soft-spoken but wry way.

And so it was that one of South Moresby's major players found himself not so much drawn but drawing his way into the issue. With the same meticulous attention to detail he showed in his artwork, JB became one of the IPS's most detailed researchers and articulate spokesmen. "Huck, like his namesake Huckleberry Finn, has a way of getting people to whitewash his fences for him," John Broadhead once wrote in the *QCI Senior Citizens' Journal*. But if he felt duped it was knowingly so; more than any persuasion on my part, it was the logging-related destruction of JB's favourite fly-fishing streams that really set the hook for his engagement. The issues Ghin and I raised were not academic in John's eyes. He had witnessed the ravaged landscape battleground on Graham Island and could imagine all too well that the war in South Moresby was real.

John not only joined the cause and has stuck with it to this very day, he allowed me to renovate a small chicken coop in his Masset backyard to use as a temporary residence. He even let me run a wire from his art studio stereo system so I could enjoy whatever classical music he was listening to in his living room in my little hut. The coop was only 1.5 metres wide and 2.5 metres long—just big enough for a bed, a small writing table and a tiny airtight stove to ward off the damp chill from Masset Inlet, just a stone's throw away through a cedar grove. Had any logging industry PR people seen my humble abode in those years, they might have thought twice about calling the IPS a well-funded lobby group.

JB had a special way with people that drew them in. Years later, when asked to reflect on the contributions to the cause from some of South Moresby's key players, Ghindigin said of JB, "I guess he's the one who blew in their ears."

Word of the Moresby struggle was already piquing the interest of the press and bringing unexpected support from far afield. The Pacific Seabird Group became the first international organization to lend its unconditional support to the cause, although I still have no idea how they even heard about it. I had not envisioned the need for an international, or even national, campaign. Surely, I thought—naively—once an environmental impact assessment is carried out and the BC government sees the world-class wildlife and recreational values of South Moresby, they will take prudent measures to protect it. I couldn't have been more mistaken. A letter from an Eastern supporter proved a more accurate prediction: "Congratulations on your South Moresby stand! Don't expect the government to move quickly on this—it may take decades. Don't give up the fight!"

But by 1977, just as the Moresby campaign was gaining momentum, the Islands Protection Society was overwhelmed by a more pressing issue: the proposal to make Kitimat, BC, a superport for Alaskan and overseas crude oil. Alaska supertankers were already plying the west coast waters of Haida Gwaii between Valdez, Alaska, and Washington State. To bring additional tankers through Dixon Entrance and Hecate Strait, destined for a new port in Kitimat, would put Haida Gwaii at the busy interchange of some of the world's heaviest oil-tanker traffic with staggering potential for spills in some of the world's richest marine waters. The IPS suddenly found itself allied with other Indigenous nations and commercial fishers who organized a blockade of oil port proponents and of government officials taking a promotional tour aboard BC Ferries to Kitimat.

We also found ourselves cutting records, making posters and appearing on national television. Randy Low and Sue Leonard, both IPS supporters and exceptionally talented musicians, recorded an anti-supertanker song at Vancouver's Little Mountain Sound recording studios. I was in Vancouver at the time getting immunization shots for a trip I was planning to South America when I suddenly found myself before the bright lights of CBC Television being interviewed about the Kitimat oil port. The reaction I was having to the typhoid, polio and tetanus booster shots combined with the lights of the TV studio made for a very effective, teary-eyed interview. When the Kitimat Oil Ports Inquiry was set up to receive public input, the IPS was awarded "intervener" status with funding by the federal government, and it at once became more legitimized and better organized. We opened an office in a former private home in Masset and started an extensive intertidal inventory to get pre-spill data for future oil-spill litigation. I was appointed director of the project and enjoyed the distinctly satisfying feeling that the IPS had finally made it into the big time. I had always wanted to see our grassroots eco-group be taken seriously, both on and off the Islands, and now it was operating in the big leagues. It had come of age.

Oscar Wilde wrote that "when the gods wish to punish us they answer our prayers." By 1978 the IPS office had become a lightning rod for every issue under the sun. People brought us dead birds fried on power lines, cats run over by cars and oil globs washing in on the Great North Beach. Abalone were being seriously overfished, geoducks were the next to go, beach buggies were destroying the dunes near Rose Spit, and some of the world's most magnificent cedar trees were being cut down at the head of Masset Inlet. The litany of environmental concerns on Haida Gwaii seemed endless and overwhelming—and then there were the global concerns of overpopulation, carbon emissions, tropical deforestation, biodiversity loss and others. The mountains of mail we received on these issues from concerned NGOs worldwide was enough to cause sleepless nights and hair loss, if not cancer and suicidal depression. One day I couldn't take it anymore. With my desk covered in the latest delivery of oil globs from North Beach, I closed the office and walked down to the Masset fuelling docks for some fresh air. This was even more depressing, with oil and gas floating on the water surface. A few drunks under the dock were smashing beer bottles on the rocks; they invited me to join them, and why the hell not, I thought. The drunken babble was mindless; just what I needed. The only issue for my drinking buddies was killing the damn "beavers" as they poked their heads up out of the water. There were no beavers there, of course; this was ocean water. The ebbing tide was gradually exposing intertidal rocks that, with the right frame of mind induced by an alcohol-laced bloodstream, might be interpreted as beavers. "Look, there's another one! Kill the damn thing," my drinking buddies implored. A few beers, and a number of dead "beavers" later, and I felt whole again. It's amazing how a simple human endeavour can ground one back to reality. A good no-deposit-no-return romp on the wild side was the medicine I needed to rededicate myself to the cause. A few days later I organized a glass cleanup along the beach.

If there was a casualty of the IPS's more universal approach to issues, it was the very issue that brought us together in the first place. Ghin and I had to keep pushing South Moresby lest it become lost in the morass. We had managed to get the NDP government in Victoria to commit to forming the first of what would become four government-appointed planning teams. The Environment and Land Use Committee (ELUC) Secretariat was the first fancy title for a government ploy designed to buy time. We saw these for what they were—government attempts to stonewall public concern and opposition while logging carried on with business as usual. We took part in this process only because it gave us access to information we wouldn't otherwise have had, and it made us appear reasonable in the eyes of government officials and the public. But in our heart of hearts we knew, as did the BC government, that planning teams would never resolve the Moresby issue. Our proposal was too radical. Never before in BC history had a single hectare of a tree farm licence been set aside for higher use. The industry representative was right when he told Ghin and me, "It'll never happen. You guys are just pissing into the wind."

And Ghin also had it right when he responded, "Yes, but if we piss there long enough, the wind will change." And it did.

CHAPTER V

The Master Abstractor
and the Prime Minister

t was mid-May 1967 and David Phillips, the self-proclaimed Master Abstractor, had waited just about long enough. Dressed in a green tweed suit for which he'd had eight fittings, Master Phillips had just spent three horribly dull days stowed away in a paint locker aboard a Greek freighter bound for China. The freighter was loading grain at the Prince Rupert grain elevators, where railcar loads of Canada's golden cargo had been hauled in from the Prairies. One can listen to the waterfall sound of grain being loaded for only so long and still retain some semblance of sanity. Disembarking in frustration, David had come to the decision that an aristocratic gentleman like himself should henceforth travel in style. Thirty years later, when he did finally get to China, he flew first class.

But these were leaner times, and David had to borrow $15 for a float plane flight to Masset. It was the closest to China he'd ever been since leaving his Toronto home and stowing away on the ship, and he was determined to get closer yet. He loaded a trunk with his tuxedo, fine English bone china, linen tablecloths, the best silverware settings, and cream-coloured gentleman's gloves and set off from Masset harbour by rowboat into the setting sun. A salmon trawler in a deadly tide rip off Shag Rock rescued him. "I didn't know what it was," the Torontonian said of the tide rip. He was only fifty-six hundred nautical miles short of his goal and barely outside Old Massett village.

David settled into the Graham Island communities, fitting in well among other eccentrics and bringing his considerable culinary skills and distinguished taste to many local functions. It wasn't until 1973 that the Master Abstractor, as he dubbed himself, ran into difficulties and notoriety.

David had been hired to lead a Canada Works program to clean up garbage along Graham Island's newly completed highway. A two-plank elevated road just wide enough for one car at a time had been the historical transportation link between Skidegate and Masset. Now an all-weather sealed surface had suddenly brought the Islands into the twentieth century along with its associated consequences: speed, head-on collisions and highway litter. David was determined to deal with the latter. He cleared a ten-mile stretch of roadside by putting the trash directly in the centre of the highway: beer bottles, insulation, plastic bags, blown-out tires, whatever. "I'd look back occasionally and see a sea of garbage on the road," David later commented proudly of his handiwork. Motorists and the RCMP saw things differently. There was already an Island-wide warrant for his arrest by the time he bunked down in Queen Charlotte City for the night.

Like Alice entering Wonderland, things became "curiouser and curiouser" for David the next morning. He found himself in Skidegate Landing sitting amid chopped-down cherry trees in full bloom. The small orchard was being cut down to make a playground for children. For David, suddenly every petal of every blossom became the crying face of an abused child. Many of the faces were Southeast Asian, David said. The Vietnam War was in its full napalm glory days so David deduced that the real problem was America, with its Southeast Asian arm of imperialism. He grew angry and looked for someone to help do something about the situation. On the right-hand side of the Skidegate Landing dock was a boat called *Millionaire*, and on the other side a boat called *Survival*. Through David's eyes, the *Millionaire* boat embodied the USA, and the *Survival* boat was the Third World—and it was leaving dock. David stopped a passerby "as a witness before God" and declared war. He headed straight for Masset to inform the commanding officer of the Canadian Forces Station that World War III had begun. Halfway up-Island, it struck David that he wasn't properly attired for such a historic undertaking, so he stopped in the little community of Port Clements at the head of Masset Inlet to get outfitted at a friend's house as an officer. Now fully fitted with a captain's hat and a double-breasted officer's coat, he tore a picket from the Mayer farm fence, stuck it through an old car's rusted-out headlight socket for a sword and charged north.

Captain David arrived in Masset with a sword of righteousness that could have rivalled Archangel Michael's. He paused at his home a moment to collect himself and fill his pack with seashells and fine linen napkins so he could present himself properly. At the reviewing stand in front of the CFS Masset headquarters, he propped up his fence-picket lance and draped his cream-coloured cloth glove atop it "to let them know they were dealing with an officer and a gentleman." He then proceeded directly to the base hospital and presented himself.

"I am Captain Master Abstractor David Lawrence Phillips, on loan to the United Nations," he told the head nurse. "I report to you whole and uninjured; I have all my wits about me." The nurse appeared dumbfounded as David continued. "I'll be in the officer's lounge. Would you please have your United Nations representative attend to me?"

The Canadian Forces Station in Masset in 1973 was no idle posting. This was still the height of the Cold War, and this base was the intelligence centre for a huge radar dish on North Beach that tracked and monitored all Soviet nuclear subs in the North Pacific. CFS Masset was a vital strategic link in America's NORAD Distant Early Warning System, but something as simple as a request for the military base's UN representative was enough to throw the whole system into disarray. As David himself said, "The military doesn't work well when it doesn't understand the line of command or the nature of the enemy."

Captain Master Abstractor was pushing the system to the max. In the officer lounge, he wrote orders in the daybook dismissing all officers and reassigning them to the S'eegay—Masset's notorious wino hangout. Captain Phillips then laid out his seashells and fine linens "to set the proper ambience and to feel at home." Not receiving any response to his distinguished presence, he grabbed a phone and reamed out the top brass. "I'm not used to waiting around," he growled. Shortly thereafter, a six-foot-eight-inch military police officer filled the doorway and asked David for his authority. The base had gone on Red Alert; the whole NORAD system may have gone on Red Alert. "They took me seriously," David said.

With an uncanny comprehension of the military mind, Captain Master Abstractor adopted its fundamental teaching that the best defence is a good offence and confronted the imposing military police officer. "If you're going to talk to me like that, I'm leaving," David snapped convincingly. The burly MP quietly stepped aside while David gathered his seashells and fine linens and with an air of indignation marched out the door.

Word of the intrusion had now spread throughout the base, but some saw the developing drama less as a threat to "free world" security than as comic theatre. A dozen French Canadian solders sipping beer on a balcony applauded David as he paraded across the parking lot. "I felt like Montgomery coming out of North Africa," David said later.

Walking toward the boundary between the Village of Masset and the CFS base, David now witnessed a civilian authority versus military authority standoff. An RCMP squad car came peeling out of police headquarters while a military police vehicle raced across the base, meeting bumper to bumper with the Mounties, who were, as always, determined to get their man. While the RCMP patrol car slowly pushed the military police car back to its proper side of the jurisdictional line, the ensuing standoff allowed David to quietly slip into the S'eegay pub and out the back door. But the noose of the law was closing in. The RCMP, still furious over the previous day's highway obstructions, were in hot pursuit.

David was now fleeing the law in bare feet. It wasn't part of any escape strategy; he'd simply forgotten where he left his shoes. He wandered over to Robin Brown's house and then along the beach of Masset Inlet to Main Street, where he stopped to have tea with Clarence Martin, a respected senior in the community. Finishing tea, he borrowed $5 and went next door to Delmas Co-op to pay half his annual membership fee—paid to Co-op #165, Middle Hill Hatchery, David's holding company. He walked out the front door into the waiting arms of the RCMP, who flew him to Prince Rupert for three days of "psych containment" and later sent him the bill for the services.

The gallivanting days of Captain Master Abstractor had come to a sudden ignoble end, and David discovered for himself the

David Lawrence Phillips, Master Abstractor and master chef, welcomes guests to a typical beggar's banquet at his Copper Beech House home featuring Haida Gwaii baked halibut, Dungeness crab and razor clam fritters.

consequences of stepping outside society's definition of the straight and narrow. A doctor in Prince Rupert had David committed to an obligatory one-month term at Essondale mental institution in Coquitlam, BC. He was put on a tranquilizing therapy cocktail of six to nine drugs, then gradually withdrawn from them a few days at a time to measure his recovery from drug withdrawal. "It was psycho-pharmacology at its worst," said David. "You have to be able to go into a psychotic state to give them an opportunity to analyze your madness so they can begin to program your wellness." David short-circuited the system. He was told that within his institutionalized thirty-day term he would have to do a project to demonstrate his wellness. David loved projects. He organized everyone in his craft class to get dressed up in suits and dresses "like respectable people." He called in the media and had all the inmates gather on the steps of the administration building with banners and placards to stage a protest against electroshock therapy.

A nearly brain-dead victim of this treatment was held up to the press as living evidence of the barbaric practice. The patients began a hunger strike in protest and David was shipped back to Masset, the town he forever after called "Essondale West," well before his term of care was up. A dozen years later David ran for mayor of Masset and swept 25 per cent of the vote. In 1976, just three years after his romp with the CFS, the RCMP and Essondale Mental Institution, he found himself in charge of organizing the first visit in history to Haida Gwaii by a Canadian prime minister. He was, after all, a master abstractor.

Never one to mince words or gestures, Pierre Trudeau had created a bit of a stir in the early 1970s with his inference that there was no such thing as aboriginal title, and if there ever was, it was extinguished at the time of confederation. First Nations across Canada were in an uproar over the statement, and their wrath had the potential to unseat a few Liberals in key ridings. Paramount among these was the largely Indigenous riding of Skeena, which includes the Queen Charlotte Islands, and which happened to be the riding of the feisty Iona Campagnolo, the anointed president of the Liberal Party later destined to become the lieutenant-governor of British Columbia. Campagnolo had been trying for some time to get the prime minister into her riding to smooth ruffled feathers, but prime ministers from Quebec are usually as loath to cross the Rockies as are the eastern subspecies of the beaver. Trudeau himself would later show his love for the West by flipping the bird to his loyal subjects from the window of a touring railcar. That little gesture may have done more to fan the flames of a Western separatist movement than any political differences.

An invitation to address the United Nations Habitat Conference in Vancouver in 1976 offered Trudeau the global stage he loved so much, and it provided Campagnolo the opportunity she needed to stage an event in her riding. Masters of the staged public spectacle, the Liberals always know how to put together great events to meet their political agenda. Campagnolo was no slouch in this regard, and she conspired with her strategists to find the most suitable venue.

The Queen Charlotte Islands Museum Society had been working for decades to raise funds for a new building to showcase the Islands' extraordinary natural and cultural heritage. The opening of the museum was now rushed to coincide with Trudeau's visit to British Columbia.

David Lawrence Phillips, the Master Abstractor, just happened to find himself on the board of directors of the museum society at that fateful moment in history, and he spun his magic to further entice the Trudeaus to extend their visit to the Misty Isles. Engaging the talents of the QCI Artisans Guild, he created an intriguing and uniquely Islands invitation. A carved red cedar box was filled with Islands treasures: sand dollars and scallop shells, photos of alluring scenery, fresh cedar boughs, an argillite Haida carving and an anthology of Islands music. The box was strapped with a custom-made miniature crowbar and shipped to Iona Campagnolo, who personally escorted it to 24 Sussex Drive for a luncheon engagement with Margaret Trudeau. As she pried open the magic box, the Vancouver-born wife of the prime minister was instantly transported back to her West Coast homeland and the decision was made, then and there, to turn Pierre's museum-opening function into a full family weekend.

The wheels began to turn quickly now. David frantically set up the itinerary and accommodations while Campagnolo's office staff made inquiries of their own. Wouldn't it be wonderful and politically astute, they reasoned, to have the prime minister meet with Indigenous leaders at the location of the first contact between Europeans and First Nations on the West Coast of Canada? The location, of course, would be Haida Gwaii, just offshore from the old village site of Kiusta. Here, in 1774, Spanish explorer Juan Perez accidentally came upon the archipelago when a storm blew his ship toward an unknown shore. Perez had been commissioned by the Spanish viceroy in San Blas, Mexico, to sail as far north as Sitka, Alaska, to lay claim to the entire Pacific coast before another Vitus Bering, or any other Russian expansionist, crowded in on these lands granted to Spain by the Pope. Perez's voyage had been miserably rough and so blown off course that the crew had not spotted land north of Monterey, California. The northwestern extension of Haida Gwaii reaches out into the north Pacific like a great arm and catches all manner of flotsam, jetsam and lost European explorers. And so it was in July 1774, after more than twelve thousand years of continuous occupation by the Indigenous peoples, that Haida Gwaii was officially "discovered."

Perez engaged with the Haida in some token trade, noted the latitudinal bearings in his ship's journal and pulled anchor just as another North Pacific gale started brewing to blow him back down the coast. The intrepid explorer died at sea in 1775 on another northern journey. Two centuries later, the Liberals were looking for a somewhat different outcome.

"If the weather should force us to stay overnight at Kiusta, what's the best accommodation available?" a spokesperson from Campagnolo's Ottawa office asked the Massett Band Council by phone.

"That would be Huckleberry's house," they joked.

"Fine, book that," came the response. It is not always easy for an Ottawa-based bureaucrat to realize that a site abandoned for more than a century and grown over in rainforest can still be listed as a place name on a map. Huckleberry House had to be one of those trendy titles for some new boutique hotel out there in Lotus Land, they must have assured themselves.

David Phillips sent word to me at Lepas Bay that the prime minister and his family would soon be joining me for dinner. It had to be a joke, I thought. While I carried on with my usual daily functions of gardening and clam digging, beachcombing, showering and laundering, the Islands' communities were abuzz in preparation for the big day. Finishing touches were going on at the museum for the ribbon-cutting ceremony. The Canadian Forces Station soldiers were rehearsing their drills for a prime ministerial review and beefing up security to keep out any more Captain Master Abstractors. They needn't have bothered, as they were simply a sideshow; David was already running the circus.

David had arranged for a small log house along the lovely Tlell River to be the Haida Gwaii version of 24 Sussex Drive for the Trudeaus' visit. He borrowed the finest antique furnishings from all over the Islands to create the ambience of the pre-war era, a sort of understated elegance where imported English bone-china tea settings were laid out on fine Irish linen, and moon snails, beachcombed from the tide line, served as candy trays. Only a few staunch NDPers refused to loan their family heirlooms for the visit of the great rose-in-the-teeth Liberal.

The Trudeaus—Pierre, Margaret and their young boys Justin, Alexandre (Sacha) and Michel—were completely charmed and totally chilled by Tlell. They spent the evening and night hunkered down under a bed of comforters as David's impeccably detailed preparations had left one item unattended: the propane heater didn't work—a minor oversight.

The next day dawned gloomy but the Trudeaus were in good spirits, horseback riding and hiking through the lush, moss-draped countryside for which Tlell is legendary. After a delightful brunch they flew aboard a Ministry of Transport Sikorsky helicopter low over the east coast beaches of Naikoon Provincial Park, then north along Dixon Entrance to Masset. On landing in the ball field in front of

CFS Masset, Trudeau performed his one official function, reviewing the troops and the equally regimented Boy Scouts and Girl Guides. Two dozen long-stemmed red roses were presented to Margaret before the official party was whisked off by car to Old Massett to meet the Haida chiefs and elders. The Sikorsky helicopter caught up with the party in the ball field beside the Ed Jones Haida Museum, and the entire entourage then headed twenty minutes west to the ancient village site of Kiusta for a tour of the archaeological dig and totem poles, escorted by Nick and Trisha Gessler and Haida summer students.

I've been told that I was named after the Apostle Thomas—"the doubting one," my mom would often remind me—so the possibility of there being any truth to David's message about the prime minister coming for dinner was almost nonexistent. Peter Norris, a good friend of mine with whom I had recently scaled the mountains called the Lions in North Vancouver and kayaked in Mexico's Sea of Cortez, was visiting at the time and we had just finished hand-washing a week's

In May of 1976, after a tour of the surrounding area, the Trudeau family arrives at CFS Masset and Prime Minister Pierre Trudeau disembarks the helicopter holding his seven-month-old son, Michel, while three-year-old Sacha (wearing a toque) chats with Justin, age five. PROJECT KIUSTA PHOTO COURTESY DAVID PHILLIPS

worth of dirty laundry, which we'd strung up in the cabin to dry as the weather was so foul. Having been cooped up much of the day, we put a pot of brown rice on the stove to slowly simmer and headed down the beach for a nice long walk. We were both dressed in ragged, throwaway clothes, having laundered everything better, and Peter actually had the entire crotch ripped out of the old shorts he wore. We were both joking about how embarrassing it would be if the prime minister actually did come when suddenly we heard the deep and unmistakable thump-thump-thump sound of a large helicopter's rotary blades coming over the treetops. We could only start laughing; it was too absurd.

It was late in the day and the Trudeau family were already tired when they finished their tour of the ancient Kiusta Village site. David had promised the Haida students working at Project Kiusta a ride in the helicopter to Lepas Bay from where they could return by trail. I was told that after Pierre Trudeau looked at David and said wearily, "What next?" he heard Isabel Adams, one of the Haida archaeology students, plead, "Come on, David, you promised."

David Phillips (with basket, centre) leads the "picnic on the beach" procession to Lepas Bay with MP Iona Campagnolo (far left), Prime Minister Pierre Trudeau (in beret, centre left) and Haida students Billy Bedard (in toque, left) and Oliver Bell (foreground, right), who were working the Project Kiusta archaeology dig.
PROJECT KIUSTA PHOTO COURTESY DAVID PHILLIPS

Far too many people disembarked from the MOT chopper that evening. The first view I had from the far end of the beach was the security detail running out to check the alder grove along the shore, either as a security measure or to relieve themselves—it was hard to decipher which from my vantage point. Next came the Master Abstractor and the prime minister in his trademark beret; both were laden with baskets of buns and raw Dungeness crab, garden salad and clam fritter batter. Iona Campagnolo emerged dressed in the *de rigueur* "Liberal red" and a gaggle of kids from Kiusta—Billy Bedard, Oliver Bell, Isabel Adams and others—filled out the procession along with Margaret, the Trudeau children and a small press corps.

One look inside the rustic driftwood cabin with wet, dripping clothes hanging everywhere was enough to tell even a Miss Manners detractor that nobody was expecting company. Pierre Trudeau was walking back down the beach toward me as I approached the cabin site. "I'm terribly sorry we've barged in on you like this," he apologized while offering his hand in greeting. "Obviously we weren't expected."

"It's no big deal," I assured him nonchalantly. "People drop in unexpectedly all the time." A warm smile came over the prime minister's face. He adjusted his beret and accompanied Peter and me back to the cabin. We chatted aimlessly as we went. Was this a botch-up by his handlers? A public moment with no official expectations? A comedy of errors in an overscripted play? Trudeau seemed to love it, and when I offered to take him on a short hike to Lookout Point, one of my favourite places, he enthusiastically agreed.

The security service and press corps tried to follow. "I'd prefer not to have this place sensationalized in the press," I said, and Trudeau caught my sentiment.

"We'd like to walk alone," he told his entourage and the seas slowly parted. A few bodyguards looked concerned, but the prime minister reassured them with the words, "I'll be fine. We'll be back shortly."

I'd never seen Lepas Bay so dreary. The sky was overcast and darkening, the tide was well out and the great expanse of normally glistening white sand was covered in the putrefying sludge of rotting seaweed. For Trudeau, however, this was paradise. "What's the name of this island here?" he asked of the inner island connected to the beach at low tide.

"No name," I replied.

"How about the island farther out?"

"No name also," I said. Trudeau couldn't imagine a place so wild that the most prominent geographic features were still nameless. "Do you think they should be named after prime ministers?" I chided.

He laughed. "Most certainly not."

As we worked our way out over large, slippery beach boulders, I couldn't help but admire this very personable, unpretentious man who just happened to be a head of state, despite my issues with some of his policies. I liked him from the start for two very down-to-earth stands of his early administration: "There's no place for the state in the bedrooms of the nation" and his ban on pay toilets. Like most Canadians who either loved his style and politics or took deep offence to one or both, I too had disdain for him invoking the War Measures Act nationwide for the kidnapping in Quebec of a British diplomat and the Quebec labour minister. I was also deeply troubled about the increase in oil-tanker

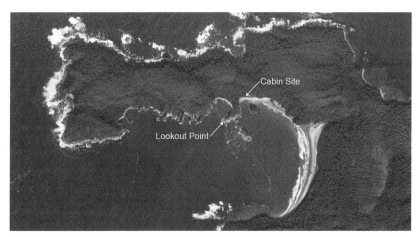

A satellite view of Lepas Bay shows the cabin location and Lookout Point where I took the prime minister for a private chat. MP Iona Campagnolo later referred to our talk as the "Supertanker Summit." GOOGLE EARTH PHOTO

traffic by Alaska supertankers along Canada's Pacific coast, and I couldn't understand why the federal government allowed US single-hulled tankers the right to pass through Canadian waters.

These troubling thoughts were going through my head as we climbed the steep, rocky promontory I had come to know as Lookout Point. "Let me help you," I said, reaching down to Trudeau for the last slippery step before the summit. I pulled him up with one strong jerk and stood there holding his hand firmly as he teetered on the brink of an eighty-foot vertical drop. He looked startled, as if he suddenly understood why security should always be by his side. "Pretty scary, eh?" I said as we gazed down at the huge Pacific breakers exploding on the granite headland below us.

"Stunning!" he replied. "Absolutely stunning!"

Kaindus Koon, the Haida name for Cape Knox, stretched out before us, a spectacular array of high cliffs and lush hanging gardens of coastal vegetation. A Peale's peregrine falcon swept down from its aerie and a bald eagle cried in defiance at our proximity to an eagle's nest where she was incubating her eggs. To the south, the Haida's legendary Tidalang Kun (Newcombe Hill) rose 152 metres above the shoreline and we could see all the way to Lavendar Point.

"That hill to the south is the basalt plug of an ancient eroded volcano," I pointed out. "It's incredible to realize how long this coast has been here, a rare ice-free refugium during the Pleistocene. Life has carried on here uninterrupted longer than almost anywhere else in Canada." My talk was, of course, leading up to the subject of federal regulations on supertankers and the need to protect areas like South Moresby. I was wearing my Islands Protection Society cap in a symbolic sense, and the prime minister was now well aware that he was being lobbied.

We sat chatting together on that narrow promontory for a long time before we realized it was growing dark. "I know a shortcut back through the forest," I offered, and Trudeau followed. We were halfway back to the cabin, walking along a deer path through the lush coastal rainforest, when a bird sang a perfect single note. "What a lovely song," my guest exclaimed, "What bird is that?"

"It's a varied thrush," I answered. "Sit down for a minute and you'll hear it call again." We sat on a fallen log twenty centimetres deep in damp, luxurious moss. All around us was a fairyland forest of moss and lichen and massive trees in a million shades of green. The thrush sang again, in a different note.

"Lovely," he said again as he rose to leave.

"The full range of notes takes five to ten minutes to complete and repeat. Wait awhile," I encouraged the country's busiest man. Neither of us spoke after that; we just sat and listened and listened and listened. The bird's song spoke to the soul, it poured over us like sunshine pours into trees. It seemed nearly dark when we returned to chaos at the cabin. The Sikorsky helicopter had departed for Langara Light Station because they couldn't get radio contact from Lepas Bay. The security agents were alerting Ottawa that the prime minister of Canada was missing on the westernmost extension of the Canadian coast and was last seen with a questionable-looking character named Huckleberry.

The cabin scene was a madhouse: packed with press corps, security men and Project Kiusta kids. Iona Campagnolo was pressed in beside the glowing-red barrel stove frying clam fritters. Her face was flushed the same ruby red as her clothing and she appeared more a character out of Dante's *Inferno* than the cool leader of the Liberal Party that she was. Trudeau observed the chaos with the calm of a war correspondent. He said quietly to anyone willing to listen, "I wish you could have shared that moment with us in the forest."

Ready for the prime minister and American ambassador... "Huckleberry House" on Lepas Bay opens its hobbit-sized door to the world.
RICHARD KRIEGER PHOTO

No one was listening. Everyone was too preoccupied with their personal needs: hunger, warmth and a dry place to hang out until the helicopter returned to rescue them. David, the mastermind behind the "picnic on the beach," was trying to feed the masses in an octagonal driftwood cabin only three metres in diameter. "It's a good thing you had a pot of rice on," he said to me later. Maggie Trudeau was a true sport, sitting out in the drizzle on the beach and trying to get a hot enough fire going with wet driftwood to boil the Dungeness crab. My friend Peter was helping her with the fire tending. She joked about the very relaxed, hang-loose ambience of the scene, but kept sending her young sons, Justin and Sacha, to be with their father while she cuddled baby Michel. Suddenly Peter remembered that the shorts he was wearing had a ripped-out crotch seam, and scurried off, totally embarrassed, in search of safety pins.

The guests were all laughing and cracking crab when the Sikorsky returned. Suddenly everything seemed official again. "Gotta go now," security beckoned authoritatively as the entourage boarded the helicopter.

"Nice bouquet," I said to Margaret as she boarded beside the two dozen roses she'd received earlier in the day from CFS Masset. "Looks like a funeral arrangement," I quipped.

"Oh, do you like it?" she teased back and started tossing roses out the doorway one by one as the helicopter lifted off. My last sight of Pierre and Maggie Trudeau was seeing them wave through a whirl of swirling sand and red roses falling from the heavens. It was somehow a fitting departure for a prime minister who captivated the world with a rose held between his lips and a wife who would soon leave him because she wanted to be "more than a rose in my husband's lapel."

I went back to my quiet, solitary summer on Lepas Bay, but the visit had made waves in Ottawa. My parents in Michigan and I both received letters from Pierre Trudeau saying how much he enjoyed his visit. Iona Campagnolo wrote to say that she had a long and frank discussion with the prime minister about US oil-tanker traffic following what she called our "Supertanker Summit" at Lookout Point. Not only did Pierre Trudeau ban tanker traffic through all coastal waters north of Vancouver Island, he went on to expand the ban to include all offshore oil and gas activity. Decades later, when his oldest son Justin became prime minister, he too pledged to put Dixon Entrance, Hecate Strait and Queen Charlotte Sound off limits to tanker traffic.

CANADA

PRIME MINISTER · PREMIER MINISTRE

O T T A W A (K1A OA2)
August 10, 1976

Dear "Huckleberry":

        Margaret and I very much enjoyed meeting you during our visit to the Kiusta ruins and the beach at Lepas Bay. The scenery was magnificent, the dinner was delicious and the company was pleasant indeed. It was a memorable afternoon and we thank you for your hospitality.

                        Yours sincerely,

Mr. Tom Henley
    c/o Mr. David Phillips
    Queen Charlotte City
    Queen Charlotte Islands, B.C.

P.S. I received a nice letter from your parents a few weeks ago. I was very glad to know them, as I was to know you.

Prime Minister Pierre Trudeau sent this personal letter to me shortly after his visit to Lepas Bay in May of 1976. The handwritten note says "P.S. I received a nice letter from your parents a few weeks ago. I was very glad to know them, as I was to know you."

It was apparently at a formal diplomatic function in Ottawa in 1976 that the Trudeaus encouraged Thomas Enders, United States ambassador to Canada, to book a stay at Huckleberry House. And so it was, the following summer, that the Master Abstractor was called on again to spin his uniquely absurd magic and put together another high-level tour.

Thomas Enders was no lightweight American diplomat sent off to the north woods in Canada. He was a hard-core Nixon administration man who had played a forceful hand in America's illegal and undeclared war in Indochina. These were critical times in US–Canadian relations, with threats of Arab oil embargoes and the security issues surrounding moving Alaskan crude through Canadian waters. Enders was the man the Nixon administration could count on to get the job done. Why the prime minister of Canada felt that Enders needed a three-day stay at Huckleberry House, the hippie shack of an American war objector, was anyone's guess, but Trudeau was noted for his pranks and sense of humour.

The official delegation was made up of five people: US Ambassador Thomas Enders and his wife Gaetana; Hobart Luppi, consul general of the Unites States in Vancouver; Ghindigin, interpreter and host for the Haida Nation; and David Lawrence Phillips, Master Abstractor, impresario and other self-proclaimed titles. The RCMP were just about the last to know what was going on, and when they found out, they tried to stop it.

I had hiked over the Kiusta trail one afternoon to dig littleneck clams for dinner when I could have sworn I heard a float plane land on Lepas Bay. I returned at once but there was no sign of any aircraft. Footprints led up from the waterline of the rising tide to my cabin and back down to the beach. It remained a mystery to me until the Enderses eventually arrived and explained how the US embassy had received an emergency message from RCMP security: "Huckleberry House is a hippie shack unfit for human occupation." The RCMP had used taxpayers' money for that little gem of intelligence while the Enderses, once they arrived, proclaimed my cabin to be "one of the most charming places" they'd ever stayed at in the world.

It was June 1977 when the high-level diplomatic mission arrived on Lepas Bay via the Kiusta trail. The tide was high when the dignitaries arrived, so it was well after dark before they could get around the cliff at low tide to reach my cabin. Ghindigin helped ease the hours of waiting with a beach fire and a gallon of cheap Calona red wine. He slung it over one shoulder to take a swig then passed it to the American ambassador, a wine connoisseur who had a private cellar of some of the world's finest vintages. Thomas declined, but his petite and sophisticated wife, who wafted the scent of a fine Italian perfume, took the bottle and a good guzzle without wiping the rim. Ghindigin was impressed, and he and Gaetana became instant soulmates, kicking back most of the gallon before the tide dropped.

Consul General Hobart Luppi arrived on crutches and struggled over the kilometre-long trail through the forest and down the long, sandy beach with the determination of a soldier storming Normandy.

He was given a fishnet and driftwood cot on the main floor to bunk down on once the party reached the cabin for the night. The Enderses had the honour of the half-loft directly above him. The loft could only be reached by negotiating the wobbly teakwood and rope ship's ladder that had washed in from a Chinese junk. Beside the double foam pad that was to be the Enderses' deluxe suite for two nights, I had placed a slab of driftwood as an end table. It was adorned with a glass kerosene lamp, a small vase of wildflowers and two purple olive snail shells in a simulated mating position. Ghindigin and I retired to tents to give the foreign

The day I finished building a sleeping loft in my Lepas Bay cabin I was amazed to find a teakwood and rope ladder from a Chinese junk washed in on the beach with just enough rungs to reach the loft. RICHARD KRIEGER PHOTO

diplomats the privacy of the cabin. We could hear them laughing all night at the utter absurdity of their predicament. Pierre Trudeau must have been having some chuckles back in Ottawa himself knowing where the Enderses were spending two nights.

Thomas Enders was an imposing man, a six-foot-ten Connecticut Yankee who could have played for the NBA rather than the Nixon and Reagan teams. He carried a large black briefcase that he never let out of his sight. Ghindigin suspected it might be a concealed automatic weapon. We never asked him what was in the bag, but he appeared to guard it with his life. One day he nearly fell from a steep ridge we were climbing to get to the north shore of Cape Knox, but even as he was struggling for a handhold he wouldn't let me assist him by taking that black bag. He spoke of security and seemed to feel vulnerable with us—Ghindigin, David and me—with no body-guard at his side. I told him that security for me was knowing where to get abalone, octopus and clams and which wild plants to eat. "That's interesting," Enders responded. "For me security is turning the switch to start my car and feeling relieved I haven't triggered my own bomb." I felt sorry for him after that.

Ghindigin has a disarming way with words. We were all sitting around one evening enjoying one of David's masterful clam fritter concoctions when Ghindigin blurted out in his matter-of-fact style, "Well, I guess America's on its way downhill now."

Enders—the blunt-spoken conservative graduate from Harvard and Yale, nearly choked on his dinner. "What do you mean by that?" he challenged. Ghindigin cited America's loss of the Vietnam War, the relinquishing of economic power to Japan and Germany, and inner-city decay. Enders wanted none of it; he was dipped and dyed red, white and blue.

We ate as much food from the sea as we could muster and never missed an opportunity to raise the issue of US oil-tanker traffic. The new proposal to make Kitimat a superport for Alaskan and overseas crude was still in the works, and Thomas Enders was the highest-level American ear we were going to find in Canada. There was method to our madness, and the Enderses' departure from Lepas Bay on day three made us seem like moderates compared to the heavy lobby they got from Greenpeace's flagship the *Rainbow Warrior* that had arranged to transport the US delegation from Kiusta to Masset. Waiting at the dock in Masset was Wilfred Penker, an Austrian immigrant to the Islands who carved huge, bizarre cedar masks. Wilfred was part of a guerrilla theatre skit depicting sea creatures dying in a massive oil spill. Gaetana was truly frightened by the episode, while Thomas clutched his black bag tighter than ever. It was all spontaneous theatre, though it must have appeared well orchestrated to the Enderses and a strange foreshadowing of things yet to come—the Exxon Valdez oil spill in Alaska.

I never saw the Enderses after their three-day visit, though I did receive thank-you letters and Christmas cards for several years after. Ghindigin and his sons Gwaai and Jaalen, along with his spouse Jenny Nelson, had a pleasant dinner at the US embassy with the Enderses during an Ottawa visit.

For me, on Lepas Bay, the visit was another phantom experience. Like Margaret Trudeau's roses wafting down from the sky, Gaetana's fine Italian perfume masked the usually smelly outhouse for days after she left. These were strange times when unlikely lives crossed paths and reverberations of those passing connections were felt for years to come.

The Trudeau visit had created a conflict for me with a person I didn't even know. Dorothy Richardson, the matriarch of Tlell's oldest homesteading family, was outraged that a Liberal prime minister would shun lifelong Islanders and Liberals to dine with "some immigrant hippie on the West Coast." She had every right to feel slighted; I didn't blame her.

Some months after the Trudeau visit I knocked on her door. "Are you Dorothy Richardson?" I asked politely.

"Why, yes," she said, surprised.

"Hi. I'm Huckleberry and I hear there are some hard feelings."

"Please come in, dear, and have some tea and cookies," she said warmly, but was obviously taken aback by my approach. We never touched on the sensitive subject then or any time after.

Not long after their visit, Maggie Trudeau was grabbing more international headlines than her husband. Tired of playing second fiddle as the obedient wife of the prime minister, she started acting her almost-twenty-nine-years-younger age in trendy hot spots, hobnobbing with the likes of Mick Jagger at Studio 54 in New York.

I recall a six-month winter sojourn I made to South America where I always received the same response to friendly chit-chat that began with "Where do you come from?"

"I come from Canada," I would reply. Even answering the question in Spanish didn't calm the ensuing confusion over the word *Canada,* followed by a pleased look of comprehension. "Ah, Canada, *entiendo* (I understand)—Maggie Trudeau and Mick Jagger!"

The last word about the Trudeau visit didn't reach me until twenty years later when I happened upon the Redheads, the light-station keepers at Race Rocks, just outside Victoria. They had been the lightkeepers at Langara Light Station during the time of the Trudeaus' visit and had been drawn into the drama of Huckleberry and the missing prime minister when the PM's helicopter flew to their station to notify Ottawa that the prime minister was missing. They were delighted to see me again, and Mrs. Redhead even knitted me a bold black-and-white-striped watch cap with a red-top tassel— just like the painting on the Race Rocks light tower.

"Do you recall telling the prime minister that MOT helicopters were disturbing the falcons at Lepas Bay when they logged training hours?" she asked me.

"Yes—but how could you have known that?"

"Well, shortly after Trudeau's visit to your cabin we received a memo sent out nationwide," she said. She told me it read:

By order of the Office of the Prime Minister, all MOT helicopters are barred from any unwarranted landings on Lepas Bay. Huckleberry believes it disturbs the falcons, and it most certainly disturbs Huckleberry.

—Pierre Elliot Trudeau,
Prime Minister of Canada

CHAPTER VI

Rediscovering

By 1977 the Save South Moresby campaign was starting to gain real momentum, at least with provincial and national conservation groups and a growing number of non-Indigenous people. "Where are the Haida on this issue?" I would often challenge Ghindigin.

"Hell, most of them are stuck in front of their TVs eating Cheezies and wieners. Almost no one goes out on the land anymore," he would reply with frustration. Ghin, on the other hand, was spending more and more of his time food foraging—gathering and drying seaweed, digging clams and cockles, jigging for cod and halibut, trapping crabs and hunting deer. More important to him than living more self-sufficiently, I came to realize, was providing traditional foods to Haida elders who craved it but could no longer get it on their own. Nothing endears you more to elders than bringing them traditional foods and medicines, and in his own quiet way Ghin was building a Haida Nation-wide support base by reminding people what mattered most—sharing, caring and protecting food and medicinal resources.

I too was living largely off the land in the summer months, when I would return to my cabin on Lepas Bay after eight months residing in Masset or Port Clements while working for the IPS. One day, after being totally alone at my cabin for several months, I was surprised to see three figures rounding the headland near the creek and hiking along the broad, sandy beach to my cabin. Ghin, Dan Helmer (Tinker) and John Yeltatzie from Old Massett had all decided to pay me a surprise visit. Nothing was that unusual about the discussions we had over several days as we gathered food from the land and sea and explored abandoned Haida village sites that once supported the highest density of people on Haida Gwaii, but somehow our casual talks planted a seed that didn't take long to germinate.

The Project Kiusta archaeological excavation had drawn to a close, so Haida youth no longer had a program to get them out of town for the summer. Many of these young people told me how much they missed that experience and how lucky I was to be able to return to my cabin on Lepas Bay. Surely there must be a better way to connect kids back to the land, I thought, than having them spend endless hours in excavation pits digging up the clamshells and salmon bones discarded by their ancestors. Although anthropology and archaeology were my fields of study at Michigan State University, I came to realize what a serious white-man obsession excavating ancient human habitation sites tended to be. What if these same Haida kids could bring back a piece of their past so they knew more fully where they'd come from and where they were going?

I recalled my best experiences growing up in Michigan, where the Boy Scout program was the only real outlet I had for my love of the outdoors. Unfortunately, it did not provide a lot of outdoor time; folding the American flag in the church basement and standing at attention while some self-absorbed former Marine drill sergeant barked out orders consumed most of my scouting time. The same paramilitary origins still plague Outward Bound and other outdoor adventure programs that approach nature as a boot camp. What if a new type of outdoor adventure camp could be created that focused on Indigenous peoples' relationships with the land? What if kids were taught to see the outdoors not as a savage wilderness but as a homeland that nourishes their bodies and souls; a landscape they had a responsibility to steward? What if we could stop our obsession with conquering nature long enough for children to rediscover it— be embraced by it?

These were the thoughts that increasingly consumed me when I returned back to town that October. Passionate as I was becoming about this, it didn't take long to enrol others. Masset in 1977, with the dubious distinction of having one of the highest per-capita juvenile crime rates in Canada, was especially receptive to the idea. The Corrections Branch was the first to back a proposal I put together. Jim Fulton, who would go on to become the Member of Parliament for Skeena and later executive director of the David Suzuki Foundation, was the QCI probation officer at the time and he threw his full support behind the proposal. The Office of the BC Attorney General and the federal solicitor general provided three-year pilot project funding, but they wanted the program to be for boys only. I wanted it to be for boys and girls.

I next approached Indian Affairs, and this federal agency also wanted to back the program, but for Indigenous youth only. I wanted it to be a camp for everyone, Indigenous and non-Indigenous youth, both boys and girls, those in trouble with the law or abused as well as those with no apparent issues. This holistic approach meant that Rediscovery, as this project would become, would forever fall through the cracks of specialized funding agencies, but in the end it was also the key to its success and longevity.

It was in the kitchen of Dulcie McCallum, the public health nurse for Haida Village, that we came up with the name "Rediscovery" for the fledgling program. Dulcie would go on to become the first female ombudsperson in BC history. Two other key players were Bev Collinson and Eloise Jones, the legal information counsellors employed by the Haida Counselling & Legal Assistance Society (HCLAS). Eloise would later become David Suzuki's executive assistant. Bev and Eloise were both instrumental in seeing that Rediscovery had a sponsor in HCLAS until it became a society of its own. Given the calibre of people being drawn to this initiative, I felt Rediscovery had real potential in creating a paradigm shift for the way outdoor programs addressed issues of youth in crisis and First Nations cultural identity.

After more than a century of apartheid in British Columbia, we were breaking all the moulds by putting Indigenous and non-Indigenous kids together in the same summer camp to eat together, sleep together, overcome challenges together and make that all-important discovery: "Hey, your dirty socks stink too!" Schools had been integrated in British Columbia only a decade earlier, and segregation was still the norm outside of school hours. Once, when I was asked by the press to sum up the Rediscovery experience in just a few words, I rather cheekily replied, "It's a white residential school without the abuse."

In one of the early Rediscovery camp sessions, a Caucasian boy from one of the Islands' logging camps summed up the attitude of the time when he told the staff on arrival, "If I knew this was going to be a stinking Indian camp, I wouldn't have come here."

Without overhearing any of this, a Haida boy the same age commented, "If you think I'm going to spend two weeks out here with a bunch of Yatz-Haida (white men) 'honkies,' you're crazy!"

"I'm glad you're both here together," I told them privately. "You can share the same two-person tent and two-person kayak for the next two weeks." It took some time to overcome the ingrained prejudice put in these kids' heads from birth by their families and communities, but they became the best of friends in the end. I truly believe that Rediscovery contributed significantly to Haida Gwaii becoming Canada's showcase for integrated First Nations and non-Indigenous communities. The Rediscovery program was even recognized as a global model for reconciliation at a conference in Northern Ireland titled "Peace Building in Chronically Divided Societies."

Over the years there were some political ploys to change Rediscovery. Some born-again members of the community wanted it be become another Bible camp, like so many faith-based youth programs in BC. Others tried to make it an exclusively Haida program, but in the end the original mission statement prevailed and it was Haida elders such as Nonnie Ethel Jones who always put it back on the original path of its mission statement: "Drawing from the strengths of Indigenous cultures and with a love and reverence for the land, Rediscovery aims to help youth of all ages and all cultures discover the world within themselves, the cultural worlds between them and the natural world around them." It was a simplistic, yet all-encompassing mission statement that has guided Rediscovery camps worldwide for nearly forty years.

One of the greatest strengths of the Rediscovery program, one that set it apart from so many others, was the fundamental role Haida elders played. In the first few years, it was difficult convincing elders to take part. Some dismissed Rediscovery as a hippie-back-to-the-land program, while others found the remoteness of the camp too extreme for the needs of elderly people. But once the first bold Haida elders came out to be part of the program they quickly became central to it and forever elevated and legitimized what we were doing. Had it not been for the loving, guiding role played by Haida elders like Ethel Jones, Mary Swanson, Nora Bellis, Alfred and Rose Davidson, Louise Dixon, Adolphus Marks, Rufus White, Lee Edenshaw, Emma Matthews and Grace Dewitt in those early years, Rediscovery would never have become the global model it is.

The elders became Rediscovery's guiding hand, ensuring that protocols were properly conducted, stories correctly told, traditional skills reacquired and Haida youth were instilled with the cultural pride and respect for all living beings their ancestors had. They became such loving grandparents to all the kids in camp that everyone, regardless of ancestry, called them Nonnie and Chini, the Massett dialect Haida words for grandmother and grandfather. Quite often elders brought grandchildren in their care to the camp and in doing so, inadvertently recreated the traditional social order of the Haida extended family. A Rediscovery camp session could have an age range from three to eighty-three with all the complexities of care-giving and social cohesion that required. In the end, the Haida elders provided such a safe and supportive place for participants to confide their feelings and be counselled and encouraged

Elders Nora Bellis, Mary Swanson, and Alfred and Rose Davidson wear their formal regalia to a Rediscovery closing ceremony night to honour the youth attending camp.

in their lives that many kids sought them out in their communities after the summer camp program ended. In this way, the program re-established an important cross-generational bond that had been deliberately broken down in many First Nations communities through the residential school system that tore Indigenous families apart for decades. Rediscovery radically refuted more than a century of forced assimilation.

Every time I'd refer to Rediscovery as a program, Ghindigin would be quick to challenge me. "It's not a 'program,' Huck. These kids are already too programmed—we're trying to deprogram them." He was right, of course, but we were both wrong in thinking that the wild west coast of Haida Gwaii would invite kids to explore it on their own in the way it inspired us. This was the television generation with twenty-minute attention spans—a disconnect with nature that was already decades ahead of the age of digital addictions. Instead of having to hold them back from going too far afield in their wilderness explorations in 1978, we couldn't get them out of their tents. During the all-too-frequent drizzly days in camp, participants would

Guujaaw plays his guitar for children visiting the Rediscovery camp on Lepas Bay. RICHARD KRIEGER PHOTO

huddle together under cover with dirty, wet clothes playing cards and complaining of boredom. Clearly some type of structure was called for. As the second oldest of nine siblings I knew a thing or two about organizing group activities that could cross the gender divide and engage youth of different ages and interests. Years of living off the land had also honed my bush skills enough to share that acquired knowledge and passion with others. Athena George, the eldest daughter of Paul George, who was a founding director of the Western Canada Wilderness Committee, came out to camp as a staff person and brought with her a great range of skills acquired while she worked with Sunship Earth, an outdoor environmental education program in the United States. Dick Wilson from Skidegate, also known as Wanagan (and later Captain Gold), was a senior guide on the program in 1978, along with Shirley Adams. Both brought with them a wealth of knowledge on Haida cultural protocols and history. Wanagan introduced the concept of a thirty-minute quiet time each day at sunset when participants would find their own spirit spot to commune privately with nature. This came to be known as "Wanagan Time"—a

Rediscovery's first staff team: Shirley Adams (left), me (centre) and Dick Wilson (right)—also known as Wanagan and, later, Captain Gold—pose in front of the original camp cookhouse.

A Rediscovery Forest Appreciation workshop is an all-day affair combining lessons with fun. Here I am with four Haida kids (Archie Samuels, Daryl Amos, Wayne York and Wendell Williams) studying a quadrat of the forest floor for micro-diversity. RICHARD KRIEGER PHOTO

Rediscovery kayakers paddle into Ninstints on Red Cod Island during a two-week voyage of discovery.

daily introspection that has been a hallmark of Rediscovery camps to this day.

The beauty of the structure that we eventually brought to camp was that it was humane, not regimented, and it addressed every aspect of a young person's development. We all knew that real growth needed to start with a better understanding of and empowerment of oneself. Wanagan Time, eagle-feather sharing circles around the council fire and opportunities to spend quality time alone during a twenty-four-hour voluntary "solo" in nature and the wilderness were all designed to further self-awareness. Skills acquisition, like learning to kayak for the first time, to hunt for octopus, gather abalone, dig clams, gut a deer, tend an organic garden, light a fire on a rainy day and trek fifty-five kilometres along a wilderness coastline—all were important components of personal development.

The hiking expedition along the coastline and solo experience were especially powerful for personal growth, as both were so challenging—the toughest thing these kids had ever done. The five-day expedition not only served to bond the group, it sometimes exposed

Rediscovery participant Carol Edenshaw helps a fellow camper prepare for a dance with a raven mask carved by her uncle, Guujaaw. RICHARD KRIEGER PHOTO

A banner proclaims the Rediscovery camp on T'aalan Stl'ang (Lepas Bay). Massett elders and hereditary chiefs have granted the program the exclusive use of this bay each summer since 1978. LANGARA FISHING ADVENTURES

With the generous assistance of the Vancouver Foundation, Haida Gwaii Rediscovery was able to commission Guujaaw to build three miniature Haida longhouses for girls, boys and staff at the Rediscovery camp on Lepas Bay.

deep cultural divides. I can recall a personal revelation while hiking down the coast during one of our first camp sessions in 1978. A family of river otters emerging from the sea took all of us by surprise, and while the otters sought protection under a huge boulder, the hikers dropped their backpacks at once. While the Caucasian kids were fumbling through their gear to locate cameras, the Haida kids were running down the beach covering their ears and biting their knuckles. "Slugus, you guys, run! They're Slugus!" they screamed back at us in panic once they reached the safety of the far end of the beach.

The Haida and non-Indigenous youth looked much the same and were dressed the same, but they may as well have been coming from different planets. To the non-Haida kids the otters were cute, cuddly photo subjects. To the Haida kids they were dangerous transformers that could appear as your best friend and lure you into the woods with hypnotic stares and whistles, where you might reappear as a Slugu yourself. Elders had taught their kids to break the spell by

An organic garden, fertilized with seaweed washed up on the beach, provides the Rediscovery camp with healthy fruits and vegetables all summer. Senior guide Danny Stewart is seen harvesting fresh peas and lettuce for a camp dinner.

biting their knuckles to create pain and covering their ears to muffle the alluring whistles. When Slugus appear in human form, the Haida say, they usually try to hide their faces so people don't see their nose whiskers and cover their hands to hide the fur between their fingers. Sitting around a Rediscovery campfire, it was not uncommon for me to notice Haida kids paying very close attention to this type of behaviour and looking for these kinds of features on the person sitting beside them.

Haida Gwaii Rediscovery was not only one of the world's most remote wilderness camps— located eighty kilometres by air

In the mid-1970s, I was in charge of the first-ever eagle nest inventory on South Moresby, where we discovered one of the world's highest nesting densities. The massive Sitka spruce tree I'm resting beside was the average size a tree needed to be to support the two- to three-thousand-kilogram nests. JEFFREY GIBBS PHOTO

The old Haida village of Ninstints on S'Gang Gwaay Llanagaay (Red Cod Island) is now a UNESCO World Heritage Site, but when I first paddled there in 1973 it was still wild—like coming upon ancient Tikal or Angkor Wat before the archaeologists arrived to cut back the jungles. RICHARD KRIEGER PHOTO

Burnaby Narrows, separating Moresby and Burnaby islands, presents one of the richest and most colourful intertidal zones in the Canadian Pacific. Had South Moresby not been saved from clear-cut logging this would have been the site of a log dump and sorting grounds. JAMES THOMPSON PHOTO, OUTER SHORES EXPEDITIONS

Langara Light Station marks the northwesternmost extension of the Canadian coast. It was from here I made my abortive attempt to cross Dixon Entrance to Alaska in 1973 and it was here the Trudeau family's helicopter flew to report that the prime minister was missing and last seen with a character named Huckleberry. LANGARA FISHING ADVENTURES PHOTO

A rainbow shines bright over Lepas Bay (T'aalan Stl'ang) where Haida Gwaii youths have gone for nearly four decades to discover the world within themselves, the cultural worlds between them and the natural world around them through the Rediscovery program.

Pillar Bay takes its name from a conglomerate rock column that stands proud above the rocky tidal zone and is said to have a shaman's bones resting atop it.
GEORGE FISCHER PHOTO, THE WEST COAST FISHING CLUB

T'aalan Stl'ang (Lepas Bay) was my wilderness home from 1973 to 1985. I'd spend the spring, summer and early autumn each year in my small cabin then return to Masset for the winter months. In all of my travels there has never been a place that so fully captured my spirit. LANGARA FISHING ADVENTURES PHOTO

This is the view of Lepas Bay and Lookout Point that the 1976 Trudeau delegation would have seen from their helicopter as they departed from my cabin nestled in the bight behind the inner island. LANGARA FISHING ADVENTURES PHOTO

The design of the Navajo-style octagonal roof I put on my cabin at Lepas Bay allowed me to lift manageable-sized logs in place while being completely on my own for three months. A clear plastic roof cover allowed for a very bright interior, and I used bamboo washed in from Asia and split into strips to protect plastic windows from blowing in during Pacific gales.
RICHARD KRIEGER PHOTO

(*Below*)
I never imagined when I built this little Hobbit House on Lepas Bay that it would one day entertain the prime minister of Canada; house the US ambassador, his wife and the US consul general for two nights; or serve as staff quarters for the Rediscovery program for decades.

Senior guide Alfie Jeffries of Coast Salish descent shows kids the triple mortuary pole at Kiusta, an ancient village site near the Rediscovery camp. The remains of the chief would have been placed in a bent cedar box and entombed in the chamber at the top of a fourth uncarved pole.

The backpacking expedition down the wild west coast of Graham Island is for many Rediscovery participants the toughest thing they have ever done in their lives. That's me on the left, in the late '70s, leading the way for one of several small groups of hikers. Following behind me are an unidentified participant, Ralph Stocker (second from right) and Wendell Williams (right). RICHARD KRIEGER PHOTO

The spectacular Seven Sisters mountains rise nearly three thousand metres above the seventy-hectare property of the Soaring Spirits Camp, where staff are trained every summer in skills needed to operate healthy and safe Rediscovery camps.

RCMP officers deliver an injunction to Haida demonstrators during a peaceful protest over logging on South Moresby Island in November 1985. Four respected elders were the first to be arrested at the blockade site and the dramatic scene was broadcast on national television. ANN E. YOW-DYSON PHOTO, GETTY IMAGES

Now on friendly terms, Mounties and Haida chiefs celebrate the signing of the South Moresby Agreement at Windy Bay in 1988. Following the 1993 Gwaii Haanas Agreement between the Canadian government and the Haida Nation, the entire archipelego and surrounding waters became protected and were renamed the Gwaii Haanas National Park Reserve and Haida Heritage Site.

It's traditional for Haida commemorative poles to have three watchmen figures near the top to symbolically guard over the village, but pole carver Jaalen Edenshaw lent a comic twist to these watchmen figures. He put gumboots on their feet to commemorate the seventy-two Haida who stood in the mud of a logging road facing arrest to save Athlii Gwaii (Lyell Island) from clear-cut logging.

For the first time in over 150 years, a new pole is raised in the Gwaii Haanas wilderness in 2013 to commemorate the twentieth anniversary of a historic agreement signed between the Haida Nation and the Government of Canada.

Lootaas (*Wave Eater*) looked regal as it was paddled through the protected waters of the Inside Passage, making its way north through nine hundred kilometres of the British Columbia coast in 1987.

Guujaaw, beating his drum, leads a paddling song as *Lootaas* arrives at Hartley Bay on the northern BC coast. Bill Reid designed the vests the paddlers are wearing and each puller was responsible for painting their own Haida-styled hat worn for ceremonial arrivals at villages along the way.

Like a scene from an Edward Curtis film, the *Lootaas* paddlers are greeted in 1987 in front of Alert Bay's famous big house, the largest feast house on the coast.

I was completely alone at Muir Glacier, nearing the end of my three-month paddling expedition in 1973, when a Glacier Bay National Monument patrol boat came by and the crew graciously offered to take this photo of me in my kayak with my camera.

My month-long trip to Antarctica aboard the National Geographic *Endeavour* was a dream come true. For me, a lifelong lover of wilderness, this was the world's greatest.

While kayaking in Mexico's Sea of Cortez in the 1980s, my good friend Peter Norris took this photo of me with our dinner catch.

In one of the most extraordinary feats of self-determination I have ever witnessed, the Moken rebuilt homes for over two hundred people within weeks of having two of their villages completely destroyed by the 2004 South Asian tsunami.

After living with a Balinese family for several weeks in the 1970s, I was dressed in a sarong and invited to take part in a village full moon ceremony.

During my trans-Africa journey we had the good fortune to come across a band of Mbuti Pygmies crossing the road in the Ituri Forest of the Congo River basin. They invited our group to spend the night in their camp and we jumped at the opportunity. Here, an oversized Mbuti hut is being erected for oversized guests.

While crossing the Grand Erg Oriental of the Sahara Desert during my six-month trans-Africa journey, I was drawn to the tops of the world's highest dunes each morning and evening to watch the sunrise and see the sunset.

This was the "Trans-African Highway" in the early '80s—a quagmire of potholes, mud and river crossings we had to make in our Bedford truck. My five companions and I spent endless hours laying out metal tracks stored on the side of the truck as we crossed the shifting sands of the Sahara.

My travels to over 130 countries and all continents have been a great blessing. Here I'm wrapped against the chill atop Mount Sinai at sunrise having spent a sleepless night riding a camel. To keep my mind active so I wouldn't doze off and plunge over a ledge to my death, I imagined ten new commandments for the twenty-first century that address the way we've been disrespecting the earth.

from the nearest town, road or telephone—it may also have been the wettest. We were forever trying to dry out clothing and sleeping bags around the fire, especially during the five-day expedition. On one trip the participants left their hiking shoes so close to the fire to dry when they bedded down for the night that all the plastic and rubber on their shoes had melted and some burned to ashes. We were at the farthest point from our base camp and looking at two to three days of hiking to get back. The kids couldn't possibly go barefoot over the jagged rocks and barnacles, so I sent my fastest staff person (Alfie Jeffries of Coast Salish ancestry) off at first light to head back to camp and call into town to send out an order of new shoes. This was going to take days, so we all got together to discuss rationing our food provisions and look at wild-food foraging options in the area. We were still contemplating how best to deal with the dilemma when Alfie suddenly returned, shouting, "There are shoes, you guys! Shoes everywhere—come look!" There, spread out along the entire length of Beresford Bay, were runners washed in overnight from a cargo container that must have capsized in a storm somewhere out in the North Pacific. The kids didn't all get matching colours, but they all got properly fitted for size. Call it serendipity, coincidence, fate, divine intervention or Raven up to his old tricks; there's a reason people talk of the magic of the Misty Isles.

Rediscovery was never intended to be a program for anyone beyond the shores of Haida Gwaii, but word of its success started spreading up and down the coast, piquing the interest of communities facing similar situations with their youth. As the founder of the program, I was frequently called upon to give presentations throughout BC, other parts of Canada and eventually the world. None of the anthropology courses I took at university could have possibly prepared me to work with Indigenous peoples in the role in which I suddenly found myself. MSU's Department of Anthropology at the time had viewed Indigenous peoples only as objects for study. By contrast, Ghindigin immersed me in Haida teachings and protocols from the start. I quickly realized that every encounter with Indigenous peoples was the same as my first day of school.

I'll never forget the first potlatch I attended in Old Massett. The Haida are the world's most gracious and hospitable people when it comes to a potlatch. Not even a total stranger is excluded from such an event, and all guests that come to bear witness enjoy the same feast foods as the chiefs and share in the wealth during gift giving. I had recently arrived on the Islands and was unknown to most, but still I was treated royally and given gifts. At the end of the night the MC asked for volunteers to help in clearing tables and cleaning up the hall. Having grown up in a large family and with a strict list of household chores to attend to, I knew my calling and immediately pitched in.

"Stop that right now," Ghindigin commanded me. "Pick up your gifts and walk out of the hall with your head held high,"

"But they asked for help," I protested.

"Do as I say," came the reply with the firmness of a parent speaking to a child. Outside the Old Massett Community Hall where the feast was held, I got a scolding I will never forget.

"You never do that, Huck, unless you've been adopted and your clan is hosting the event," Ghin told me firmly.

"And if I do?"

"They'll think you're a slave," came the unexpected reply.

It was true—the Haida had practised slavery in the past and to this day know which families on Haida Gwaii descended from slaves. Over time, as I became better known to the Haida community, I was invited to be seated at the head table with chiefs and matriarchs. Other Yatz-Haida (white people) who arrived on the Islands even before me were seated at the back of the room or on the bleachers and expected to clean up after each event. They had already inadvertently established slave status for themselves.

No anthropology course in the world could have taught me that lesson, and there were many, many more I learned from my new teacher, Professor Ghindigin, and the Haida elders I came to know as dear friends. When I was invited down to the Four Corners region of Colorado to introduce the Rediscovery model to a group of Pueblo, Navajo, Lakota and Ute peoples, I found myself sitting before a distinguished group of their elders. I knew from Haida Gwaii to give

A Rediscovery participant being honoured as "Stone Ribs" is led by camp guides Danny Stewart (left) and Pat Stephenson (right) in a torchlit procession to the council fire. RICHARD KRIEGER PHOTO

only a very gentle handshake while avoiding eye contact so as not to appear aggressive or as if I were trying to steal their souls. I had also been taught not to speak until the elders spoke first. After making the obligatory round of gentle handshakes, I sat down and waited ... and waited and waited for an elder to speak. At least twenty minutes passed in complete silence before an old Ute elder said, "This is good. We can work with you." Had I opened my mouth, I would have failed the job interview.

Over the years and at many different locations, I saw events at Rediscovery camps that transcended logic and scientific explanation. Right from the start on Haida Gwaii it was common for Haida youth attending the program to see and feel the presence of their ancestors. I recall sitting by the council fire one night on the beach at Lepas Bay when participants were sharing deeply as they passed the eagle feather. No one had the right to speak until they held the feather, and those who held it that particular night felt everyone would think they were crazy if they told what they were seeing. Only a dozen of us were passing the feather, but a much larger crowd of shadow figures had gathered in close beside and behind us. The weird thing about their presence was that they could be detected only from the periphery of each person's vision; if you tried to look directly at them, they would not be there. The feather had gone all the way around the circle before anyone had the courage to speak up and a general discussion ensued.

"Did you guys just see the shadow people I saw?" a boy asked.

"Yes," came the emphatic answer, whispered from everyone at once. It was only then that I knew my own mind was not playing tricks on me.

Another night on Haida Gwaii Rediscovery, when the final embers had extinguished from the council fire, we'd retired to the dining hall for hot chocolate before the kids' bedtime. Everyone in camp was accounted for inside the building when someone suddenly said in a hushed voice trembling with fear, "Who's dancing around the fire? Who put more wood on?" We all rushed to the plastic window to see many figures dancing around the fire we had just left, even though those of us in the dining hall were the only people in a fifty-mile radius. We turned off our kerosene lamps to see better, and every person in that camp saw the same illusory beings. When the ghost dancers ended and suddenly vanished we went out to inspect the site, and there on the ground were small dark footprints, not indented in the sand, but appearing as if they were shadows on the surface. The next morning they were still there but fading, and they disappeared quickly with the rising sun.

When the first Rediscovery camp opened outside of Haida Gwaii, I was called down to Crestone, Colorado, to oversee the first session of Rediscovery Four Corners. The setting for this camp was the spectacular San Luis Valley bordering the Great Sand Dunes National Monument in the Four Corners region of Utah, Arizona, Colorado and New Mexico. Plains Indian tipis had been secured to represent the culture and heritage of the Ute peoples who had once occupied these lands at various times, along with the Pueblo and Navajo. On the evening before camp we were erecting four tipis to house the participants arriving the next morning. A Pueblo elder,

Frank Martinez, was monitoring the careful placement of the structures, as they had to be aligned exactly north, south, east and west. It was near sunset when the last cover went up and over the poles of the east tipi. As we were placing the ground cloths inside the tipi, a staff member brought my attention to a serious problem. A colony of red fire ants was hidden in the prairie grass that was to be the floor and sleeping area. We could not possibly bed kids down on a fire-ant nest site. "Hey, you guys," I called out. "We've got an issue here. We've got to move this tipi, which means we have to move them all or else they'll be out of alignment." The staff sighed with exhaustion because they knew that meant an all-night work ordeal by lamplight.

"Everyone is too tired, Thom," Frank Martinez said to me. "Let me talk to the ants in the morning." I knew not to challenge an elder or question sensitive cultural beliefs, but safety has always been Rediscovery's top priority, and that responsibility fell squarely on my shoulders as program director.

"Can you talk to the ants now?" I asked with typical white-man impatience.

"No," Frank replied as if he were speaking to a child. "The ants would bite me if I disturbed them now. Just wait until morning."

I had little faith in ants' listening skills after being bitten by them many times, so I quietly instructed the staff to close off the east tipi until we could drop it and rearrange the set-up of all four tipis when the campers went on a hike in a few days' time. They would simply have to double up sleeping arrangements in the three available tipis until then. Pretending not to sense my cynicism or notice my staff instructions, Frank invited me down to the campsite for the first-light ceremony he would conduct the following morning.

I was anticipating an elaborate ritual with drums, smudging and chanting, but instead the ceremony was little more than a simple request. As the sun was just beginning to brighten the eastern horizon, Frank placed a pinch of cornmeal beside the entrance hole of the colony, gently laid his head on the ant mound as though it were a pillow and whispered down the ant tunnel, "Dear ants, I'm sorry to wake you so early this morning. I have brought you a gift of cornmeal and ask a favour of you in return. We have made the mistake of erecting a tipi over your home and the children need to move in today. Can you please move your home?"

The ceremony was every bit as charming as it seemed to me naive, but I knew from my anthropology courses that this was probably just cultural protocol for the Pueblo, who believe they once shared the underworld with ants. According to legend, the ants provided most of their food to the Pueblo people so they would grow large enough to emerge into the upper world while the ants remained small, forever making their homes in the underworld. I also knew from my biology background that ants stretch, yawn and wash themselves when they wake in the morning just like humans, but that's as far with anthropomorphism as my Western-moulded mind was willing to go.

I made a juniper wreath to place over the tent flap both to respect the Pueblo traditions and to caution the arriving participants to not enter the east tipi. An hour later the students arrived, and while I was explaining the doubled-up sleeping arrangements, Frank Martinez quietly signalled me to come over to the backside of the east tipi. There, before my eyes, the last ants in the colony were hauling away their larvae to a new nest site well away from the tipi. Frank did not gloat or chide me but humbly spoke to his ant relatives. "Thank you, brothers and sisters."

It was growing increasingly clear to me, the co-founder of Rediscovery, that I was the one doing much of the rediscovering. I had been so conditioned to the denial of anything that could not be scientifically explained that I was like a horse with blinders, unable to see peripheral realities. I struggled for a rational explanation. Perhaps ants don't tolerate having their homes shifted from bright light to shade, I told myself as I tried to rationalize the event I'd just witnessed. But again and again, Rediscovery confronted me with situations that seemed inexplicable and far from coincidental.

I was called up to Fort Ware in northeast British Columbia one summer to assist with the start-up of a new Rediscovery camp for the Sekani peoples. Fort Ware had been riddled with youth violence following the federal government's removal of the people from the land (allegedly for better access to government services like schools and medical clinics, but also conveniently getting them out of the way of massive deforestation, mining proposals and hydroelectric dams). A new generation of youth with no job prospects found themselves condemned to a cycle of poverty and a life of boredom. Not surprisingly, they were seriously acting out.

The elders wanted to get the kids back onto the land. Their idea was to set up Suze Kanutsa, an Awakening Rediscovery camp far up the Finlay River from the community. The Sekani elders still had many of their traditions intact even if their young people were sliding down the slippery slope of assimilation. I recall one elder telling the young men and women about to go off on their twenty-four-hour solos that a spirit guardian might come to them that night just as spirits had come to their ancestors in the past.

One troubled teenaged boy, a member of the wolf clan, was told that a guardian might come to him who would be his spirit protector for life. I recall dropping this young man off at his solo site and being impressed by how quickly he got a fire started and began building a suitable shelter. He's going to do fine, I thought as I left him.

When he returned to base camp the next morning, the tale of his encounter stretched the boundaries of credibility. As he told it, he was sitting by his dying fire in the middle of the night, too scared to go inside his shelter as he had heard movement in the bushes. It was too dark to search for more firewood, and he was upset that he had not gathered more. Suddenly, he saw two yellow eyes peering at him from the edge of the fading firelight. It was a female wolf, and she cautiously approached the terrified boy. He tried to calm his mind with the words of the elder, reminding himself that the wolf might be a spirit guardian coming to him in an animal form.

The night was growing cold, but the boy's shivering probably had more to do with fear than temperature when the she-wolf curled up beside him to keep him warm. When he awoke the next morning the wolf was gone, but he swore it was not a dream. "Yeah, right, man," the other kids said, teasing him mercilessly. "What kind of berries and mushrooms were you eating, dude?"

"Holy shit," one kid said, suddenly speaking up above the roar of the teasing boys. "Look, you guys—he's got wolf hair all over his jacket!"

And so it was, with one experience after another, Rediscovery stretched my narrow definition of reality and blew it to smithereens. My teachers were no longer accredited professors at a prestigious university, but kids and elders shadow-dancing with ancestral spirits, talking to ants and snuggling up with wild wolves to keep warm. If I didn't exactly comprehend how any of this was possible, I was at least broadening my mind to possibilities and rediscovering some of my own Indigenous roots. As Ghindigin always said, "Rediscovery offers non-Natives experiences to which they are just more generations removed."

Nearly forty years after Rediscovery began on the shores of Haida Gwaii, I was still very actively involved with all the camps through the Rediscovery International Foundation (RIF), which had been set up to act as a support organization to train staff and link the camps together through shared experiences. For over twenty years I was the lead RIF facilitator at United World College of the Pacific (Lester B. Pearson College), where the RIF conducted a two-week intensive training program that helped Rediscovery trainees acquire the qualifications and gain the confidence they needed to run a camp. Wilderness First Aid, Bronze Medallion Lifesaving and Flat Water Levels 1 & 2 canoe courses were combined with workshops on conflict resolution, cross-cultural awareness, protocols, respect and boundaries, camp scheduling, fundraising and over a hundred Rediscovery games and activities the program had developed over the years. Youth from around the world took part in this training, many of whom went off to start Rediscovery camps in their home countries. Most importantly, the training program created a united sense of purpose and ensured that all camps using the Rediscovery model met the same health and safety standards.

In addition to running the annual RIF Leadership Development Training, the foundation organized annual gatherings and special events that brought many camps together for shared adventures. It was while I was in Northern British Columbia at such an event that I shared a recurring dream with a Gitksan elder sitting around a campfire one night.

Dreams have always held special significance for me; from my earliest years I was held in their thrall. I had a secret "dream box" as a child that I would use to store my dreams in. I used to think that the crust that formed on the edges of my eyes each night from the air pollution of the Oldsmobile factory just across the Grand River from my childhood home in Michigan was the physical form of the dream from the night before. Every morning I would carefully record on paper what the dream had been about and place the crust in a little box with the note. Any time I wanted to repeat a particularly pleasant dream, I would read the note, carefully set the crust back in my eyes and have the same dream. It worked brilliantly until my older brother caught me doing it and told me it was stupid. There's nothing like an adult reality check to destroy the magic of childhood.

Even without my fantasy dream box there was something very unusual in the recurring dream I recounted to the elder by the fireside that night. It was simple but profound in the sense that it kept repeating even when I was in Southeast Asia, far away from the location the dream spoke to. Like a movie that repeats a scene for dramatic effect, the dream has me sitting in a one-room log cabin drinking mint tea and writing at a small table beside a window. The view from the window is stunningly beautiful, with seven granite mountain peaks covered in snow looming into the sky. Suddenly, someone knocks at the door. I cannot make out who it is from the angle of the window, so I put down my tea and walk around the table to open the door. As soon as I do this I wake up. Even though this dream reoccurred dozens of times, I have never discovered who is knocking at the door.

"Pay attention to that dream," the Gitksan elder advised me. "It's sending you an important message."

"Is it death at the door?" I asked.

The old woman paused for a moment, closing her eyes for some time while the last embers of the fire extinguished. "I don't think so," she said at length. "But it sounds like the place in your dream is somewhere in our territories."

Several years later, I was invited by the Kispiox community in Northern BC to help train local staff for their Anspayaxw Rediscovery camp along with Haisla youth from Kitimat. I flew from Victoria to Smithers, rented a car at the airport and drove the back roads for several hours to reach their remote Kuldo camp beside a lake in the wilderness. "Where are the Haisla youth?" I asked on arrival.

"Their driver was sick today so they couldn't come," came the reply.

"Why don't I drive down to Kitimat and pick them up?" I offered. "Who knows when I'll get up this way again?"

Doreen Angus, the director of the Gitksan program, thought that was a good idea.

And so I set off on a six-hour round-trip drive south to Kitimat. I never like to drive more than a few hours without stopping to stretch, so I pulled off Highway 16 onto an old logging road just before crossing the bridge over Price Creek. As I rounded a corner of the dirt road to be well clear of the highway traffic, I almost drove into a Kermode bear with her two cubs. I was stunned. Like most people, I had never seen a Spirit Bear before in my life. The Kermode, or Spirit Bear, is a genetic variation of the coastal black bear that has evolved a white coat similar to a polar bear; it is sacred according to Indigenous traditions and has never been hunted. This region of the Skeena Valley is the farthest inland these bears have expanded their range from the coast.

I had left my camera back at the Anspayaxw Rediscovery camp along with my gear, so all I could do was watch in amazement as the mother Kermode taught her cubs how to turn over rocks in search of insects. It was not until the family of bears wandered back into the forest cover that I got out of the car to stretch my hamstrings on the front bumper. While doing this I noticed a movement in the bushes on the hillside beside me. It was not a bear this time, but an old woman picking soapberries. When our eyes met she said calmly, "Go down the highway a little farther and turn right."

"Why?" I asked.

"Just a little farther," she replied before absorbing herself again in her berry picking.

There must be a garbage dump down the road where bears gather, I thought, and I followed her instructions. The dirt road she had spoken of did not take me to a garbage dump at all, but ended in a large wildflower field beside the Skeena River. A small log cabin that stood nearby looked strangely familiar. When I turned to see whether there were any bears in the area, I was floored to see the seven mountain peaks depicted in my dream looming nearly three thousand metres above the valley and crowned with hanging glaciers and snow. I could not believe my eyes. I stood there completely transfixed and dumbstruck until my attention was drawn to an old farmer driving toward me on a tractor from an adjacent hayfield.

"So you've come to buy the land?" he said before even offering a hello. "I was wondering how you found the place, as it's only advertised in the local paper and there's no For Sale sign on the highway."

I assured the farmer I had not come to buy any land, but standing there in the location of a dream that had called to me from the other side of the planet, I began to wonder if maybe I had. The old farmer must have sensed my uncertainty and said before parting, "Well, if you change your mind, my house is just the other side of that far field."

Years later in the summer of 2004, I was invited up to the region again to help organize a canoe expedition from Kispiox to the coast in traditional Northwest Coast canoes. By this time the knock-on-the-door dream had stopped recurring, but I could not get the image of that land out of my head. The Rediscovery canoe journey, which was called Retracing the Ancestral Highway, was designed to bring together all the Indigenous nations living in the Skeena watershed to have their youth paddle from Kispiox to the sea. The Babine Carrier, Wet'suwet'en, Gitksan and Tsimshian Nations all had Rediscovery camps in their traditional territories so it was easy to enrol enthusiastic paddlers for four of the twelve-person canoes. A fifth international canoe was manned by Indigenous youth, some of them refugees, from Thailand, Guatemala, Burma, Brazil, Mongolia, Malaysia and Mexico. Together, sixty young men and women with very little in common negotiated the fastest navigable river in North America on a historic and epic journey to the sea.

The canoes arrived in Kitwanga village on the second day of the paddle and had a layover day due to a death in the family of Roy Henry Vickers, the celebrated Indigenous artist and lead skipper for the expedition. I awoke very early that morning and decided to drive six kilometres up the highway to see the land I had stumbled upon years earlier and had not been able to get out of my head. Arriving at the wildflower meadow as the rising sun was illuminating the Seven Sisters mountain range in a red alpine glow, I said to myself, "If I'm supposed to buy this land I need a sign right now." Just then a black bear came walking out of the woods directly toward me, stopped twenty metres away, stared at me and returned to the forest.

A few minutes later I found myself knocking on the door of the owner's farmhouse. "Do you remember me? Have you sold your land yet?" I asked.

"Not yet," the man replied, "but now that we've got it advertised on a website we're getting a lot of interest, and I think it will sell soon."

"I'd like to buy it if you're willing to sell," I found myself saying, having no idea at all how I was going to finance it. Fortunately, I learned later that my home in Victoria had increased in value enough to extend the amortization and secure a loan to purchase the property.

He shook my hand, agreeing to his original asking price of $1,000 per acre, but told me to return later that night to sign the papers as the land was in his son's name and the son needed to sign after he returned from work at the local sawmill. I escorted all the canoe quest paddlers up to the Salmon Glacier on a day trip, dropped the hungry youth off at the Kitwanga community hall for a Gitksan feast, and returned to the farm that evening. The son, whom I had never met before, was fixing a tractor with his dad when I arrived, but neither he nor the older man said anything to me. I waited a long time for some recognition and was about to depart when the old man said, "Son, go in the house and sign those papers on the kitchen table."

"Are you sure, Dad?"

"Yup, we've gotta do the right thing here," his dad said.

None of this made any sense to me until the old man said, "You consider yourself a pretty lucky fella, don't you?"

"I guess so. I've never felt unlucky," I replied, but I was confused by the question.

"Do you know what happened twenty minutes after you walked out of here this morning?" the old man asked. "I got a call from a doctor in Montana who saw the picture of the mountain view on our website and offered me $2,000 an acre—that's double your price."

"So it's already sold?"

"I shook your hand, didn't I?" he countered. "I figure a man's gotta be good for his word. We just hope you'll be a good neighbour."

And so it was, against all odds, that Soaring Spirits Camp came to be. A spectacular seventy-one-hectare property bordering two kilometres of one of the world's great salmon rivers was secured for all time as a place for youth from local communities and the global community to discover the world within themselves, the cultural worlds between them and the natural world around them. Like the Moresby campaign, Rediscovery seemed guided by spirit.

CHAPTER VII

Islands at the Edge

B y the late 1970s several Canadian luminaries and internationally renowned figures had begun lending their support
to the Moresby cause. Among them were celebrated artists
like Bill Reid, Robert Bateman and Toni Onley, national broadcaster and geneticist David Suzuki, internationally acclaimed
undersea explorer Jacques Cousteau, as well as royalty like Prince
Philip and Prince Charles. As one might expect, Bill Reid, of
Haida ancestry on his mother's side, was one of the first celebrities
to do so.

My first encounter with the master carver came in the summer
of 1976 one morning at dawn after I'd spent a night curled up
beneath the dogfish pole Bill had been commissioned to carve for the
front of the Skidegate Band office. Ghindigin was assisting Bill with
the carving, and he wanted me to meet Bill to help persuade him to
support our cause. By the time I hitchhiked down from Masset to
Skidegate Landing where the pole was being carved, Bill had already
put down his tools and gone home for the day. Ghindigin suggested I
sleep under the pole in a bed of cedar shavings to get a better feeling
for their creation and to be in position to meet the esteemed artist
first thing in the morning.

I have no idea what Bill thought of me as I emerged somewhat groggily from beneath the pole, my wool shirt covered in shavings, to greet him when he arrived at work that morning. He struck me as a man of few words as he went about his business, seemingly uninterested in what Ghin and I had to say. Supernatural beings were slowly being released from the fine-grained confinement of centuries-old cedar, and Bill seemed silent almost out of reverence as he chipped away at the great log. Ghin and I did our best to persuade him to back the Moresby cause, but at the end of the day he left us with a single

The dogfish pole carved by Bill Reid and Guujaaw stands proudly in front of Skidegate's longhouse.

thought: "The way I see it, boys, is you're going to be living together on these islands with those you oppose for a long time to come."

It was true, we would be, and there was certainly wisdom in his words. With only five thousand Islands residents at the time, everyone pretty well knew everyone else's business on Haida Gwaii, especially when it was none of their own. The Islands' grapevine was faster than a superconductor, and we had to be careful to not alienate potential supporters. Still, Bill must surely have heard what we had to say—he was reminded of it day after day as I continued to meet with Ghindigin at the carving shed to discuss strategies.

The scourge of Parkinson's disease, diagnosed six years earlier, was slowly taking its toll on Bill's body. It is hard to imagine a worse fate to befall a master carver, designer and goldsmith than to lose control of motor functions in the hands. Ghin once told me that he was carving on the pole one day and encouraging Bill to let him carve voluptuous breasts on a female figure. Bill, who was having an especially bad day with Parkinson's, would not consent. After fumbling hopelessly with his carving tools, he finally set them down in disgust. "You keep carving, Ghindigin," he said as he headed off for home. "I'm feeling about as useless as a tit on a totem pole." In the end, Bill Reid's contribution to elevating Rediscovery and the South Moresby cause was anything but useless, for once he was on board with us he threw the full power of his esteemed position behind our initiatives and donated prints and artwork to help fund the efforts.

There were so many important events in the years leading up to the Lyell Island blockade that it is difficult to recount them all. The All-Island Symposium in 1980 certainly set the stage for bringing Queen Charlotte Islanders on board. Using the stunning images of professional photographers Richard Krieger and Jack Litrell, and with a musical score produced by artist Lark Clark, a slide presentation on South Moresby's world-class features wowed the crowd at the Queen Charlotte Islands' new museum. Even the logging industry spokesman at the conference commented, "The Islands Protection Society does a consistently fine job of presenting their bias."

In 1977, earlier in the campaign, to help ease tensions, Paul George and Richard Krieger suggested that I make a trip to the logging community in Powrivco Bay that would be shut down if our wilderness proposal met with success. Having worked a short stint as a logger myself, and being a firm believer in the power of dialogue to diffuse differences, I took Paul and Richard up on it.

We first presented a slideshow with Richard's images showing the values at stake and the impacts logging can have on ancient forest-nesting seabirds like auklets and murrelets. We spoke of the impacts of increased sedimentation from road building on salmon streams and intertidal life, and we expressed alarm at the soil mass wasting from landslides triggered by logging steep slopes on islands with high seismic activity and heavy rainfall. It all might have fallen on deaf ears, because the first question that came up after my presentation was "Do you have some kind of a hard-on for IT&T?" International Telephone & Telegraph, give or take a name change,

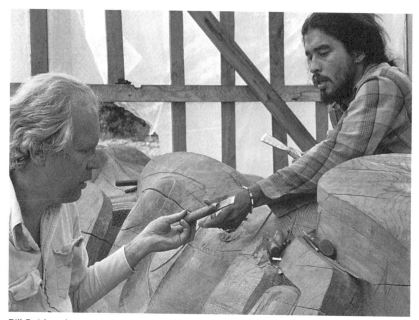

Bill Reid and apprentice carver Guujaaw work on the dogfish pole in a makeshift carving shed in Skidegate. RICHARD KRIEGER PHOTO

was the multi-billion-dollar corporate owner of Rayonier (B.C.) Ltd. at the time, though that was the first time I was made aware of it.

In 1983, John Broadhead shared my vision of producing a publication that would elevate the Moresby campaign to the national and international level. We had already collaborated successfully on the production of *All Alone Stone*, a magazine for the local communities, and we were bold enough to think we could now produce something much bigger—a book! We quickly put together a prospectus and began soliciting experts in various fields to write specific chapters. Bill Reid agreed to write the compelling opening chapter, "These Shining Islands," and his French wife Martine, while in Paris, managed to solicit a foreword by none other than the world's most celebrated undersea explorer and co-inventor of the self-contained underwater breathing apparatus (SCUBA)—Jacques Cousteau.

John and I wrote several chapters of the book and enlisted the professional help of Bristol Foster, director of the BC Ecological Reserves program, to write a chapter on Queen Charlotte Islands endemic species. Jim Pojar, a professional forester, wrote a chapter on the ecology of ancient forests, David Denning of the Bamfield Marine Sciences Centre wrote a chapter on marine life and Wayne Campbell, an ornithologist at the Royal BC Museum, composed the chapter on seabirds. It all looked pretty impressive, but we had no publisher.

It was Bill Reid who opened the door to this unorthodox publication being considered by Western Canada's largest publishing house at the time, Douglas & McIntyre. Bill had been publishing most of his works through this house, and he suggested he might go elsewhere if the owner, Scott McIntyre, didn't meet with me and John to review our manuscript. We met with Scott at his Vancouver office, but much as we tried to persuade him of the growing support and potential audience for this book, he remained reluctant to buy in. "I have a whole warehouse full of my optimism," he told us. Further lobbying on the part of Bill Reid finally persuaded Scott to take it on. Because we were in a rush to publish and all of Douglas & McIntyre's book designers were tied up with other projects, Scott reluctantly agreed to let John Broadhead and I design the book.

Paul George, Guujaaw and I pose for a photo during a reconnaissance trip to South Moresby in the early days of the struggle to protect Hdaida Gwaii from clear-cut logging. RICHARD KRIEGER PHOTO

Co-authors and designers John Broadhead and I present a copy of our book, *Islands at the Edge*, to Prince Philip.

JB's artistic skills seamlessly wove together both images and artwork donated by several acclaimed Canadian artists. The style was unorthodox but bold enough to set a new trend in BC publishing. *Islands at the Edge: Preserving the Queen Charlotte Islands Wilderness* became an instant, award-winning success. Alan Twigg at *BC BookWorld* had this to say about it:

> The turning point for recognition of Haida Gwaii as a separate culture—the book that, more than any other, made it acceptable and even preferable to refer to the place as Haida Gwaii—was *Islands at the Edge: Preserving the Queen Charlotte Islands Wilderness* (1984), a co-operative project largely engineered and written by Thom Henley. Later renamed *Islands at the Edge: Preserving the Queen Charlotte Archipelago*, this political milestone was accorded the first Bill Duthie Booksellers' Choice Award in 1985.
>
> At the gala event on Granville Island, Henley asked artist Bill Reid to give an acceptance speech. Reid's riveting denunciation of modern BC society was not only the highlight of

an evening that marked the coming of age of BC writing and publishing with the creation of the BC Book Prizes, it signalled to the mainland that Haida culture would henceforth aggressively seek self-definition. Quivering with Parkinson's disease, Reid reminded the audience of the ravages of white civilization, calling it "the worst plague of locusts."

Islands at the Edge was a powerful ambassadorial force in the successful preservation of South Moresby Island as a park. Its success begat a string of well-researched coffee table books to protect the environment, notably *Stein: The Way of the River* (1988) by Michael M'Gonigle and Wendy Wickwire, and *Carmanah: Artistic Visions of an Ancient Rainforest* (1989), spearheaded by Paul George, who had produced a similar book about Meares Island in 1985.

The person who paved the way for the success of our book and created a national customer base was none other than Dr. David Suzuki. *The Nature of Things* documentary on Windy Bay that aired nationwide on January 27, 1982, had already made South Moresby a household name three years before the book was released.

I, like millions of Canadians, Americans and Australians, was a huge fan of Suzuki's courageous, pull-no-punches broadcast style. From a little-known geneticist at UBC to one of the most respected men in the country, his ascent arose from his humble but passionate commitment to protecting the planet and human rights. It was a great honour for me to be invited aboard his helicopter in the autumn of 1981 and fly down to Windy Bay to complete a shoot for an upcoming *Nature of Things* program. David's film crew had been stormbound in Windy Bay for several days prior to our arrival, and it was clear from a falling barometer and darkening sky that another autumn gale was fast approaching.

"David, you don't have time to go into the forest. We've got to get this shot and leave ahead of the storm," a member of Suzuki's crew told him as we disembarked on the beach and ran out under the swirling rotary blades of the helicopter to the forest edge. "This is the most spectacular forest we've seen anywhere in the world," his crew member added. "You've got to tell people that, David."

I have never before seen such a level of professionalism as when David very calmly sat down on a beach log that day, looked straight into the camera and delivered an eloquent and heart-felt testimonial. I was filmed for the show, as was Ghindigin, who was now called Guujaaw. David later took on a devil's advo-cate role with Guujaaw, asking him why saving the area was so important to the Haida. Guujaaw had spoken of how the Haida's whole cultural and spiritual iden-tity was tied to the land. "So what are you trying to tell me?" Suzuki

David Suzuki, renowned geneticist, broadcaster and conservationist, gave the Moresby campaign a huge boost when his *The Nature of Things* show featured the area's natural wonders. According to Suzuki, this episode got more letters and calls than any other show he's ever done. JEFFREY GIBBS PHOTO

challenged. "Will you no longer be Haida if they log these islands?"

Guujaaw confessed to me later that he was a bit stumped for a reply, so he just answered, "Nope, we'll still be here. We'll just be a bit more like everyone else."

That reply, David Suzuki told me later over dinner at his house, totally floored him. My God, he thought, these people really see themselves as different. It was the seminal moment that moved him into an entirely new direction in his life—becoming a champion for Indigenous people's rights worldwide. But Suzuki wasn't popular everywhere, and he came under increasing threats from the logging community in Sandspit following the Windy Bay broadcast.

What really set the Moresby cause apart from all others and started a new national trend was the close alliance that was forged between the Haida in asserting their rights and a conservation

SOUTH MORESBY RALLY

As logging proceeds on Lyell Island, Canada stands to lose an outstanding national park in South Moresby. The time for public action is now. You are urged to take two hours to help save South Moresby—for your children's children.

ROBSON SQUARE
TUESDAY   MARCH 24   12 NOON
12:45 walk to Western Forest Products Ltd.
at 1140 West Pender Street for
SPECIAL EVENTS
SPEAKERS
DAVID **SUZUKI**
BILL **REID** and others

Bill Reid and David Suzuki were guest speakers at a Vancouver rally for South Moresby. JEFFREY GIBBS PHOTO

community placing their bets that Haida stewardship would easily trump the BC government and federal agencies in protecting the area. The bet paid off.

There is an ancient name for Haida Gwaii that translates roughly as "Islands Emerging from (Supernatural) Concealment," reflecting the mythical origins of the Haida archipelago. Scientists have their own myth based on tectonic plate movements. The Haida Islands are considered geological gypsies, cast adrift aboard a plate that has been slowly shifting northwestward from an area that is now Baja, Mexico.

Now perched on the very edge of the continental shelf and pressed against the howling gales of the Pacific, the 150 islands that make up the archipelago are said to have the highest-energy coastline in all of Canada—a scientific analysis based on factors such as wind speed and wave action. We knew all of this, of course, when we titled our book *Islands at the Edge* and intended the double meaning with the logging threats to South Moresby, but no one at the time recognized our movement was on the edge of effecting change on a global scale.

CHAPTER VIII

Gumboot Diplomacy

B y the summer of 1985 things were heating up for the Moresby campaign. Beban Logging, the local contractor to Western Forest Products (the new tree farm licence holder), was starting to feel the pressure of growing opposition to its logging plans. No longer content to sit back and scoff at our "feeble" attempts to have a portion of TFL 24 set aside for higher use, the industry people now felt threatened. They hired a media consultant and persuaded Jack Webster, a popular BCTV broadcaster in Vancouver, to take up the pro-logging cause. Not only did Webster find himself on the wrong side of this issue, he inadvertently helped to push it to a dramatic conclusion in a direction opposite from his intent.

Elizabeth May, an outspoken environmentalist from Cape Breton Island who later became the head of the Green Party of Canada, had unexpectedly been appointed as an aide to Tom McMillan, the newly appointed federal environment minister. Through her considerable powers of persuasion she arranged for McMillan to make a trip to South Moresby to see for himself what was at stake. I had already met Tom McMillan quite by accident at the 1985 Parks Canada Centennial Conference in Banff, Alberta, during a bit of a scuffle. Colleen McCrory, a fellow environmentalist and strong South

Moresby supporter, was also attending the conference in Banff to lobby for the creation of more parks. After we'd listened to hours of self-absorbed and self-congratulatory speeches about Parks Canada's past but with no apparent vision for the future, Colleen and I challenged each other to take the stage. Unannounced and definitely uninvited, we walked down the centre aisle of the Banff Conference Centre onto the stage and took command of the microphone just before the keynote speaker was to be introduced.

As I was making a hasty but impassioned plea to the delegates to do something truly significant to mark a hundred years of national parks in Canada by saving South Moresby, the federal environment minister entered the room and observed the commotion onstage. Up until this point, Parks Canada had never once supported the South Moresby Wilderness Proposal. They wanted to save only Hotspring Island and De la Beche Inlet, incredibly small areas bordering both sides of Juan Perez Sound with no commercial timber values. At planning team meetings they spoke of maintaining "the illusion of wilderness" in South Moresby as had been attempted in the pathetic logging leave strip that is now Pacific Rim National Park. We saw this as cowardice on the part of a federal agency that should have been the strongest supporter of the cause.

Just as Colleen McCrory and I were about to be unceremoniously dragged from the microphone, Tom McMillan appeared onstage, his presence stopping the embarrassing scuffle about to ensue. Fortunately, I had a copy of *Islands at the Edge* in hand. It was fresh off the press, and the moment seemed opportune to present it to Canada's minister of the environment. Making the presentation suddenly legitimized my presence onstage and helped everyone save face, so security was held back for the moment.

"Honourable minister," I began, "we beseech your help in protecting this area of national and international significance, because without your immediate intervention, South Moresby, portrayed through the words and images in this book, will be little more than a memory in the libraries of our nation." McMillan seemed moved, and he diverged from his prepared speech to tell the Centennial

Conference that he would make saving South Moresby a top priority of his office. He received a standing ovation.

Just a few months later I was to have my second encounter with Tom McMillan, who was an old school buddy of Brian Mulroney, Canada's acting Conservative prime minister. As Tom disembarked his flight in Sandspit, the Islands' only airport at the time and a logging community and hotbed of resentment to the Moresby cause, he was greeted by an angry crowd waving signs and shouting, "Tom McMillan and Thom Henley, go home!"

"You didn't tell me you were walking me into a lynch mob," McMillan said to me when I greeted him. He was visibly shaken.

"We never said this was going to be easy," I replied. "It's going to take courage and commitment." We boarded a helicopter with Guujaaw and flew south into the proposed wilderness area with its shining islands, emerald mountains and primal forests. Tom was now enthralled and in a very spirited mood when we landed on Hotspring Island. We were alone on this paradise isle set like a jewel in the middle of Juan Perez Sound, and it was Guujaaw who suggested we enjoy one of the Islands' geothermal pools for a soothing soak. None of us had brought along swimsuits, but no women were present so we saw no reason why underwear couldn't suffice. It must have been the helicopter pilot who mentioned this incident to the Beban Logging team in Sandspit. The next morning Tom McMillan did a BCTV interview in Vancouver before flying back to Ottawa, and Jack Webster's belligerent first question was, "So, Mr. Minister, I hear you were skinny-dipping with the hippies on Hotspring Island yesterday?"

"Actually, Jack, I was wearing underwear," McMillan replied calmly. "I wouldn't call that skinny-dipping—would you?"

"Not skinny-dipping," Webster replied, somewhat embarrassed. "Next question."

Jack Webster seemed annoyed that he had been set up to look unprofessional with a stupid question, but apart from this error in his usually stellar reporting he made a much more serious mistake. He and other members of the press had begun to imply that the Haida

The logging of Lyell Island was massive and relentless for years. Images of expanding clear-cuts helped mobilize support across the country. RICHARD KRIEGER PHOTO

were being used as stooges by a well-funded and organized environmental movement in pursuit of its conservation goals. He could not have been more wrong, as anyone with background knowledge in the history of this struggle knew. The Haida had actually spearheaded the movement with the concerns of the Skidegate Band Council over logging Burnaby Island in 1973, and Guujaaw had built the cause every step of the way from that day forward. But now the insinuation that the Haida were not in control of their destiny on this issue forced the Haida Nation to take centre stage. It was a national and international stage more than a decade in the making and built by people from all walks of life, but for now it was the Haida's stage. After ten years of sitting on the sidelines, attending one South Moresby planning team session after another while Lyell Island was being logged, the Haida were about to go back to their warrior roots and take a stand to stop it. I am convinced to this day that South Moresby would never have been saved without this action.

For thousands of years the Haida gained a reputation as fierce and sometimes merciless warriors in raids and skirmishes against mainland tribes and between their own villages. Often referred to as the "Vikings of the North Pacific" by European explorers, the Haida are known to have traded and raided for slaves and bounty from Alaska to California and possibly farther. The first European explorers were dumbfounded to find potatoes, a food crop native to South America, growing on Langara Island. Many of Haida Gwaii's neighbours were equally fierce in battle—the Tlingit, Tsimshian, Gitksan, Heiltsuk, Nuxalk and Nu'Chal'nuth. And yet, surprisingly, none of these Indigenous tribes ever sought a military solution to European colonizers stealing their lands. Against superior firepower it seemed more astute to settle differences in the feast house. Although genetically predisposed to battle, the Haida, in historical times, have also chosen the path of nonviolent but determined resistance.

Knowing the nature of your enemy and employing the element of surprise in battle have long been standard war strategies known to the Indigenous nations of the Pacific Northwest. Unlike the standoff at Oka in Eastern Canada, where the Mohawk stood in armed opposition to the RCMP and Canadian military in protecting a sacred burial site, the Gitksan once stood their ground over a fishing rights dispute on the Skeena River by pummelling heavily armed RCMP and federal Fisheries officers with marshmallows. Armed with nothing but puffed confectionery, the Gitksan made government authorities look ridiculous on national television. When asked by the press about the incident that came to be known as the Marshmallow War, the Gitksan simply replied, "We thought it was a pretty good strategy until we saw some of our young warriors eating all the ammunition."

When the Haida took up the call from Buddy Richardson, president of the Haida Nation Council, to blockade the logging road on Lyell Island in the late autumn of 1985, they too confounded the authorities with a strategy that could not have been conceived in any conventional war room.

Far from orchestrating and financing the Haida blockade on Lyell Island, the environmental community was taken completely by surprise when Buddy Richardson made the announcement, as was I. All of the conservation groups supporting the Moresby cause were asked to stay back until there were no more Haida left to be arrested before they would be invited to join ranks. Only MP Svend Robinson from Burnaby disregarded that request, and he was the only non-Haida to be arrested. The Haida, as a united people, were asserting themselves for the first time in a very long time, and for most young Haida the blockade marked the beginning of the movement to protect South Moresby, even though the campaign had already been around for years.

Once in front of the Masset Courthouse, where Haida youth were routinely lined up facing charges of vandalism and drunk and disorderly conduct, I commented to Guujaaw, "You know, Guuj, when the first Haida is arrested for standing up for the land instead of this, it will change everything." It did. The Lyell Island blockade became the overnight catalyst for reawakening the Haida Nation; it engaged young Haida feeling trapped in a cycle of poverty, unemployment and hopelessness and empowered them in a way that no youth program ever could.

As Guujaaw said about the battle lines he and I drew on the map in 1974, "Though easy to draw a line, holding the line is what counts."

The blockade site was set up almost overnight as the Haida mobilized their war effort. Haida-owned fishing boats became the nation's navy, moving people and supplies from the Skidegate command post to the front lines on Lyell where a cabin was erected to shelter blockaders from the autumn gales. The RCMP had to scramble and invest huge resources to catch up. They brought in a mobile command unit from Vancouver with high-tech capability to intercept all Haida communication between Skidegate and the blockade camp. But just as the Navajo were used by the US military in World War II to communicate secret messages that the Germans and Japanese could never decipher, so too did the Haida circumvent the entire RCMP surveillance system by relaying all messages in Haida—a language no Canadian official had ever bothered to learn in over two centuries of contact.

As more and more media found their way to the 1985 Lyell Island blockade, the South Moresby cause moved to the theatre of high drama, perfectly suited for television news. JEFFREY GIBBS PHOTO

Seeing the mangled slopes of Talunkwan and Lyell islands rallied the Haida and people throughout the world to put a stop to the destruction in South Moresby. RICHARD KRIEGER PHOTO

The Moresby cause had now moved to the theatre of high drama, which was perfectly suited for television news. A decade of lobbying, releasing news reports, producing magazines, attending meetings and publishing a book on the cause now paled in comparison as the campaign to save South Moresby entered every Canadian living room on the evening news. Over the course of cold, wet weeks, while Haida in gumboots held their ground in the ankle-deep mud of a wilderness logging road on the most remote body of land in the country, every Canadian could see it. Through the gruelling November gales, no Haida fist was raised in anger and no words were shouted in rage; the Haida Nation conducted itself with the dignity called for at a chief's function. In spite of news hype that encouraged confrontation, the blockaders set the tone for a nonviolent response to a state that was fully armed and held the monopoly on violence.

Respected elders Nonnie Ethel Jones and Chinny Adolphus Marks from Massett, joined by Nonni Ada Yovanovich and Chini Watson Pryce from Skidegate, showed up at the blockade site the night before the first arrests. To the surprise of everyone, and over the objections of many, the four of them insisted they be the first to be arrested the next morning. Taught to always respect their elders, the young warriors had no choice but to blacken their faces in mourning and stand silently by.

"Please don't put us in handcuffs," Nonnie Ethel asked hereditary chief Alan Wilson, the First Nations RCMP constable assigned to the task. "Just put your arm out as if you're leading Ada and I into the feast house," she said.

Plank benches had been set across the logging road, and a small fire was built to keep the elders warm from the November chill. They were dressed in their finest ceremonial regalia but wearing gumboots in the mud for the arrest. Ada and Ethel, both devout Christian women, had their Bibles in their hands and were quietly praying when the orders were read to them that they were under arrest. They then solemnly rose and walked with Constable Alan Wilson through a line of Haida protesters, who were shaking rattles and singing a mourning song as the elders were led to the paddy wagon. Tears

Three of the elders who changed everything with their arrests at the 1985 Lyell Island blockade. From left to right: Ethel Jones, Watson Pryce and Ada Yovanovich are seen here relaxing at Ninstints after the Moresby battle was won.

were flowing down the faces of the arresting constable and the young Haida lining the road. Later that evening the dramatic scene was broadcast nationwide.

I recall exactly where I was that evening as if it were the first news of the Kennedy assassination, or the hotel lobby in Istanbul where I sat with two Muslim clerics watching the second plane fly into the World Trade Center on a barely working television. There are moments in life indelibly etched with places and events.

I was sitting in a Victoria hotel room with Ethel Jones's best friend, Nonnie Grace Dewitt (formerly Wilson), and several other Haida. We had been attending a rally on the grounds of the Parliament Buildings in support of the Haida blockade and had just returned to our hotel when the national news came on television. Grace was the mother of Alan Wilson, the RCMP constable who was seen arresting her best friend on national television, and she could not hold back her tears. I comforted her with the words, "It's all over, Nonnie Grace, it's all over now," for I was fully aware of the transcending moment we had just witnessed. Peaceful senior citizens had been arrested on national television while holding their Bibles. Somehow I knew that iconic image would shame a nation into saving South Moresby.

CHAPTER IX

All Aboard!

The seventy-two Haida arrested on Lyell Island in November of 1985 had definitely elevated the cause for the Moresby campaign, even if the objectives were somewhat different. As Haida Nation president Buddy Richardson stated at the time, "The Haida objectives are very simple and very clear. The first is to protect Gwaii Haanas [Islands of Wonder] in its natural state in perpetuity, the second is to bring about recognition and respect for Haida title to Gwaii Haanas."

Both causes were still a long way from resolution in the year of the blockade, though the tide was about to turn. While the BC government was referring to the arrested Haida elders as common criminals, I sensed that this was not the sentiment across the country. Jack Webster had done an amazing job of keeping the blockade in the spotlight with daily footage on his 9:00 a.m. TV show. Although totally opposing the protest and supporting the loggers, Jack inadvertently made South Moresby a household name across Canada like never before.

I started contemplating ways we could show national support for the cause in a more public and dramatic fashion than letter-writing campaigns and petitions. The Canadian Nature Federation

(CNF) was Canada's largest conservation organization and the nation's equivalent of the American National Audubon Society—basically, bird lovers. When I was soliciting images and contributors for the *Islands at the Edge* book, I had approached Wayne Campbell, who worked in ornithology at the Royal BC Museum. Not only had Wayne graciously contributed the chapter "Down on the Water," but I recalled him telling me that birding was the number-one hobby in the world—much more popular than stamp, coin, butterfly or seashell collecting. South Moresby had a quarter of the nesting seabirds in the Canadian Pacific, which was one reason the international Pacific Seabird Group was the first organization to lend its support to our cause. It also had the highest eagle-nesting density in Canada and second-highest in the world. It suddenly struck me that we needed to enrol and engage the birders.

I met with Gregg Sheehy, the conservation director of the CNF, to discuss ways to involve their members in the Moresby campaign, at least more directly than sending letters to the editors of newspapers. On one of my lobby trips to Ottawa, Gregg happened to mention that Gary Clarke, president of the Tourism Industry Association of Canada, had suggested to him that the South Moresby campaigners should take a train across the country to support the cause. Gregg did not take the offhand comment as a serious proposal, but I did.

In most people's minds, the railway was the link that first connected Canada and gave it a strong sense of national purpose and identity. Never mind the fact that it was built on the backs of Chinese coolie labour, using land obtained for almost nothing (or outright stolen) from the Indigenous people, and capital raised for the most part in Britain. It was a symbol of national unity, or as historian Daniel Francis wrote, "We know that the railway no longer holds this country together in fact, but we suspect it is the one thing that holds it together in our imagination." I was now excited about the prospect and determined to organize a national train caravan to bring Canadians together on the Moresby issue.

As the founding director of the Islands Protection Society, I was not used to having my proposals so quickly and soundly rejected.

"That's crazy, Huck," I was told when I took the idea back to BC. "What if nobody or only a few people show up? We'll just look weak."

"The government already thinks we're weak," I replied. "What have we got to lose?" My argument dissuaded no one from their position, so I decided to seek support elsewhere.

On a subsequent visit to Ottawa in December, I told Gregg Sheehy to start organizing the CNF troops—we were going to do the train trip. "I think it was a bit like you calling a bluff and putting me on the spot, which is probably a good way to influence people," Gregg wrote to me decades later. He took the proposal to the CNF and with his considerable powers of persuasion, solicited the board's approval and started mobilizing the various chapters of the CNF from St. John's, Newfoundland, to Vancouver with a mass mailing. Unfortunately, this was in the days prior to the internet and social media, and Canada Post delayed the bulk mail so long that the train had already passed before most CNF members received their notifications.

At first there was no support in BC for my hare-brained idea, but that just prompted me to push it harder. But once the ball started moving with the CNF endorsement, others came to support the caravan. Paul George, director of the Western Canada Wilderness Committee (WCWC), had been pivotal in the Moresby campaign. Had he and photographer Richard Krieger not photo-documented Windy Bay and proposed it for a BC ecological reserve, it would have been the first place on Lyell Island to be logged. Paul got his entire WCWC media machine behind the caravan to ensure it had a big finish in Vancouver even if it had a weak start out East. Jeff Gibbs, one of the founders of Canada's Environmental Youth Alliance, also mobilized his students in support of the train. They brought a youthful energy that would rock Vancouver for the grand finale.

We had no operating budget and certainly could not afford to rent an entire passenger train, so we advertised a schedule of stops across the country where supporters could board and ride a segment of the route, or join special events in major cities along the way in

St. John's, Moncton, Halifax, Montreal, Ottawa, Toronto, Winnipeg, Regina, Calgary, Edmonton and Vancouver. Only Gregg Sheehy and I would ride the train the entire distance from coast to coast. Anticipating how easily our small contingent could get swallowed up in the hustle and bustle of a whistle stop, I asked Vancouver artists and South Moresby supporters Evelyn Roth and Hannelore Evans to design a large eagle puppet for the caravan. They crafted a magnificent, theatrical piece—a giant eagle with a twenty-foot wingspan that could be quickly assembled, hoisted at every train stop and disassembled before moving on. The eagle always drew a crowd, making our contingent look larger than life. We now had a made-for-television-and-news-photos mascot to identify and promote our cause.

John Broadhead also raised the caravan's profile by designing a beautiful button for supporters to wear that quickly found its way from train conductor caps to the suit lapels of government officials. The design on the button was a Canadian National train heading south to Lyell Island, bringing Canada symbolically to Gwaii Haanas and the site of the Haida blockades, under the watchful eye of Raven and a full moon.

John Broadhead designed this button for the Save South Moresby Caravan. It depicts the train heading for Lyell Island under the watchful eye of Raven. JOHN BROADHEAD PHOTO

A Canadian National Railway conductor proudly wears the button supporting the train caravan cause. GREGG SHEEHY PHOTO

During the launch of the eagle kite at Signal Hill, Newfoundland, at the start of the Save South Moresby Caravan in the spring of 1986, an Atlantic gust caught the large fabric wings and nearly carried us west ahead of our train. GREGG SHEEHY PHOTO

It was a blustery day on March 4, 1986, when Gregg Sheehy and a handful of local supporters, including Canadian folk singer Valdy, joined me to first unfurl the eagle mascot atop Signal Hill National Historic Park in St. John's, Newfoundland, to mark the start of our journey. A strong Atlantic wind caught the giant wings, nearly lifting us all off the ground and threatening to fly us west ahead of our train. Gregg said that had the CNF had more time to notify their members we would have seen much bigger crowds at the outset. Unfortunately, time was of the essence, for by the time we had garnered enough support for the idea, we were running dangerously close to the date the BC government's Environment and Land Use planning team would make their final decision on the fate of South Moresby. We needed to demonstrate that this was no idle endeavour; it was, in fact, the largest environmental campaign in Canadian history.

One group that did take the train caravan very seriously was the logging industry—two forest industry representatives who were trying to turn every rally into a debate tailed us the entire way. Meeting with the Canadian Sealers Association in St. John's,

The Save South Moresby Caravan started out in Newfoundland where enthusiastic crowds cheered us on. There were no train links from St. John's so we travelled aboard a CN Roadcruiser Bus. GREGG SHEEHY PHOTO

the Chainsaw Twins, as the two came to be lovingly known, told the sealers that Greenpeace was behind the Moresby campaign (which it never was) and that they should come out in force to ride us out of town (quite literally and ironically) "on a rail." A global Greenpeace campaign had all but shut down Newfoundland's sealing industry at that time, and tensions were strong. Nobody's fools, the Newfoundland sealers did a little research of their own and came to our opening rally, not heckling and threatening the "goddamn environmentalists" but wearing caravan buttons in support of the cause.

With no train links from St. John's, the caravan had to start out aboard a CN Roadcruiser Bus. A CBC van riding beside us had a cameraman filming our passage from an open side door. He was hanging so far out with his heavy camera that Gregg and I feared he might fall and become the first casualty of the thirteen-year campaign.

Until 1969, when CN Rail curtailed all passenger train services in Newfoundland, rail travel had a real romantic appeal. Before roads were built across Newfoundland, the train's dining car was said to have been the finest restaurant on the island as passengers chugged their way along North America's longest narrow-gauge rails.

Once we did climb aboard the train in New Brunswick, I must confess to hearing echoes of some of the doubters back in BC when I went to bed in my sleeper car that first night. It was well past midnight when the train slowed for something or someone on the tracks; the slower clickety-clack sound of the rails beneath the carriage woke me. I lifted the blinds beside my bunk to groggily peer out. There, standing in knee-deep snow in the middle of the night, was a crowd of several dozen South Moresby supporters waving banners and balloons and wildly cheering us on. The train was running behind schedule, I learned later, and this group, members of the New Brunswick Federation of Naturalists, had been standing in the frigid cold for over an hour. I couldn't believe my eyes, or their dedication, and I wondered how many other supporters we might have passed in the dark. Canadian nature lovers are a hardy lot, and from that moment on there was never a doubt in my mind

Supporters turned up out of nowhere in small and large groups as the Save South Moresby Choo Choo train caravan steamed across the world's second-largest country. GREGG SHEEHY PHOTO

that average Canadians were on board with this issue.

Support came from the least likely places. An Air Canada pilot, Ernie Beauchesne, built a travelling display for our events and flew from city to city all the way to Vancouver to set it up ahead of the train's arrival. The wife of a Canadian judge donated the $1,000 needed to rent St. Paul's Anglican Church for the caravan's event in Toronto. Bagpipers showed up at the CN Rail station in Ottawa to escort federal Environment Minister Tom McMillan onto the train wearing his VIA Rail hat with a Save South Moresby

A bagpiper showed up to support the train arriving in Ottawa and escorted federal Environment Minister Tom McMillan as he boarded the ride to Toronto. GREGG SHEEHY PHOTO

button attached. Even well-known celebrities like Pete Seeger, Bruce Cockburn and Long John Baldry lent their time and talents to fundraising events along the way.

Every day and at every stop more and more supporters came aboard. The Save South Moresby Caravan was becoming the party you didn't want to miss. People boarded with musical instruments, composing lyrics and singing songs to the tune of "Chattanooga Choo Choo." Revelling in the company of fellow Canadians united in purpose, supporters brought aboard food to share from their respective regions—maple syrup, bannock, smoked fish and Quebec's contribution to low-fat diets, poutine: french fries smothered in gravy and grated cheese.

By the time the train reached Montreal, the press was following the story closely and members of Parliament were tripping over one another trying to get aboard the ride into Ottawa. Former prime minister Pierre Trudeau came out strongly in support of the caravan cause, as did Tom McMillan, House Speaker John Fraser and former Liberal environment minister Charles Caccia. It was snowballing and time for the Haida Nation to join in.

Our event in Toronto was scheduled for St. Paul's Anglican Church and the Haida Nation flew in the elders arrested on Lyell Island four months earlier to be part of it. As the train pulled into Union Station, Guujaaw was on the platform pounding his drum along with a strong delegation of Haida in ceremonial blankets supporting their elders Ethel Jones, Ada Yovanovich, Watson Pryce and Grace Dewitt. They held big banners proclaiming, "You Can Kill a Tree but Not Haida Nation!" The church was packed that evening with an estimated seventeen hundred people as Pierre Berton, the esteemed Canadian historian, prepared to deliver a speech in support of the cause. He called the logging of South Moresby "an act of vandalism, a national disgrace." Strong as his delivery was, it was not the highlight of the evening. That moment was reserved for the Haida elders' entry.

The entire assembly rose in a spontaneous standing ovation as Nonnie Ethel Jones, Nonni Ada Yovanovich and Chini Watson Pryce (Chief Gaahlaay) walked down the centre aisle of the church to speak at the podium. Branded criminals by the BC government, these elders were getting a hero's welcome in a major church in the nation's financial capital. "It's just wonderful how people across Canada are with us," said Ethel Jones, who was scheduled to appear in court on April 16 in Prince Rupert to face charges and a possible jail sentence. "We know our fight is just beginning. We're not stopping now," she told the cheering church assembly.

It was one thing to bring environmentalists and bird lovers to the cause, but the elders had now brought the backing of church groups right across the country, making the movement so mainstream I knew there could be no turning back for the provincial and federal governments. In retrospect, the message must have been painfully clear for the authorities; you don't arrest peaceful senior citizens holding their Bibles in front of national television cameras.

Former federal environment minister Charles Caccia spoke at a train stop press conference in support of the Moresby campaign. GREGG SHEEHY PHOTO

No environmentalist backroom planning session could have ever come up with such a strategy; it was pure serendipity or, as the Haida would see it, Raven working his mysterious ways. It seemed to me now just a matter of time and political willpower to seal the deal. Tom McMillan told me later that the Save South Moresby Caravan and the event in Toronto gave him the political clout he needed to prove to Ottawa and Victoria that this was truly a national issue.

Another major event in support of the train caravan and Moresby cause was held in Vancouver, organized by none other than Master Abstractor David Lawrence Phillips. He secured works from celebrated Canadian artists for a caravan support raffle and had Bob Rae at the piano and other well-known performers for a $100-a-plate fundraising dinner. What really grabbed the attention of the media was not the event, but the aftermath. Never one to waste good food and a lover of throwing spontaneous "beggar's banquets," David hired a food truck to transport all the leftovers to feed the city's homeless. "Hundred-Dollar-a-Plate Dinners Served on Skid Row" the newspapers blared the next morning. The Moresby campaign was now reaching every segment of Canadian society.

As the Save South Moresby Choo Choo (as it came to be lovingly known) roared its way across the second-largest country on earth, excitement mounted. A huge First Nations powwow was held in Winnipeg in support of the Haida's stand on Lyell Island and major events were held in Regina and Calgary before the train route split in Calgary so Edmonton could be included on the northern route. Gregg Sheehy rode with supporters on the southern route along with Colleen McCrory and famed bear biologist Charlie Russell, while I headed north with an excited throng of supporters to Edmonton for another big event. The train really filled up in Jasper for one of the world's most scenic rail journeys through the Canadian Rockies all the way to Vancouver.

The Save South Moresby Caravan Supercontinental #3 train pulled into Vancouver's CN Rail station at 1:30 p.m., March 15. It was greeted by over two thousand cheering people crammed into the

Haida elders who rode the train from Toronto to Vancouver are welcomed by banner-waving and cheering supporters at the journey's end. RICHARD KRIEGER PHOTO

station and in front of the building as the caravan supporters disembarked from Edmonton. Calgary supporters, having arrived at 9:30 a.m., were already on the platform to welcome the second train. As Gregg Sheehy and I unfurled the giant eagle for the last time, we could only quietly smile at each other. From when we had first done this in St. John's just ten days earlier, our numbers had swelled a thousandfold. The train caravan had become more than a success; it was a seminal event.

After some preliminary speeches in front of the train station, a parade ensued through downtown Vancouver all the way to Burrard Inlet. The Western Canada Wilderness Committee had secured a parade permit from city hall so we could legally make our march. As Guujaaw drummed the elders through the streets, I hoisted the eagle kite at the front of the parade route. There was a festive air to the march; it was more than a protest, with red and white balloons dancing in the fresh spring breeze, heartfelt banners and homemade signs all following a giant eagle kite beneath which Haida in full regalia sang celebratory songs.

Thousands of supporters in front of the CN Rail station welcomed the train's arrival in Vancouver. RICHARD KRIEGER PHOTO

The Save South Moresby Caravan parade swelled in numbers as it proceeded from the CN Rail station to Canada Place on Burrard Inlet. RICHARD KRIEGER PHOTO

After leading the Vancouver parade with the eagle kite at the end of our historic train journey, I never saw our eagle mascot again. RICHARD KRIEGER PHOTO

I don't believe we ever got an estimate of the crowd size that continued to swell as we marched across the Cambie Street Bridge through downtown Vancouver to Burrard Inlet, but it was enormous by the time we reached Canada Place, the federal government's newly built showcase for Expo 86. It seemed a fitting place to end a historic journey to raise awareness for the Moresby campaign and Haida rights. Expo 86 was, after all, scheduled to be a World Exposition on Transportation and Communication.

At the Canada Place rally, Buddy Richardson said it was a day of celebration, "celebrating South Moresby as an important part of the earth." Jim Fulton, MP for the region and the person who introduced the guest speaker, noted that a bald eagle was circling the gathering. "It's symbolic!" he said, and indeed it was. It seemed as if the eagle kite mascot that had just travelled with us seventy-five hundred kilometres across Canada had finally freed itself of its inanimate form, and true to the Haida tradition of transformation, it just sort of disappeared. I have no idea what happened to it after that event.

Some years later, Jim Hart, Chief Eidansuu (Edenshaw) from Old Massett, was telling me of a time he was carving near Masset Inlet and saw a raven land on a spruce branch near the water's edge. "The poor thing had its beak stuck in a white Styrofoam fishing float," Jim said. "I thought it would starve to death, but I had no idea how I could help it." While he was pondering the dilemma, a flock of surf scoter ducks flew in to dabble along the water's edge. Seeing them, the raven suddenly swooped down with outstretched wings and scattered them in all directions. The raven then returned to the same branch it had been sitting on, effortlessly threw off the fish float and cawed as if it were laughing. "That rascal was pretending to be an eagle," Chief Edenshaw told me. "He could never have startled the ducks as a raven, but he scared the hell out of them with the white 'head' of a bald eagle."

Perhaps the Save South Moresby Caravan's eagle puppet was Raven in disguise all along.

CHAPTER X

Raven Walks Around the World

Passionate and obsessed as I was with Rediscovery and the Moresby cause, they were never enough to contain my wanderlust. I have the gypsy gene in me. "You can't go away now!" fellow conservationists would plead. "Everything hangs in the balance in the next few months." Somehow I always knew that was not the case. While the governments, planning teams and the press wanted us to believe that line, the movement was always outside of their predictions and control. It had a life of its own, something I had felt from the start. Far from distracting me from the cause, my mid-winter journeys between November and April always reinforced my beliefs and rededicated me to the cause.

It was easy to fall into the trap of naysayers in British Columbia telling us that South Moresby was no different than anywhere else on the coast, that there were "way nicer areas" in need of protection. "Why be stupid?" people would ask. "No one is going to defer a tree farm licence for higher use in BC anyway. Do something more constructive with your time."

Had I stayed put in BC twelve months a year I might have started to believe such defeatist attitudes. I remember Guujaaw once commenting, "The gift that Huck brought to Haida Gwaii was putting everything in global perspective."

Having travelled throughout much of the world, I learned that it's pretty hard to hold onto provincial attitudes when you return home. I can recall returning to Victoria after a six-month trip across the African continent where I witnessed people starving in the Sahel, but the big issue in BC's capital that was burning up the talk-show lines and grabbing newspaper headlines was the fake heritage decor of the new Eaton's shopping mall. So much of what we concern ourselves with seems trivial compared to greater global issues, but my travels always served to put things in perspective and reconfirm my first impression of Haida Gwaii and the South Moresby cause. It was an area of global significance; we just needed to convince Canada of that.

Even as a child I had this insatiable wanderlust. I can recall a spontaneous hike I made during my high school years. I was standing on the beach of Lake Michigan where our family had a summer cottage when I was overcome with a desire to follow the shoreline much farther north than my normal strolls.

"How long do you think it would take me to hike north to Ludington?" I asked my parents.

"About three days," my dad answered matter-of-factly.

"See you then," I replied as I set off, foolishly barefoot. As one of nine kids, I was never sure if my folks were trying to support my passion for adventure or simply trying to thin out the herd, but there they were three days later waiting for me in a beach parking lot as I crawled the last kilometre of my forty-eight-kilometre beach ordeal with horribly blistered feet.

To be honest, there were times when my youthful quest for adventure bordered on the reckless and absurd, if not the suicidal. On two occasions, were it not for the intervention of what I can only call guardian angels, I wouldn't be here today.

Even as a child attending religious classes, I could never really fathom the concept of angels. Those feathery creatures always appeared freaky to me in paintings; I was like a child terrified of clowns. Even at my elementary school, where the nuns were forever harping on the glories of heaven and the horrors of hell, the thought of spending eternity with a celestial host of those cheery cherubs stringing away on their harps had less appeal to me than the damnation alternative of fire and brimstone. My guardian angels turned out to be very different.

One cold, dark winter in my early twenties I decided to hitch-hike across the USA and down the Baja Peninsula in search of some affordable warmth and sunshine. In those days there was no sealed road running the length of the thousand-mile-long peninsula, just criss-crossing tracks through the world's most beautiful floral desert. After one long, arduous ride in the back of a cattle truck, being jostled between ornery steers and the sideboards, I was smothered in dust, reeking of cow dung and looking for any escape at all. The dirt road suddenly emerged from the desert, running beside a glorious stretch of golden sand beach with Pacific breakers fringing a deep blue sea. Water was such a welcome and unexpected sight that I immediately banged on the cab roof of the truck for the Mexican driver to drop me off. He looked confused, as there was nothing here but wilderness desert and wild Pacific shores, but I was determined to end the ordeal, and against my driver's better judgment, I disembarked.

As the truck disappeared on the southern horizon in a cloud of dust and calling cattle, I looked up and down the beach and realized I was utterly alone. Thrilled at the prospect, I stripped naked, ran down the beach and plunged into the sea. As I swam offshore, I found myself being lifted skyward as if a whale was surfacing below me. It was a monster wave, the first in a set, and I was lucky enough to be on the seaward side as it broke violently on the steep shore. "Holy shit," I thought out loud. I swam farther out to sea as I watched three more monster waves wreak their havoc on the shore. I soon realized that the big breakers were coming in sets of three to four with more moderate waves in between. I was going to have to time my exit very carefully, I realized. I treaded water and watched for some time to make sure I had the wave pattern right.

As soon as the last breaker in a big set ended its long Pacific journey on the Baja shore, I swam frantically to reach the beach. The backwash was serious, however, nearly negating my strongest strokes. I was just putting my feet down on the steep beach when the first breaker in a big set crushed me and I emerged from the tumbling dazed and with a bloody nose. I struggled in panic to regain my footing and exit the water before the next wave struck, but the undertow was too powerful and I took a second pounding. When I rose for air this time I realized I was in real trouble and likely to drown. Instead of my life flashing before me, I recall focusing on a single ocotillo cactus sitting alone on the ridge to the east of the beach and thinking how embarrassing this was. I was a good swimmer yet I was going to drown right beside the shore.

When the third wave hit me I was knocked unconscious. When I came to I was lying on my back, coated in coarse sand and puking up seawater while the wrinkled old face of a fisherman stared at me from inches away with deep concern. I had no idea where he could have possibly come from, but he had apparently rescued me from the surf after the final wave of the big set that took me down.

"*Loco! Peligroso aqui, señor*" (Crazy! Dangerous here, mister) was all he said as he tapped my forehead to make his point and went his way. I looked down the beach to see where he was heading, but there was no boat, beach hut or village to be seen and his tracks in the sand were already being washed away by the waves before I fully had my wits about me.

A few years later I was miraculously saved again in the high Peruvian Andes. I had already hiked the Inca Trail to Machu Picchu long before trekkers started crowding this trail, but I was in search of something even wilder and less well-trodden. A Peace Corps volunteer I happened to meet told me of a largely unknown Inca road that led from a high mountain pass three days down to the jungles of the Peruvian Amazon. It sounded perfect. "Where is the pass?" I asked him. The instructions I was given were as simple as they were ambiguous. I was to catch a twice-a-week local bus that travelled through the pass and get off at the summit. There I would find a large statue of Jesus with his arms outstretched. I was to hike in the direction of the statue's left arm until I came upon the carved rocks of an Inca road. From there I simply needed to follow the road down to the Amazon jungles where I would come to the village that the bus was headed to, with twice-a-week service back out.

It all seemed straightforward enough, so I set off on the appointed day to catch the bus to the pass. There was barely room for my backpack amid the crowd of villagers, crying babies and big handwoven bags crammed full of potatoes and chickens. The other passengers became concerned when I banged the side of the bus to be let off as we reached the high mountain pass. The statue of Jesus was there, as promised, but my fellow travellers were all issuing dire warnings in Spanish and Quechua and trying to restrain me from disembarking. These people have no sense of adventure, I thought as I resisted an old woman physically trying to hold me back. Of course I was wrong—no one survives in the Andes without a respect for elevation and having a sixth sense for approaching weather.

No sooner had the bus and its passengers reluctantly left me behind than it started to snow. I quickly shouldered my bag and set off in the direction Jesus was telling me to go. The snowfall quickly turned into a complete whiteout and I looked back, alarmed to see that the huge Jesus statue had disappeared. Lost, I decided to retrace my steps and make camp beside the statue until the weather cleared, but snowfall had already erased my trail. I was totally disoriented now and becoming frightened. Was I going to freeze to death in the high Andes like some mangled Inca mummy found centuries later in a glacial crevasse?

Just as the fatal mistake I had made was fully sinking in, I saw a hunched-over figure appearing like an apparition through the heavy falling snow. It looked like a huge brown bear at first, but I knew no brown bears inhabited the Andes—only the smaller Andean speckled bear. As the phantom-like creature drew closer, I could make out the figure of a barefoot old man bent under the weight of the huge pile of firewood he was hauling. He walked right up to me, said nothing, but signalled with a head nod for me to follow and continued on his way. I followed him like an obedient dog.

We hadn't hiked through the snow for more than forty-five minutes before our descent led us out of the flurry and into a large green alpine valley where I found myself hiking down the ancient sculptured steps of an Inca road. The wood hauler easily outpaced me, even with his advanced age and heavy load. Before I lost sight of him, he seemed to be heading for a rock hut set in the centre of the valley below, and I made a promise to myself to give him the most treasured food items from my backpack when I reached his house; after all, he had saved my life.

There were no trees to conceal anything in this high Andean valley, only the lone stone house that I kept my eye on as I descended, but to my surprise no one was there when I arrived. The hut had not been used in a long time, as the cobwebs covering the doorway and thick dust on the few furnishings testified. I searched in all directions for the humble man who had rescued me, but no one was to be found. This angel had no wings and was certainly not strumming a harp.

I travelled much farther afield after leaving Michigan, eventually reaching 130 countries and every continent, including Antarctica. The memories of these adventures are too extensive to relate here, but a few of my encounters had a direct bearing on my future endeavours on Haida Gwaii.

My six-month odyssey crossing the African continent in a Bedford truck with a few companions and camping out every night under the stars of the Sahara Desert, the jungle canopy of the Congo River basin and the plains of East Africa where lions roared throughout the night etched many indelible images in my mind. My companions and I had to lay out metal tracks ahead of the truck when crossing the shifting sands of the Grand Erg Oriental in the central Sahara, sometimes moving only a kilometre a day. But the slowest going was negotiating the bomb-crater-like holes in the red earth of the Congo River basin, where torrential rains would turn the dirt road, absurdly known as the Trans-African Highway, into a quagmire of mud.

Late one evening, as the five in our group were about to give up on making any further progress, a small band of Mbuti Pygmies darted across the road in front of us. They were carrying huge hand-woven jungle-fibre nets atop their heads that made them resemble lions with shaggy manes more than people. We stopped the truck to request permission to photograph them, but they surprised us by waving for us to join them deep in the Ituri Forest where they had their camp. Sharing is an instinctive response among nomadic forest dwellers, so we were invited to join in the feast of a dik-dik (the world's smallest bovine) that they had successfully caught in their nets.

It was growing dark by the time the meat was roasted on sticks for us to share. Sensing our need for shelter, the Mbuti graciously erected several much larger leaf-covered huts for their oversized guests. Even then the huts were too small for all in our party so I slept beside the fire in the centre of camp that was tended throughout the night by a young Mbuti man. Mbuti women are responsible for moving fire by day, carry a burning ember with them when they frequently relocate their settlements, and a young unmarried man is given the task of keeping the flame alive throughout the night. The flame I was hypnotized to sleep by may have been burning unextinguished for decades or centuries.

At first light, the fire keeper and I were awoken by a "honey guide"—a small bird that finds an Mbuti encampment once it has located a beehive in a

An Mbuti (Pygmy) man blackens his face in preparation for a dik-dik hunt I took part in deep in the Ituri Forest of the Congo River Basin. It is believed that some Mbuti fires have been burning unextinguished for decades or centuries.

tree. "Quick, quick—honey, quick" was the call the frantic little bird seemed to make as it danced around our fire site, desperate to get our attention. Before anyone else awoke, the young man lined a basket with fresh leaves, grabbed a thick burning stick from the fire and followed the excited bird deep into the forest with me close behind. Before long the honey guide led us to the tree where it had discovered a large beehive in a hollow twenty metres overhead. The Mbuti boy wasted no time in scrambling up the tree, smoking out the bees and filling his basket with the most succulent honey I have ever tasted in my life. Before either of us could take a bite, however, the boy was duty bound to take the choicest piece of honeycomb, replete with bee larvae, and set it ceremoniously atop a stick he drove into the ground as a gift to the little bird. I was told later that this is a uniquely symbiotic relationship between the Mbuti and the honey guides, as the birds take their message only to the Mbuti, never the neighbouring Bantu tribes.

Back in camp everyone shared in the breakfast honeycomb feast before the Mbuti passed around marijuana to smoke in preparation for another dik-dik hunt. The Mbuti grow no crops, but they trade jungle meat, wild honey and forest medicines with the agriculturally based Bantu tribes that neighbour the Ituri Forest. The Bantu in turn provide the Mbuti with "ganja," their preferred drug. As the men set off with the nets atop their heads to lay out a horseshoe-shaped trap in the forest, the women, children and dogs drove the shy and reclusive dik-diks out from their hiding places under fallen trees and into the trap. Standing just outside the nets with toylike bows and poison-tipped arrows, the Mbuti men were ready to receive the prey.

It was a hunt I will never forget. The men used only simulated birdcalls to communicate with one another while setting out their nets in the incredibly dense forest. Even if we hadn't been in a stoned state, it would have been impossible to distinguish the real birdcalls from the Mbuti calls. Sitting silently and listening to this hunt, I came to the startling realization of why so-called pygmies are the world's smallest people. They are exactly as tall as the height a dik-dik can graze when standing on its hind feet and reaching up with its neck. I had a horrible backache from bending over while trying to negotiate my way through the forest, but the Mbuti walked upright with their nets atop their heads as casually as an urbanite strolling down the street to a morning coffee shop.

We hadn't seen a lot of primary forest along the Trans-African road, as the Bantu-speaking tribes were clearing increasing amounts of forest for their expanding population and agricultural needs. It was clear to me that before long the Mbuti would no longer have a forest homeland at all, and I vowed that day to start working toward tropical rainforest preservation as soon as South Moresby's temperate rainforest was secured on Haida Gwaii.

My next encounter with some of the world's traditional forest-based societies was with the Penan people in the jungles of Borneo, followed by a month with the Asmat in the mangrove-swamp forests of southwestern New Guinea, and then a long-term relationship with the Mentawai on the remote Indonesian island of Siberut. Years of living together with the Haida had prepared me for all of these encounters, allowing me to immerse myself into distinct Indigenous cultures with relative ease. I had by now totally departed from the academic training I'd received at the Michigan State University Department of Anthropology, where it was considered unprofessional to become involved in the human-rights issues Indigenous societies almost universally face or to even form friendships on a basic human level, as such relationships might cloud one's "findings."

I can recall the first trip I made back to Borneo to introduce Dr. Wade Davis to the Penan people after he agreed to co-author the book *Penan: Voice for the Borneo Rainforest* with me. We were staying in a small, elevated hut set up for visiting dignitaries and interviewing a group of Penan when we realized it was growing too dark for them to travel the long distance back to their homes in the forest. "Why don't we all just sleep here together?" I suggested.

"That is what we really like," came the immediate reply. Ever since Rajah James Brooke annexed Sarawak for the United Kingdom by putting down a pirate rebellion, the Penan have had trade

David Suzuki (left) wrote the foreword to *Penan: Voice for the Borneo Rainforest*, co-authored by Wade Davis (right) and me (centre). It was a centrepiece and funding source for the Voices for the Borneo Rainforest World Tour that brought worldwide attention to the plight of these nomadic, forest-dwelling peoples.

relationships with foreigners. But just like the apartheid systems designed to separate First Peoples in Canada from the nation's immigrants, the British always insisted on separate quarters for their own trade ambassadors and officials. The Malaysian government has kept that apartheid policy in place to this day.

My offer to all bed down together that night, I realized in retrospect, was revolutionary and undermining a several-hundred-year-old tradition, but Haida Gwaii Rediscovery had prepared me for this to the point it seemed perfectly natural. I found myself cuddling up against the cold with a gaggle of Penan while Wade Davis, the esteemed anthropologist from Harvard, went to the far corner of the shelter to sleep alone. The next morning he was troubled by his behaviour, though no one else seemed to care. "I wonder what it was that made me behave like that?" Wade asked, almost apologetically. "Why didn't I curl up with you guys?" Academia, I thought, but didn't openly reply.

Over the decades I found myself being welcomed back home in remote parts of the planet by Indigenous peoples who had formally adopted me into their tribes and honoured me with names. I consider these titles to be the highest accolades ever bestowed on me. I was given the names Qualum (Original Path) by Napoleon Kruger of the Thompson tribe in British Columbia's Interior; Pepejek Urip (Lifting Life Upright) by the Penan people of Borneo; Utut Kunan (Forever and Always Lucky) by the Mentawai tribe on the island of Siberut, Indonesia; Tahari Ara (Big Brother) by the Newari people in the Kathmandu Valley, Nepal; Phuyai Baan (Village Headman) by my friends in Thailand; Tenzin Chdrk (Strong in Spirit) by a Tibetan friend who works closely with the Dalai Lama in Dar es Salaam; and Omulebeleze (Guardian) by the Bakiga tribe on the border of Uganda and the Congo.

Back home, the first Haida name ever bestowed on me from the elders, Skudglu, was more a translation of the nickname I arrived with than anything special. Skudglu is Haida for the red huckleberry.

I was formally adopted into the Yagu Laanas Clan by Mary Yeltatzie Swanson (seated at front, right) at her son Darin's potlatch, and was bestowed the name Yaahl Hlaagaay Gwii Kaas (Raven Walks Around the World). Doctors Richard and Becky Feldman (standing together at left and beside Darin Swanson, wearing headdress) were also adopted at this event. Crystal Swanson (front, centre) is seated beside her mother and her son, Ernie, stands beside me (back, right).

Much later, after the start of the Moresby campaign and Rediscovery, Haida elder Ethel Jones started calling me Kiljai, the Haida word for a chief. I was never comfortable with such a name, as I was certainly not Haida, much less a chief. I had no lineage rights whatsoever, so I felt greatly indebted to Mary Swanson, who formalized my adoption into her family at a potlatch where I was given the name Yaahl Hlaagaay Gwii Kaas—"Raven Walks Around the World." It is a required custom to repeat your name three times in the feast house for all to hear and then to dance once you receive it, so a simpler honorary title would have been easier for me to pronounce repeatedly. Nonetheless, it was a distinct honour to be given a name by the granddaughter of legendary Haida artist Charles Edenshaw and matriarch of the Yagu Laanas Clan—the largest of the Haida clans. Raven is held in the highest esteem by the Haida as the creator and trickster that freed the sun, moon and stars from a chief's treasure box, and released the first humans from the confines of a clamshell on North Beach at the dawn of time. Ever curious and throwing caution to the wind, Raven can find himself walking around the

I was seated in the place of honour with my Haida mother through adoption, Mary Yeltatzie Swanson, at her ninetieth birthday celebration.

world quite serendipitously. No character, mythological or otherwise, has a better faculty of making fortunate discoveries by accident.

It was nice to have a title to help excuse my gypsy ways, and none of those other names, wonderful as they were, captured my true wanderlust and nomadic spirit as fully as Raven Walks Around the World.

It was, in fact, through one of my Haida Gwaii connections that my wanderings took me to a destination I could only have dreamed about. Having lived most of my life at poverty level, I thought being able to afford a trip to Antarctica, a bucket-list destination, was a prospect that would forever elude me. Every summer when I returned from Asia to Victoria, where I had moved in 1983, I would make a point of joining Dr. Bristol Foster and Dr. Tom Reimchen (better known as "Stickleback Tom" from his Haida Gwaii genetic research days) at the Irish Times Pub for grub, a few pints of ale and a chance to catch up. Bristol Foster was the first government official to back Guujaaw and me in the early days of the South Moresby cause. Bristol was so highly regarded in academic circles that he was employed by Lindblad Expeditions to lecture aboard their cruises to Antarctica. Lindblad was the company that first opened the doors to tourism on the planet's southernmost continent, and they had now partnered with National Geographic Expeditions to offer some of the world's most exclusive sailings.

Late that evening at the pub, after more than our share of ale, Bristol told me that he could contact Lindblad's head office to see whether they might take me on if there was a last-minute cancellation. Months later, I got an email message from Lindblad saying they had an opening for me, but I had not been checking my messages frequently enough and lost out on the opportunity. I begged Bristol to ask that they put my name back on the standby list, and after some objections that they were stretching the rules, they did.

Over a year later I was on a several-day pony trek in the remote highlands of Lesotho, Africa, when I came across a small town with an internet shop. I hitched my Basotho pony to a fence and decided to check my email. There was a message from Lindblad: "An elderly couple have had to make a last-minute cancellation to their month-long Antarctica trip, but they are fully insured. The value of their trip is $56,000, but it's yours for $1,000 if you can be in Santiago, Chile, in three days." I unhitched my pony and asked my guide to take it back to his village, tipped him handsomely for his troubles and began looking for the fastest route from Lesotho to Santiago.

It was not easy getting outfitted for cold-weather gear in Santiago in midsummer, but then Lindblad gave me the details of my $1,000 trip fee. Incredibly, it included a night at the Santiago Sheraton, my flight to Ushuaia and back where the ship was docked, and my expedition parka. When adding up those costs, I realized the trip was basically free!

I had to pinch myself to believe it was really happening as I joined my fellow Antarctic adventurers on the National Geographic *Endeavour* ship. It was not a crowd for George Bush jokes, but the conservative fellow American passengers and I did share a love of wildlife and adventure so we got along well even if there was no political or financial commonality. Knowing I was the only person on board with a private room valued at $56,000, several passengers asked me, "What exactly do you do for a living?"

"I get by," I replied.

Our cruise took us out Beagle passage to the Falkland Islands and on to South Georgia Island, the world's most spectacular setting for penguins, fur seals and elephant seals, set on the edge of the rich waters of the Antarctic convergence. We then cruised to the South Orkney Islands and eventually the Antarctic Peninsula before returning to Cape Horn and Tierra del Fuego. That month-long voyage held far too many magical moments to relate here, but I will never forget the captain putting the bow of the ship right up on the Ross Ice Shelf so we could step ashore with emperor penguins, or blissfully paddling my single kayak through giant icebergs shimmering a deep blue as feeding penguins darted out of the water all around my craft. Lost in the sublime moment, I failed to hear a Zodiac power up beside me. A ship's steward was standing upright on the bow wearing his parka and white gloves and holding up a

Thermos and a large mug. "Would you prefer peppermint schnapps or brandy with your hot chocolate, sir?"

In addition to over-the-top indulgence, real research was taking place on the vessel. A marine biologist on board would launch an underwater submersible below the icebergs with a live feed to the ship's cocktail lounge. The large screens would suddenly zoom in on a new discovery and interrupt the cheery cocktail chatter for a moment. "Excuse me, ladies and gentlemen, but the brilliantly coloured nudibranch you are seeing on your screen right now has never before been seen by human eyes; it's one of over twenty-three hundred nudibranch species, but this one is new to science. Shall we name it?" Everyone would then raise a glass to bestow a slightly tipsy name on a new sea slug species.

As extravagant as my Lindblad cruise was, it paled in comparison to the opulence of the next ship I was invited to lecture aboard. After I'd given an address at the Explorers Club not long after my Antarctica voyage, a woman in attendance suggested I speak aboard *The World*—the world's most exclusive and prestigious ship. I knew nothing about this vessel until I was contacted by the head office in

Moken Sea Gypsies row their traditional dugouts beside *The World*—the most exclusive ship on the seas—where I was twice invited aboard to cruise the coast of Burma (now Myanmar) while giving lectures for some of the world's richest people.

Florida and given the terms of my engagement. I would need to sign a legal affidavit to never divulge the names of the residents on board. While some of the world's boastfully rich flaunt their wealth like Donald Trump and are addicted to media attention, the super rich are more discreet and prefer their privacy. At 196 metres in length and crewed by 260 staff, *The World* Residences at Sea is the largest private ship on the high seas. It is large enough to be a cruise ship for thousands of passengers, but instead it provides 165 living residences for its owners, some having a net worth in excess of $100 billion. I was told that Oprah Winfrey wanted to join this exclusive club but would have attracted the media attention the exceptionally wealthy go out of their way to avoid.

When I was invited aboard *The World* for a week to lecture about the Moken Sea Gypsies as we cruised through the remote Mergui Archipelago of Burma (now Myanmar), I saw an opportunity to raise awareness about Indigenous rights with people of influence and also gain access to an extremely restricted region of Myanmar where Moken peoples were facing forced assimilation. I had not expected to be treated to a level of luxury I'd never before imagined. Five years later when I was invited back to lecture again as the ship repeated the same passage, I was granted even more privileges on board. One restriction I had was to not have my wine orders exceed $250 a bottle, though there were no restrictions on the number of bottles.

How exactly did I end up here, I wondered as I awoke on board one morning to the ship's TV channel that was announcing to its elite passengers my next lecture in the theatre. From hitchhiking barefoot and penniless in Central America to cruising aboard the largest and most exclusive passenger vessel that continuously circumnavigates the globe, I'd pretty well seen it all. That's the beauty of travel—expanding the mind through transformational experiences and then returning home to put it all in perspective. Haida Gwaii, the Islands of the People, a microcosm of our planet if ever there was one, had become that perspective point for me.

CHAPTER XI

Wave Eater

O ne final act had to be performed before the curtain came down on the South Moresby show, but the actors were unaware at the time that they were even being cast for it. Bill Reid had been commissioned by the Bank of British Columbia to carve a twenty-four-metre traditional Haida canoe for Expo 86 in Vancouver. So prestigious and historical was this undertaking that the ocean-going vessel named *Lootaas*—Haida for Wave Eater—was positioned in front of the Royal Yacht *Britannia* for the opening ceremony. No one ever imagined that this cedar canoe would set the final dramatic stage for the thirteen-year struggle to save South Moresby.

Since Bill Reid had opened the door for the Islands Protection Society to publish *Islands at the Edge: Preserving the Queen Charlotte Islands Wilderness*, I had been spending more and more time with him, turning a casual relationship into a deep friendship. Guujaaw continued assisting Bill in creating his final legacy of masterpieces, so the invitation was always open for me to spend time in Bill's Granville Island studio while visiting Guujaaw in Vancouver. Watching Bill's monumental creations transform from mere sketches on scraps of paper into world-renowned works of art was awe-inspiring. There was his stunning yellow cedar sculpture *The Raven and the First Men* (1980), which

Bill Reid immortalized the Haida creation story in his carving, *The Raven and the First Men*, which now graces the rotunda of the Museum of Anthropology at the University of British Columbia.

Guujaaw sits atop a giant clamshell while working on Bill Reid's sculpture *The Raven and the First Men*. RICHARD KRIEGER PHOTO

now graces the rotunda hall of the Museum of Anthropology at the University of British Columbia, followed by the monumental bronze sculpture of the Haida Killer Whale, *Chief of the Undersea World* that guards the entrance to the Vancouver Aquarium. Some of Bill's creations were pure whimsy, like a frog with bulging eyes you could pull around on rollers that Bill called *Phyllidula, the Shape of Frogs to Come*.

Bill's thirty-year struggle with Parkinson's disease was taking a frightening toll on his abilities by the time I got to know him well. He seemed almost possessed in his determination to leave as lasting a legacy as possible before the scourge claimed his life. I watched him model and cast what may go down as his greatest achievement—*The Spirit of Haida Gwaii (The Black Canoe)*—a colossal, five-thousand-kilogram bronze sculpture commissioned for the Canadian embassy in Washington, DC, in 1989. A twin casting in 1996 called *The Jade Canoe* was created for the main lobby of the Vancouver International Airport and became such an iconic national symbol the image was used to grace the Canadian $20 banknote.

For this crowning achievement, Bill deliberately crowded all the Haida mythological creatures into the canoe facing different directions as a mischievous statement about Haida politics; he privately referred to it as the *Ship of Fools*. No one infuriated the Haida more or endowed them with greater pride in their culture than Bill Reid. His often glib comments seemed insensitive. When asked by the media how he felt about the renaissance in Haida art catalyzed by his work, he replied, "What renaissance? Most Haida don't know which end of a hatchet to hold."

From having frequent dinners together, often at his house, and assisting him in his wheelchair to various gallery openings, I knew that Bill's words often came not from his heart, but the pain and heavy medication he was on for his fatal condition. His spirit was totally with the Haida Nation, and he demonstrated that repeatedly with his support for Rediscovery and elevating the South Moresby cause. Had it not been for Bill hosting a gathering of influential

Bill Reid's famous sculpture, *The Jade Canoe* is installed in the lobby of the Vancouver International Airport. It is a replica of *The Spirit of Haida Gwaii (The Black Canoe)*—a colossal, five-thousand-kilogram bronze sculpture commissioned for the Canadian embassy in Washington, DC.

people at his house that was attended by Maurice Strong, founding director of the United Nations Environment Program, Rediscovery might never have expanded beyond the shores of Haida Gwaii: it was at a Rediscovery slideshow I presented in Bill's apartment that Maurice's wife, Hanne, invited me to Colorado to start up a Rediscovery program for the Ute, Pueblo and Navajo tribes.

Bill Reid loved the idea of a reawakening of Indigenous cultures on the coast. Even though he was refused permission to build a home and studio in Skidegate Village due to his half-Haida heritage and lack of Indian status, he used to lobby me hard to set up a Haida village on a small island just offshore from Skidegate so Haida elementary schoolchildren could have a place to go for cultural immersion and outdoor education after school hours.

The last time I saw Bill, shortly before he passed away on March 13, 1998, was when I dropped in on him unexpectedly for a quick courtesy call along with Justin Nelson, a young Nuxalk boy from Bella Coola who had been taking the Rediscovery training I was facilitating at United World College. With barely an introduction and not an ounce of intimidation, Justin walked right across Bill's living-room floor, took a masterpiece painted drum from the wall and said, "Mind if I drum you a song, Mr. Reid?" Had any of Bill's agents or art groupies been present they would have scolded Justin for his insolence and found him an unpainted drum.

Not Bill. "That would be good," he replied.

While risking rubbing off some of the priceless painting on the drum skin to warm the hide with the palm of his hand, Justin proclaimed the ownership of the song he was about to sing. "Long ago when our chiefs first came to the Bella Coola Valley, they danced down the eyelashes of the sun singing this song. It has been handed down through the generations to Chief Lawrence Pootlas." As Justin began the song in his powerful feast-house voice, Bill almost shot out of his wheelchair in excitement. Moved as much by the vivid imagery of the story as the song, he was mesmerized, with both arms banging the sides of the wheelchair and both feet pounding the floor to the drumbeat. The Chief Lawrence Pootlas song is certainly one of the most powerful and beautifully composed on the entire coast. When the song ended, Justin casually hung the now well-used drum back on the wall and said in parting, "Mind if I visit you again, Mr. Reid, and sing you another song?"

Bill was still frozen in his wheelchair, eyes as wide as saucers, when he replied what would become the last words I would hear from him: "That would be good!"

Bill always considered the carving of the fifteen-metre Haida war canoe *Lootaas*, from a massive red cedar tree, his greatest accomplishment. His monumental sculptures, prints and elegant gold and silver castings of Haida legendary beings were impressive enough to draw world admiration, but the canoe spoke more directly to the Haida as a living, vibrant, moving culture. Appropriately, it was in *Lootaas* that Bill Reid's ashes were ultimately carried to Tanu, where I attended the scattering on the soil of his mother's ancestral village.

Years before, in the spring of 1987, Bill was trying to solicit Haida paddlers to take the Expo 86 canoe back to Haida Gwaii. The Skidegate Band Council had persuaded the bank that commissioned the piece to donate it back to the Islands, home of the cedar tree it was crafted from. Originally, the plan was to transport the massive vessel aboard a barge, but Haida pride could not allow that. Frank Brown, a young Heiltsuk man who had the worst record for juvenile crime in his mid-coast community of Bella Bella, had done something that took the World Exposition by surprise. He decided it was time he gave something back to his community, so he cut down a cedar tree, hollowed it into a traditional Heiltsuk canoe, trained a crew of village kids his own age and, using beach boulders as ballast, paddled all the way to Vancouver. Frank Brown's canoe pulled into False Creek in the middle of the Expo 86 ceremonies, to the surprise of everyone. He required no bank to commission his undertaking. It was clear from this act that the renaissance of Indigenous identity on the coast was not restricted to Haida Gwaii or to celebrated artists; it was coming from all quarters.

Frank Brown's initiative would in time mark the rebirth of canoe tribal journeys from Washington State to Alaska, but for now it posed a quandary. It was a silent Heiltsuk challenge but a culturally important one, and the Haida knew they would be compelled to paddle the *Lootaas* home to Haida Gwaii. The Vikings of the North Pacific and Lords of the Coast could never bear the humiliation of barging a Haida war canoe across their ancestral sea lanes while other nations were paddling.

In the spring of 1987, during one of my many visits to Bill Reid's studio, I overheard him complaining that he couldn't get any Haida to paddle the canoe north. "They all want money," he grumbled. "I'm just trying to get the damn thing up there." Most young Haida saw Bill Reid as fantastically wealthy compared to the poverty and chronic unemployment that was their reality. Naturally, they were looking for financial compensation, but Bill had no such funds. "Hell, I'll let the Vancouver Rowing Club's women's team paddle *Lootaas* to Haida Gwaii at no cost," Bill told me in frustration.

"Don't do that," I pleaded. "I'll find you a Haida team who will pull the canoe for free."

"Where?"

"Rediscovery kids will do it!" And so it was that I got on a plane from Vancouver to Haida Gwaii with forty-eight hours to come up with a paddling team to pull a fifteen-metre Haida war canoe through nine hundred kilometres of coastal waters for the first time in over a century.

Arriving in Masset after dark and standing under a lamppost in the almost exact location I ended up after disembarking the Northland Navigation freighter on my first arrival fourteen years earlier, I was contemplating where to begin in co-ordinating the biggest Haida cultural event of the twentieth century. Just then, RCMP Constable Alan Wilson, the arresting officer of the elders during the Lyell Island blockade, pulled up beside me in his squad car. "What are you doing back on the Islands, Huck?" he greeted me warmly, extending a hand to shake.

"I've got two days to put together a paddling team to bring *Lootaas* back from Vancouver," I replied.

"Stay right here," Constable Wilson ordered me. He turned on his squad car siren and flashing lights and raced off to Old Massett

village. It was not hard for a cop to locate former Rediscovery participants; everyone knew everyone else in the village, and many of the
boys had been corrections referrals to the camp at some point in
their lives.

As soon as Constable Wilson's squad car pulled up beside me
with an excited crew of young men and women, we embraced as
Rediscovery family and Alan raced back for another carload, and
several more. I signed them all up and gave them a list of what to
bring, and in no time we had our Masset paddling team. I now
needed to enrol paddlers from Skidegate, and the Skidegate Band
Council got strongly behind the selection. The following morning
we all boarded the flight from Sandspit to Vancouver and started the
training.

To be honest, Bill was not that far off in his assessment of
contemporary Haida skills. Some of the pullers weren't sure which
end of the canoe was the bow or how to hold a paddle, but it took
little time before their ancestral genetic encoding kicked in and
these kids were ready for the high seas. I was impressed to see how
quickly the paddlers took to their task under the direction of Jim
Frank, a Haida skipper brought in from Southeast Alaska to head the
expedition.

A friend of Bill Reid's had a large heritage vessel, the *Ivanhoe*,
that he very generously offered as the support boat for the expedition. It would be large enough to bring the *Lootaas* canoe up
alongside, disembark tired and hungry paddlers, grub them up and
bed them down for the night in the rather spartan quarters of the
ship's hull. The boat owner and Bill had the staterooms on board, as
would be expected, but eventually the disparity in grub proved an
issue. Gourmet meals were being served in first class, but the steerage
passengers doing all the paddling felt they were not getting the food
they needed to keep their energy up. Anyone who has ever lived on
Haida Gwaii knows how culturally important food is and what a
contentious issue restricting it can be. Because I had a personal and
positive relationship with many of the paddlers through Rediscovery,
the Skidegate Band Council employed me to oversee the crew and

resolve conflicts that might arise between them. As most of the youth had already learned how to resolve differences by passing an eagle feather to designate the sole speaker at Rediscovery camps, the only issue that arose on the *Lootaas* expedition was the grub. In time that too was resolved to everyone's satisfaction.

We had only a few days to practise paddling and paint Haida-crest designs on paddles and woven Haida hats for the ceremonial entrances into the villages we planned to visit during the expedition. Bill Reid quickly designed canvas vests for all the paddlers to wear at these events, so the overall impression was an event much better organized than it actually was. The *Lootaas* expedition would be a historical cultural event followed closely by the press and witnessed by thousands of First Nations peoples at the seven villages where we would be welcomed along the way to Skidegate: Sliammon, Cape Mudge, Alert Bay, Bella Bella, Klemtu, Hartley Bay and Kitkatla. But it was never meant to have a political agenda like the South Moresby train caravan. At least, not until Haida Nation

president Buddy Richardson took the stage at the Granville Island launch, telling the BC and federal governments in no uncertain terms that *Lootaas* would be paddled straight to Lyell Island, where everyone aboard would blockade the logging road and the Haida Nation would call on people throughout the world to join them. This announcement came as news to most of us, and everyone was free to make their own decision on civil disobedience, but if there was a need for a final fire to be lit under the South Moresby cause, Buddy's impassioned delivery was it.

Archie Samuels practises a paddle song with Guujaaw's drum aboard *Lootaas* (*Wave Eater*) in 1987.

A short-term moratorium had been placed on Lyell Island logging to allow for a cooldown after the seventy-two Haida were arrested at the blockades in November, but now that the story had played itself out in the press, the moratorium was about to be lifted with the issuing of new cutting blocks. In other words,

Reg Wesley paints his crest on a Haida hat in preparation for the *Lootaas* canoe launch in Vancouver.

BC would be back to logging business as usual. At least, that was the plan according to the BC Forest Service.

We departed Granville Island with great fanfare, paddled under the Burrard Bridge with car-honking salutes and set a course along the edge of Stanley Park north to Haida Gwaii. Nothing like this massive canoe, pulled by twenty strong Haida men and women,

had been seen in over a century. Paddling out into the protected waters of Georgia Strait, later to become the Salish Sea, we headed straight for the Coast Salish community of Sliammon near Sechelt. Although it was now a bedroom community to the province's largest metropolis, it was still easy to visualize longhouses standing along the beach where suburban-style houses now stood. We were warmly greeted, feasted and billeted for the night. The next morning before our departure a few of the local youth wanted to experience paddling in *Lootaas*, and the Haida paddlers obliged them by

Bill Reid sees his Expo 86 masterpiece *Lootaas* (*Wave Eater*) come to life on the paddle expedition from Vancouver to Haida Gwaii in 1987.

carrying some of the girls out to the canoe on their shoulders to keep their feet dry. Seeing their young maidens hoisted onto the shoulders of Haida men heading out to a massive war canoe was not a good image for the elders.

At the same time the *Lootaas* expedition was historical and supported as a seminal Coastal First Nations event, it also had the potential of bringing up age-old animosities. Knowing this, we were careful to follow protocol by always entering a village stern first and formally requesting permission to land. The Haida's reputation on the coast as the fiercest warriors preceded us, so the paddlers had to rehearse this manoeuvre many times; a bow-first entry traditionally designated a war-party raid.

Our paddle route took us north to Cape Mudge, the boundary that separates Coast Salish from Kwakiutl territory. The screaming tide rips of Seymour Narrows gave the *Lootaas* paddlers their first real test in navigating dangerous waters. Just past the narrows we pulled into Alert Bay with a rousing welcome by the U'mista Cultural Society and all hereditary chiefs in full regalia. Paddling up to the largest feast house on the coast with its stunning house-frontal design and regally attired welcome party was like a scene out of an Edward Curtis film. With Bill Reid seated ceremoniously in the bow, the *Lootaas* pullers requested permission to land and then swung the canoe around to do so stern first as protocol dictated.

The feast, songs and masked-dance performances that night in the Alert Bay big house were spectacular, but one moment especially stood out for

Kwakiutl U'mista society dancers welcome *Lootaas* paddlers in front of Alert Bay's famous big house.

Haida paddlers in slickers—Audrey Collison, Robert Cross, Diane Brown and Neika Collison—prepare for a wet day at sea as they depart from the support vessel MV *Ivanhoe* during the historic 1987 *Lootaas* expedition.

me. Chief Archie Robinson from Klemtu, also known as Kitasoo, stepped forward and invited the *Lootaas* paddlers to his village much farther up the coast. This was not on our original paddling route, as it took us out of the way, but the invitation had been given in the proper way, announced in the feast house, and protocol made it compulsory that we accept.

Departing from the relatively safe waters of the Inside Passage, *Lootaas* now paddled out into the open waters of Queen Charlotte Sound. What could have proven one of the greatest challenges of the entire trip turned out to be a flat, calm, duck-pond day. The real adventure came days later after a wonderful stay in Bella Bella when *Lootaas* had to cross Milbanke Sound. The support vessel, *Ivanhoe*, broke down that day once the initial paddling crew had set off after breakfast with limited food and water. There was no way to do the planned crew change or get additional supplies to the canoe with the support vessel down. We always had a mixed crew of young men and women, so paddlers needing to relieve themselves had to wrap themselves in a blanket and do their business in a bucket. It was not a pretty sight. By the time we got *Ivanhoe* up and running again, *Lootaas* had crossed the Sound and was making a beeline for Kitasoo in the dark. The support vessel attempted to rush ahead to anchor offshore and disembark the documentary film crew before the canoe's arrival, but it was too late. Cussing like sailors that they were missing the most important scene on the trip, the film crew was stuck on board, but I was happy. The Haida paddlers deserved this moment all to themselves, I felt, for they had given everything they had of their spirits and bodies to get there.

Nothing like this had happened in Kitasoo, the southernmost of the Tsimshian villages on the coast, for over a century. Once Chief Archie Robinson's invitation had been formally accepted in Alert Bay, his villagers frantically prepared for the *Lootaas*'s arrival. There wasn't much of a cultural revival in Kitasoo at that time so button blankets and headdresses had to be quickly fashioned for the welcoming party. We later learned that the entire community had been formally standing on the beach, singing and waiting for the *Lootaas* since sunset; it was now nearly midnight when a Haida paddling song somewhere in the dark met the Kitasoo songs of welcome coming from shore.

As the massive prow of *Lootaas* emerged from the gloom of night, the welcoming party fell completely silent. The Haida paddlers, exhausted from sixteen hours at sea and looking as wild as their forefathers in a war raid, requested permission to come ashore only to be met with a profound and prolonged silence. At long last, Chief Archie Robinson spoke up with the words, "Haida people, it is with mixed emotions we greet you here tonight, for the last time your people arrived in the dark very few of us survived." Again there was a painfully long silence; centuries of mistrust and animosity had to be reconciled in each person's heart in the dark of the coastal wilderness. The exhausted paddlers had no idea what they were walking into when they disembarked. "Okay, come ashore," the chief finally broke the tense silence. "The food is on."

Kitasoo would experience a cultural renaissance following this event, building the most beautiful feast houses on the coast near the point where we landed and starting up their own Rediscovery program and ecotourism ventures in the Great Bear Rainforest, but for this night the Haida and Tsimshian were happy to just peacefully meet and eat together.

The daily routine involved in paddling the nine hundred kilometres up the coast made it hard to recall every high point, but a highlight for the entire expedition was spending a night camping on a beautiful white-sand beach in the middle of what would later be designated the Great Bear Rainforest. This was the mainland counterpart to Gwaii Haanas, lying directly east of it. The pristine wilderness with its many islands, deep inland fjords, climax forests and glacier-capped mountains deserved equal protection, as it was also the home of the Kermode or Spirit Bear. Guujaaw had been working with Islands residents for years trying to stop the hunting of the Haida Gwaii black bear, but to no avail. I'll never forget the phone conversation we had when I returned from a trip overseas and learned through Guujaaw that the Great Bear Rainforest had been granted protection.

"You know why they did it?" Guujaaw asked me.

"Because of the Spirit Bears?"

"Because they're white!" he answered firmly. I laughed, but his point could not be refuted.

Our overnight camp on one of the islands of the Great Bear Rainforest was especially memorable after weeks of sleeping aboard the *Ivanhoe* or being billeted in villages after late-night feasts because the paddlers were suddenly free of protocols and expectations. They played on the beach like otters and spontaneously began rehearsing a new dance to a drum song they heard carried on the wind. This would prove especially poignant at the end of the journey.

From Kitasoo we paddled north to the Tsimshian village of Kitkatla before attempting the crossing of notorious Hecate Strait. Some paddlers were falling ill by this point, and others had tendinitis in their wrists from the seemingly endless hours and days of paddling. One day I was asked to fill in for a tired paddler, but I protested. "Come on, you guys. You said this was going to be done by only the Haida."

"Hell, you're a Haida, Huck. Get in here," members of the crew replied almost in unison.

And so I did, but just long enough to see the genius in the design of this craft that rode the waves better than any fishing boat I'd ever been on. *Wave Eater* was the perfect name for a canoe that cut through each mounting crest with the ease of a surf master. *Lootaas* was buoyant but stable, with lead weights lining a groove in the hull for ballast and an automatic bilge pump to take care of any errant waves breaking over the gunwales. Safe as the vessel was, we still felt it prudent to have a few Haida seiners escort the boat on the final journey across Hecate Strait to Haida Gwaii.

Ten thousand years ago, Hecate Strait was a broad coastal plain giving access to the Haida Islands for caribou, grizzlies and other mainland fauna. The Skeena and Nass Rivers ran through this plain, providing a cornucopia of migratory fish, from the oil-rich

Lootaas cuts a proud image as it plies the coast during the long voyage from Vancouver to Skidegate.

oolichan to all five species of Pacific salmon. But then the sea levels rose at the close of the ice age, forming the shallow yet dangerous Hecate Strait. The prevailing southeasterly wind can whip up seas here in a matter of minutes, so timing was everything in making the crossing in a canoe. We waited out the weather a bit, knowing that if we missed a window of opportunity it might be our last for a week or more. A great welcome feast was being planned for the landing in Skidegate and we couldn't arrive too early—or worse, too late. On the evening of July 8, the barometer was rising and the decision was made to do the sixty-kilometre crossing in the calm of the

A Heiltsuk chief stands proudly on the bow of *Lootaas* as it arrives at Bella Bella. Arriving home in Haida Gwaii was the only time *Lootaas* paddlers could land their craft bow-first during the entire expedition. In others' tribal territories, a bow-first landing would have designated a war party.

night. It went without incident and the next morning the prow of a Haida canoe made a historic landing on Haida Gwaii. It was hard to contain the excitement of the crew, but contain it we had to, as we were not due to land in Skidegate for another two days. We hid out in a small cove south of Gray Bay on Louise Island, biding time until July 11 when *Lootaas* made its triumphant entry into Skidegate.

After Buddy's bombastic declaration at the *Lootaas* launch, delivered with all the confidence of an elected leader holding a powerful mandate from his people, both levels of government kicked into high gear. While Guujaaw and I were blissfully leading the canoe expedition through the scenic Inside Passage, the phone lines between Ottawa and Victoria had been burning up trying to reach a settlement. They eventually did on July 7—a $138-million payout to the province of BC by the government of Canada.

Raven, the trickster who makes things happen unintentionally and inadvertently, was at his very best this day. Not only was the first Haida canoe arriving from Vancouver in more than a hundred years, but a memorandum of understanding was signed the same day by the provincial and federal governments to protect South Moresby along the boundary lines first proposed by Guujaaw and me in October of 1974. It was beyond belief! As Guujaaw said later, "There were so many places where people could have quit and said we lost. We lost every battle all the way through, but won the war. The rightness of what we were doing saw it through. Everyone coming into it was new to the cause; the issue was older than any politician's term in office by the time it was done."

The moment I stepped onto the beach, congratulatory crowds and colleagues in the conservation movement mobbed me. Many of them had flown in from Vancouver and Ottawa for the celebration, but my spirit was still very much a part of the *Lootaas* team and when I was invited to sit with them in the place of honour in the feast hall, I accepted. When I was acknowledged by the master of ceremonies

From left to right: Federal Environment Minister Tom McMillan, Prime Minister Brian Mulroney, BC Premier Bill Vander Zalm and BC Minister of Environment and Parks Bruce Strachan sign the historic Memorandum of Understanding to protect South Moresby on the same day the *Lootaas* expedition arrived in Skidegate from Vancouver on July 11, 1987. BRISTOL FOSTER PHOTO

Against all odds, Beban Logging prepares its equipment to depart Lyell Island after the Memorandum of Understanding was signed between the federal and provincial governments to protect South Moresby. JEFFREY GIBBS PHOTO

and asked to stand, the *Lootaas* team started a thunderous ovation that spread throughout the hall; it moved me more than any recognition I have received in my life. "Huckleberry is pretty popular around here," the master of ceremonies said when the ovation died down. But the real highlight of the night for me came later. It was not the cutting of the celebratory cake or the distinguished dignitaries who spoke. Instead, the moment came when the paddlers were introduced and began singing the drum song that had come to them on the waves and performing the new dance they had choreographed at the island camp a week earlier. I had never seen a moment like that in all the years I'd attended Haida feasts, or any other event in the world during my travels. The entire assembly rose in unison, cheering wildly and pounding their feet on the bleachers; elders were weeping. "The land still speaks to our youth," I overheard one of them saying, choked with emotion. No longer were the Haida reaching into their ancestral treasure boxes to retrieve remnants of a culture that had been largely stolen from them. It was clear to all present that Haida culture was alive, in the moment, and moving forward with confidence. That night we were witnessing more than a landmark agreement in the history of Canada; it was the transformation of a nation.

A South Moresby celebration cake, kept frozen for years as politicians debated the fate of the area, is about to be cut by Speaker of the House of Commons John Fraser (holding cake) along with Colleen McCrory (left), John Broadhead (second from right) and Vicky Husband (right) at the historic signing of the Memorandum of Understanding and *Lootaas* arrival feast in Skidegate on July 11, 1987. JEFFREY GIBBS PHOTO

CHAPTER XII

The Global Stage

The development of the South Moresby Agreement, protecting an area following the lines of our original proposal after a decade of government planning teams cutting it apart, took everyone by surprise and forever altered the Canadian landscape for grassroots conservation initiatives. As John Broadhead was quoted as saying, "It shook Canada's tree."

Just as suddenly, Guujaaw, JB and I were being lauded as environmental heroes. I became the first person outside the United States to receive the State University of New York's prestigious Sol Feinstone Award, the IUCN International Parks Merit Award from Geneva and the Giraffe Project International Award from the US Giraffe Heroes Project for "sticking your neck out." Guujaaw and JB received prestigious awards of their own, and together JB and I received the Canadian Nature Federation's top conservation award.

The problem with becoming a media star or celebrity comes when you actually start to believe the hype that's being generated about you—that's when you're in trouble. I never pursued the South Moresby cause with expectations of being recognized. I was already aware of how the stardom game was played in our society. One of the media's favourite pastimes is putting someone on a pedestal, getting them to believe their own hype and then pulling the rug out from under them when their human frailties are exposed. We've all seen this over and over, but somehow the underlying message can often elude us: in the end we're all just people with both personal strengths and all-too-human weaknesses.

Being in the limelight can certainly be fun for the novelty of it, but I've always felt that everyone should be recognized with an award once in their life so they can have their fifteen minutes of fame and get over it. In my mind, we all need to champion environmental protection and human rights and not abdicate our personal responsibilities to special-interest groups. Some conservationists were upset that I did not capitalize on the momentum by spearheading the BC Green Party movement to lobby for change within the system, but I'd already had enough experience with the system to see the limitations of partisan politics. Would the Green Party winning a national election and holding federal office really bring about the changes necessary for a sustainable human future? Or would "green" legislation be undone with the next pro-business Conservative government that would surely replace them every time Canadian voters flip-flopped at the ballot box? Better, I reasoned, that the conservation community merge with every political party in the land so green initiatives come from all quarters at all times and debunk the us-against-them (good guys against bad guys) myth that all too often permeates the partisan political landscape.

I recall being asked to address a rally in front of the BC Parliament Buildings shortly after the Moresby campaign had reached a successful conclusion. I guess I was seen as someone who could draw a crowd at the time. Hundreds of protesters were waving placards and angrily denouncing the government when I stepped up to speak. "Anger is not a totally inappropriate response to situations we often find ourselves in with government policy," I said, "but let's not let it be our only response." Far from inflaming the crowd with the fiery rhetoric expected at a rally, my words seemed to put a damper on the event, and I was never invited to speak at a Parliament Buildings rally again. But I still stand by what I said that day. For an activist there's always a cause to inflame one's passions, but until we learn to address and control personal anger issues, we seriously curtail our ability to be effective in bringing about meaningful, long-term change.

Guujaaw, John Broadhead and I had seen how the political process works. For over a decade and through several successive NDP governments we had lobbied the party with the most progressive environmental and human-rights platform in the province, but never once could we get a foot in the door of the premier's office for a five-minute discussion on the issue. In the end, it was an arch-conservative Social Credit Party premier who signed into law the South Moresby Agreement, and it was a pro-business Conservative Party prime minister in Ottawa who did the same on behalf of the government of Canada. Quite apart from the growing national pressure for governments to do the right thing, both Bill Vander Zalm in British Columbia and Brian Mulroney in Ottawa had personal reasons to engage positively. Vander Zalm was such a diehard conservative Catholic that he would not allow the word *condoms* to be used in high school education on AIDS prevention, but the Dutch boy liked flowers. In fact, he liked them so much that he built his own private Fantasy Gardens complex atop a BC agricultural land reserve and had to eventually leave office because of a conflict-of-interest scandal. When Vander Zalm was informed that pre-ice age plants were flowering in South Moresby's alpine that were unique in the world, we found a point he could connect with and he went against the decision of his entire cabinet to sign for the area's protection. Similarly, it became personal for Brian Mulroney. After he appointed his close school buddy Tom McMillan to be the federal environment minister and we enrolled the minister to our cause, McMillan brought the prime minister along with him in his passion to protect the area. In spite of differences, people can almost always find some point of connection, and the political lesson I took away from this nearly fourteen-year struggle was how to connect those human commonality dots.

I must confess to feeling humbled, but also quite empowered, by our sudden success, and I was determined to take the lessons learned from the Moresby campaign to the larger theatre. Having made numerous trips to the tropical rainforests of South America, Africa and Southeast Asia since leaving Michigan, I had promised myself that I would devote my time to tropical forest protection once South Moresby was secure. At the time, much of North America's attention was focused on the Amazon rainforest, but even more threatened forests, older and richer in species, needed attention in Africa's Congo River basin and in Southeast Asia.

Following the success of the Moresby campaign I was on an extensive lecture circuit, and one of the invitations was from Carmel, California. There I met John Werner, a photographer for the Grateful Dead who wanted to record the music of the Mbuti Pygmies in the Congo River basin. I had already encountered the Mbuti some years earlier during my six-month trans-African journey, and it seemed a good collaboration for me to engage in a tropical forest conservation campaign. Before we could work out the logistics for this trip, Randy Hayes, the executive director of the Rainforest Action Network in San Francisco, got wind of our plans and dissuaded us from going. "There's a crisis right now with the Penan in the rainforests of Sarawak, Borneo," he told us. "The press are barred from entry and we need someone on the ground to get the story out." Instead of going to the African Congo, we found ourselves Borneo-bound.

We received some financial backing for the trip following a private meeting with the Grateful Dead's "rhythmic devil" drummer Mickey Hart in his San Francisco home and from Sandy Levy, a new-age California art-of-personal-marketing guru. It would be hard to imagine more diverse funding sources. John Werner, his girlfriend, a recording artist and I then headed to Sarawak's Mulu National Park under the guise of tourists. There we met a remarkable young Penan man named Dawat Lupung in a government resettlement site called Bukit Lawang. Dawat knew government spies were hiding in his village and did not want to talk to us on camera until we travelled across the Baram River and hiked some distance into Mulu National Park. There, dressed in his traditional loincloth and crouched in the folds of a huge rainforest tree, Dawat proceeded to tell the world his story. There was no prompting other than the opening questions posed through a translator: "What does this forest mean to you? What would life be without it?"

None of us had any idea what Dawat was saying until it was translated some days later, but we knew it was profound and the delivery so impassioned that it brought tears to our eyes. Back in the United States we presented the video testimonial to the Congressional Human Rights Caucus in Washington, DC, then lobbied the Malaysian government—to no avail—to set aside a protected forest base so the Penan would have what Dawat called "a way to stay." Dawat's testimonial was so powerful he became the recipient of the Reebok Human Rights Award, and I started to see his testimonial as the text for a new book.

The last time I had been in Washington, DC, securing a joint resolution from the US House and Senate that called on Canada to protect South Moresby, I had the Canadian ambassador's office chasing me around Power Town wanting to know why I was trying

After President Jimmy Carter granted unconditional amnesty to civilian war objectors on January 21, 1977, I was able to make a trip on my own to Washington, DC, to secure a joint resolution from the US House and Senate calling on Canada to save South Moresby.

to embarrass Canada. This time I had the Malaysian ambassador to the United States wanting to know much the same. Most people in power are confounded by those who ignore status and procedure.

For my California partners, the Penan story was now out; it had been presented to the US Congress and they felt no compulsion to press the cause further after we returned to North America. For me it was different; the plight of the Penan had grabbed me much as the Moresby cause had, and I felt certain that the same tactics that had worked so well in British Columbia could be used in Sarawak to protect their forest. I could not have been more naive.

I made five more trips back to Sarawak to meet with the Penan, each time drawing increasing attention to myself. Malaysian authorities already had arrest warrants out for Bruno Manser, a Swiss citizen who travelled to Malaysia to learn from the Orang Asli (original people) of Peninsular Malaysia. When government authorities refused to give Bruno a permit to study the Orang Asli, he joined the Mulu Caves Expedition to Sarawak, Borneo, where he first encountered the nomadic Penan as porters. When the scientific study was completed, the researchers returned home, but not Bruno; he disappeared into the Borneo rainforest along with the porters. There he lived a simple life with the Penan for six years, sketching and documenting what he learned. But as the ravages of logging pressed in from all sides, Bruno found himself forced into an advocacy position. The authorities blamed what they called an outside agitator for inciting the Penan to erect road blockades that increasingly challenged the logging companies, but Bruno said he acted only as the Penan's spokesman, getting messages to the outside world. Bruno Manser was now a wanted man and I could sympathize, having been in that position myself.

Several times the Penan I met during my information-gathering trips to Sarawak wanted to take me to meet with Bruno deep in his forest hideaway, but I knew that would only draw more attention to me and possibly give away his position. The Penan are brilliant at hiding people; had they not kept a security perimeter around Bruno for years the authorities surely would have entrapped him. The

Penan I was visiting were aware enough of government spies that they were always quick to push my head underwater whenever a boat passed by while I was bathing in the river. Still, in spite of their best efforts to conceal me as they were concealing Bruno, my movements were being followed closely by secret police.

One day in the frontier town of Marudi I was dragged into the police post for questioning after I was seen speaking with two Penan who had come to town for some supplies. "Why were you talking to those natives?" a sergeant demanded as I stood in front of his desk while he had his hand on a loaded revolver pointing at my groin.

"I met them once and wanted to ask how they were doing," I replied innocently.

The officer then went on to name every place I had been over the previous few weeks, along with the correct times and dates. "Wow, you guys are really good," I complimented him, as I'd had no idea I was being so closely followed. This response only made the authority more antagonistic, and I realized that my best defence might be a good offence. I took him by surprise by showing no fear of the gun he had pointing at me and demanded, as a tourist to Sarawak during the government's Visit Malaysia Year campaign, to phone the Malaysian Ministry of Tourism and the Canadian embassy in Kuala Lumpur. Both requests unsettled him so much that he let me go with a stern warning to speak to no more Penan. Totalitarian officials are not used to being challenged in their countries, and my boldness brought me the result I hoped for. It could just as easily have landed me in prison under Malaysia's draconian Internal Security Act, or worse, seen a tightening of the trigger.

By 1990, a strategy was emerging to bring the Penan story to the world stage. Having seen what the Save South Moresby Caravan did to elevate the Haida Gwaii cause, I felt confident that a Penan world tour would meet with similar success. This, however, would be a much more complex undertaking, as no Penan had ever set foot outside of Malaysia and they would not only need passports but a good reason to travel. The Penan association that was co-ordinating the logging resistance selected two men from different resettlement sites to represent their cause, Unga Paren, a married man in his thirties with two children, and Mutang Tu'o, a young single Penan man in his early twenties. Dean James Morton of St. John the Divine Cathedral in Manhattan agreed to formally invite these two "Christian" Penan to a church conference. The religious angle was a good strategy, as Malaysia was struggling with issues of religious freedom at the time and they wanted to appear to be fair to all faiths.

The bigger challenge was getting Bruno Manser out of the jungle to translate for them as the Penan's most knowledgeable spokesman. A female friend of Bruno's from Switzerland arrived in Sarawak as a tourist with a fake passport for the fugitive, a wig and a stick-on moustache hidden in her daypack. To complete the disguise she flew out with Bruno Manser posing as her husband. Mutang Urud, a Kelabit tribesman from Sarawak who had been assisting the Penan and Bruno, came along as an additional translator. My job was to co-ordinate a fifty-five-day blitz of twenty-eight major cities in sixteen countries on three continents.

I found tremendous support from some of our South Moresby campaign alumni. Paul George, director of the Western Canada Wilderness Committee, agreed to publish the book on the Penan that I had envisioned using the testimony of Dawat Lupung. I asked Wade Davis, whom I had first met when he was a logger in Port Clements, if he would write a foreword to the book, but he did much more, joining me as co-author. Wade's career had been launched with a bestselling book, *The Serpent and the Rainbow*, and his name certainly brought more credibility to the book than mine ever could. The book we now collaborated on was titled *Penan: Voice for the Borneo Rainforest*, and it became a central point for raising revenue and lobbying world leaders and influential people on the Voices for the Borneo Rainforest World Tour.

I first met Bruno Manser at a human-rights conference in Hawaii, just months before we were to launch the world tour with the Penan. I could see instantly why the Penan were so endeared to this soft-spoken, Gandhi-like man, as he embodied their same peaceful spirit and reverence for living things. Mutang Urud flew with the

Penan from Sarawak to Bangkok, where Bruno and I met up with them during a transit layover to Australia. To this day I regret we did not have a film crew recording this entire epic journey as the Penan first experienced life outside Malaysia. It was as though they were holding a mirror up to the modern world, showing us what we had become. Situations were often humorous but sometimes profound.

Mutang Urud told me later, when the plane departed from Sarawak, that he thought the two Penan men were having panic attacks as they pressed their faces to the window of the fuselage, desperately trying to see the tail of the plane. Trying to reassure them everything was okay, Mutang was interrupted when one of the Penan asked, "Is this the one that makes the smoke?" Ever since World War II the Penan had seen the occasional vapour trail in the sky through openings in the forest canopy, but they had never been aboard one of the big birds that made it.

Huddled together on the floor of Bangkok International Airport, the two Penan were dumbfounded by the new and novel sights they beheld, especially overweight people. They had no words in their language to describe such a thing because there are no overweight Penan. They had words for a fat Borneo bearded pig, but not for a person. "Maybe they eat, not full," was all they could say, shaking their heads in utter disbelief. It was not until the end of the nearly two-month trip that I understood what they meant by this.

Our whirlwind journey took us from Bangkok to Sydney, Canberra, Melbourne and Hobart, Tasmania. While "down under," the Penan testified before an Australian parliamentary committee on human rights. We then crossed the Pacific to San Francisco, Seattle, Vancouver and Victoria. Great events had been organized everywhere by dedicated human-rights campaigners and seventy small environmental groups and church organizations. The big guns like Friends of the Earth, Greenpeace, the World Wide Fund for Nature and the Nature Conservancy failed to support us for a number of reasons. Some feared reprisals from Malaysia, where they either already had or hoped to establish chapters. Others could not get clearance through their bureaucracies in time, as we pulled off the trip so quickly. Still others thought we were just plain nuts to be doing this.

Still on a high from the Haida Gwaii success, Vancouver residents came out in force. A packed house at the Robson Square auditorium gave a standing ovation to the Penan when they emerged onstage dressed in their traditional loincloths and holding their blowpipes. Mutang Tu'o was quickly learning enough English to speak on his own behalf and he always spoke in parables: "We are like fish trapped in a small river pool in the dry season and if the rain does not come soon, we will surely die. Can you be our rain?" he would ask the audience. People were always touched by this simple metaphorical message, and hundreds of students from the Environmental Youth Alliance in Vancouver responded by first clicking their fingers, then tapping their hands on their knees and finally stomping their feet on the auditorium floor to simulate the sound of an approaching rainstorm. It sounded so real it thrilled the Penan.

After crossing Canada through Calgary and Toronto, we headed to New York, where a whirlwind of activities was scheduled. Mick Jagger's former wife Bianca invited us to her Park Avenue residence in Manhattan to discuss celebrity support. We met with Javier Perez de Cuellar, the Secretary-General of the United Nations, who offered to undertake a good offices action to meet with the Malaysian prime minister on the issue. But the biggest event was at St. John the Divine Cathedral where many United Nations delegates worshipped. Dean James Morton wanted the Penan to speak at the altar for the Sunday service in their traditional loincloths so as not to appear as common immigrants in the city. But it was late autumn and, too late, we discovered that the cathedral was much too cold for such scanty clothing. I felt responsible for ensuring that the Penan returned to their homeland healthy and safe, so I insisted they wear something warm. All that was available in the sacristy were the elegant red robes worn by the archbishop and high clergy for midnight mass on Christmas Eve. "These will do," I told Dean Morton against his serious reservations, and when the organ played to announce the start of the service the

Penan representative Mutang Tu'o (centre, left) and translator Mutang Urud (centre, right) pose with me (left) and Jeff Gibbs (right) in front of the United Nations headquarters in New York during the sixteen-nation Voices for the Borneo Rainforest World Tour in 1990.

Dressed in robes reserved for archbishops, Penan representatives Mutang Tu'o and Unga Paren address worshippers, including United Nations delegates, at the altar of St. John the Divine Cathedral in Manhattan as part of the Voices for the Borneo Rainforest World Tour. Swiss activist Bruno Manser stands beside translator Mutang Urud at the microphone with Dean James Morton presiding.

From left to right: Translator Mutang Urud and Penan representative Mutang Tu'o present a copy of the book *Penan: Voice for the Borneo Rainforest* to Prince Bernhard, the father of Queen Beatrix of the Netherlands.

two Penan stepped out onto the elevated altar looking like Jesus on his final walk to Calvary.

Senator and later vice-president Al Gore made a heartfelt connection with the Penan in Washington, DC, and promised to do all he could to support their cause. Another supporter we met on the tour was Canadian filmmaker James Cameron, who would go on to produce the two biggest blockbusters of all time, *Titanic* and *Avatar*. Cameron promised us that he heard the plight of the Penan and totally empathized with it. "I will tell this story in cinema one day," he told us, "but you may not recognize the Penan at first." In *Avatar*, Cameron took the Penan's beloved forest Tong Tana to another planet and brilliantly portrayed the industrial world's insatiable appetite for resources by naming the mining compound they sought *un-obtain-ium*.

We arrived in Europe for a multi-nation tour of Sweden, Denmark, Holland, the United Kingdom, France, Germany, Austria and Switzerland. Everywhere environmental and human-rights groups had prepared the way and organized events for us. Rainforest Group Nepenthes, a handful of dedicated university students in Copenhagen, went so far as to build a model Penan village on the main floor of the national museum and had students from every school in the country tour it to learn about the plight of the Penan before our arrival. They also conducted the best press conference on the entire tour, with reporters from every news and media outlet in the country in attendance. Who says small is not beautiful?

While in Denmark, we were invited to a palace to meet Prince Bernhard, the father of Queen Beatrix of the Netherlands. A hunter himself and intrigued by the Penan's blowpipes, Prince Bernhard asked for a demonstration and Mutang Tu'o quickly obliged. Spotting the darting movement of a rabbit in the garden through the window in the reception room, the opportunistic hunter was out the door and taking deadly aim from the palace balcony within seconds. "Please, please!" The prince rushed after Mutang Tu'o and pleaded before the dart left the chamber, "Those are my pets!"

The Penan met with the minister of the environment in Austria, where they were saddened to see the houseplants in the minister's smoke-filled office dead from lack of water and light. They were nearly moved to tears when they saw hardwood floors, walls and elevator panels made from the trees of their homeland. Although Penan tradition makes it taboo to cut a large tree, they knew what the cut wood looked like from making blowpipes from sections of living trees and from the stump ends of the loggers' cuts.

The Penan had met with members of the Grateful Dead in San Francisco, but now they were invited to join them for a live concert in London's Wembley Stadium. Wearing large headphones to prevent them from going deaf, Unga Paren and Mutang Tu'o walked out onstage to the cheers of a stadium full of "Dead heads." Unga wondered how the people there would ever again be able to hear a bird call in the forest. They probably wouldn't.

The last leg of our journey took us back to Asia and Japan, where most of the Penan's forest was ending up through powerful

Sososhogas who signed corrupt deals with the chief minister of Sarawak and the Chinese concession holders. The media generated a huge story around our arrival and even showed a diagram on national television for the Japanese to understand the scale of the destruction. With revered Mount Fuji as a comparison point, the diagram showed the annual volume of plywood being cut from Sarawak trees as ten times higher than the mountain when laid flat, one piece atop another. It was staggering—the most rapid rate of deforestation the world has ever known.

Funding for the Voices for the Borneo Rainforest World Tour had all but run out by the time we reached Yokohama, Japan. Book sales and donations had kept us going until now, but we needed another infusion of funds to complete the two-month tour. A rainforest benefit concert put on in Tokyo by the Rainforest Action Network did the trick.

I will never forget sitting with Unga Paren and Mutang Tu'o one final time at Narita airport as we were about to part ways. I was curious to know what they considered the most memorable parts of the tour.

"It makes my head hurt to think about it," Unga replied. He had mastered enough English to speak without a translator by now.

I pressed the question. "What is it that makes your head hurt?"

"The buildings that disappear into the sky," came the reply. The Penan had stood at the base of the World Trade Center in Manhattan eleven years before it would be demolished by the most brazen terrorist attack in history. Low-level haze had obscured the tops of the Twin Towers that day so they appeared to extend into the heavens.

"So it's hard to imagine living so high off the ground compared to your *sulap* shelters in the forest?" I asked.

"No," Unga replied. "It makes my head hurt to see such high buildings with so many rooms and so many buildings just like them, but no place to sleep for the people on the street under the newspapers." They saw right through us.

For the forest-dwelling Penan it was unthinkable that a society would not care equally for every member. When a Penan hunts a fish or animal, no matter how small, an unwritten code dictates that all must share it equally. I had been concerned that the Penan might not want to return home after the trip. As the saying goes, "Once they've seen the lights of the city you can't get them back on the farm." But I couldn't have been more wrong. The Penan were eager to return home, to be back in a place where everyone cared for everyone else, even if their world was being dismantled before their eyes by the ravages of corrupt logging. It was hard for urban dwellers to grasp the full horror of what was happening in Borneo, so we had to put it into perspective for them during the world tour presentations. Imagine an alien force arriving on earth and destroying every home, school, supermarket, pharmacy, cemetery and place of worship, then forcing you into relocation camps as you watch your ancient culture being obliterated. Only then would you know what the deforestation of Tong Tana and forced resettlement sites meant to the Penan.

I had one last question for Unga and Mutang Tu'o before they boarded their return flight to Kuala Lumpur and Sarawak. "What do you mean by 'eat not full'?" I had heard this expression a number of times—when the Penan first saw overweight people in the Bangkok airport, when they would enter an especially opulent room or when they saw a shopper overburdened with bags. For nomadic peoples possessions are encumbrance, restricting them in their freedom to move. This time it took the aid of our translators to get the full meaning of Unga's reply. Before this trip he thought everyone in the world lived like the Penan, sharing equally. But now he had seen a world where no matter how much food people put in their stomachs, how many consumer goods they crammed into their homes or how much money they hoarded in their bank accounts, it wasn't enough. It never would be; it just created the desire for more. It struck me as a profound revelation, but it really shouldn't have been. Somewhere buried deep in our own cultures we have the same lessons. "Thou shalt not covet thy neighbour's goods" has certainly become the most violated of the Ten Commandments, and the Buddha's teachings "desire causes pain" has all but been lost on Asia's new generation of consumer addicts.

It was a sad parting of ways after months of travelling together. While the Penan returned safely to their communities in Borneo and Bruno Manser to Switzerland, Mutang Urud and I would soon discover that we had become official enemies of the state of Malaysia. For me, living in Canada, there was no danger, but for Mutang, continuing his activist role in Sarawak proved perilous. With a brutal banging on his door near midnight on February 5, 1992, Mutang Urud was arrested under an emergency ordinance, imprisoned and held in solitary confinement for one month. On his conditional release, he fled across the border to Brunei and eventually found asylum in North America, first through Reverend Dean Morton at St. John the Divine in Manhattan and later he secured refugee status in Canada. That was certainly not the intended outcome of our world tour efforts, but by no means had we given up.

While in New York on a follow-up trip, Mutang Urud and I met with Dawn Zain, wife of the Malaysian permanent ambassador to the United Nations, who had been a friend of Taib Mahmud before he became Sarawak's chief minister. She told us how Taib used to sleep on her couch at her Park Avenue address when he came to visit in Manhattan before he became wealthy enough through logging-concession kickbacks to purchase any Park Avenue residence he wanted. During one of his visits Taib shared with her Prime Minister Mahatir Mohamad's secret ambition of one day becoming the United Nations Secretary-General. This was information we could work with. We devised a strategy that had the potential to bring about a more unequivocal result than the Voices for the Borneo Rainforest World Tour. We quickly contacted as many international conservation groups as we could to see how many of them might be willing to bestow their highest awards on Malaysia's prime minister at the upcoming 1992 Earth Summit in Rio de Janeiro. To qualify as the world's newest environmental and human-rights hero, all Mahatir had to do was announce a biosphere reserve that would protect the Sarawak rainforest and the Penan's traditional way of life. This would be a global stage to display stature and make Mahatir a more likely candidate to be nominated for the UN post after his term ended as prime minister. The bait was dangled before him and he may have nibbled, but he never took the bite.

The federal government of Malaysia has exclusive rights to all the revenues flowing from Sarawak and Sabah's oil fields; in return, the two states of East Malaysia rely on timber revenues to support themselves. The plan was for the Malaysian federal government to use some of the record-breaking oil revenues flowing to Kuala Lumpur at the time to compensate the state of Sarawak for deferring the cutting in the proposed UN biosphere reserve. Unfortunately, Mahatir was about as arrogant, intransigent and insufferable as they get. His response to the Penan's desperate plea for a home-land and an opportunity to raise his own stature on the world stage was the glib and ethnocentric remark, "I'd rather see them eating McDonald's hamburgers than the unmentionables they eat in their forest." He was clearly not the person for the UN Secretary-General position.

It was even worse in Sarawak with Chief Minister Taib Mahmud, whose oligarchy controlled the awarding of all timber concessions and was obscenely profiting from them. In British Columbia, we had Tom Waterland, Minister of Forests, Lands and Natural Resources, forced out of office when it became public that he had vested inter-ests in Western Forest Products, which was logging Lyell Island while he was approving the cutting plans. Unfortunately, the rules that apply in the West are largely lost in Asia, allowing Taib Mahmud to amass such a fortune that he is rated one of the world's most corrupt officials, often compared to Suharto in Indonesia and Marcos in the Philippines, each of whom raised the bar to Olympian heights for nepotism and cronyism. Although both Mahatir and Taib wrap themselves in their religion whenever it's politically expedient to do so, they clearly have no regard for one of the fundamental teachings of their faith: "Those who oppress will learn what misfortune has been prepared for them." (Koran 26:227)

Malaysia is a strange state with no meaningful historic links between Peninsular Malaysia and its two eastern states of Sarawak and Sabah on Borneo. The British claimed these distant territories and simply threw them both into the pot when granting Malaysia independence in 1947. In keeping with the British sense of fair play, the government allowed a Malaysian publishing house to buy the rights to our book *Penan: Voice for the Borneo Rainforest*. It was put on sale in all of the nation's bookstores and Kuala Lumpur International Airport after the world tour, but under Malaysia's restrictions on free speech, Wade Davis and I were blacklisted for writing it.

After the magical success of the South Moresby campaign, the Penan cause was proving to be the greatest disappointment and sense of failure in my life. During the tour, Bruno Manser and I had been given Penan names by Unga Paren. Ukap Urip (Opening Life Up) was the name bestowed on Bruno, and Pepejek Urip (Lifting Life Upright) was the complimentary name I was given. We both fervently wished we could have fully lived up to the honours. Sadly, Bruno had no better ideas than I did on where to go next in turning things around for the Penan. We met a few more times and did a wilderness adventure trip together in the Canadian High Arctic, along with Mutang Urud, to see whether the purity of the air and landscape might lead to further inspiration. In the end, Bruno disappeared in April 2001 trying to sneak back into the homeland of the Penan. The questions surrounding his mysterious disappearance and presumed death may never be answered. Did the authorities murder him, or did he succumb to a fatal accident in a forest that would have quickly consumed all evidence? Either way, it was a tragic ending for a person who had devoted most of his adult life to environmental and Indigenous human-rights causes. The only solace for those attending his many memorials from Switzerland to Canada to Sarawak was in knowing that Bruno was certainly where his heart was when his life appeared to have ended.

I would continue bringing the Penan message to the world with every opportunity presented to me to lecture on the global stage, and I would continue to lobby on their behalf as do the Bruno Manser Fund and Mutang Urud to this day. But the campaign to save the Penan's homeland through our efforts in the late 1980s and early '90s seemed a tragic failure in the end. The Penan's beloved forest home-land, Tong Tana, was not only logged, but the secondary scrub forest is increasingly giving way to oil palm and rubber tree plantations, so there is no hope of the forest ever growing back. The series of happy accidents that surrounded the success of the Haida Gwaii campaign has yet to unfold on the island of Borneo.

CHAPTER XIII

A Tsunami of Change

Every culture has its creation story, and the Haida version eerily mirrors the opening of the Bible in Genesis 1: "And God said, 'Let there be light,' and there was light." The Haida legend, however, is considerably more intriguing in describing how light came to be.

No anthropomorphic deity exists in Haida culture—just Raven, the trickster. A story older than the Bible and carefully handed down through oral rather than written tradition tells of Raven transforming himself into a spruce needle and falling from a tree branch into the water just as a chief's daughter was about to take a drink at a stream. The princess inadvertently swallowed the spruce needle and became pregnant with Raven in human form. As a child crying in the chief's house because he was not allowed to play with a bentwood cedar box containing light, Raven one day grew impatient, transformed back into his bird form and stole the light from the box. It is said that Raven was white at the time but had eaten so much of the chief's food he became temporarily stuck in the smoke hole in the roof of the longhouse during his escape and his feathers turned black from the smoke and soot. Freed at last, he flew into the dark heavens, releasing the sun, the moon and the stars. Let there be light ... and there was light.

Eons of time later and after more than two centuries of colonization, Haida leaders gathered around a bentwood cedar box—much like the one from which Raven stole the light—removed the lid and shouted into it, "Queen Charlotte Islands." The lid was quickly replaced and tied with cedar-bark rope so the name could not escape as all present announced, "The real name is Haida Gwaii," meaning Islands of the People. The box was ceremoniously given to outgoing BC Premier Gordon Campbell, who became Canada's representative in England, to present to Queen Elizabeth. Through this simple but brilliant cultural act, the Haida returned the name bestowed on their isles in 1787 by Captain George Dixon, who was the first European to circumnavigate the archipelago (with the likely exception of Sir Francis Drake more than two centuries earlier) and who named the islands after his ship and queen—the wife of King George III. The governments of Canada and British Columbia had no choice now but to change the name on every map, chart, news broadcast and weather report from that day forward. The Queen Charlotte Islands had been symbolically stripped of their colonial yoke; they would henceforth be called Haida Gwaii.

And so it was in the aftermath of the Moresby campaign that a renewed nation emerged. Guujaaw told me that his uncle, Percy Williams, to whom I had presented the eagle during my kayak journey in 1973, was deeply moved by the name change. "Uncle Percy said that when he heard that the name was Haida Gwaii a tear welled up in his eyes, a lump in his throat. All these years in politics he said he remained emotionally detached, determined that emotion was for the family, but he said he thought back to the days when they had no influence over anything—when it was the white man's world."

Guujaaw had also once written to me: "Consider when you came. Our people—the island people, for that matter, had nothing to say about anything; the Haida people had no influence over anything."

Like Bill Reid, Guujaaw was inspired by the ancient poles carved by his ancestors and found at abandoned Haida village sites. RICHARD KRIEGER PHOTO

All of that changed with the 1985 Lyell Island blockade and the signing of the Gwaii Haanas Agreement in 1993. The fact that a Haida name was used to designate Western Canada's most significant national park reserve and Haida heritage site spoke volumes about who was now calling the shots. I can recall a meeting with Parks Canada I was asked to attend with Guujaaw and Diane Brown, both champions of Haida rights and cultural identity. The meeting was to discuss the possibility of a new Rediscovery camp for Swan Bay, in the very heart of the national park reserve. "You can't put a Rediscovery camp at that site," the Parks Canada official said with authority. "Lots of kayakers will want to use Swan Bay for camping."

"Well, they're not going to be camping in Swan Bay when our kids are there," Diane responded even more firmly, with the authority of a protective mother. "Who knows who these people might be—axe murderers or Catholic priests?"

Asserting Haida rights was the name of the game now and with no legal basis to fall back on, the province of BC was at a loss over what to do with this unprecedented assertiveness. A treaty, a conquest or a purchase of Haida territory had never before existed so there was no legal leg for the province to stand on in claiming these isles, even under British law. The fact that Haida Gwaii, the most isolated archipelago in Canada, had no competing territorial claims from neighbouring tribes gave it an unusually strong and unique position in the land claims and title debates raging across the province. Every time the Haida asserted their rights to the land and surrounding waters, they threw a monkey wrench into the workings of government. Something had to be done, as BC was courting foreign investments, especially from China, and everything remained uncertain when title questions were unresolved.

In 2009 the BC government signed a reconciliation agreement with the Haida Nation designed to create greater certainty in land-use decisions, and as Guujaaw said, to "lay the groundwork for an era of peace." Through shared decision-making, revenue sharing and responsible economic and sustainable development, it was hoped that this agreement would increase prosperity for both the province and the Islands. It included $10 million for the Haida Nation to buy out forest tenures and further committed to renaming the Queen Charlotte Islands as Haida Gwaii. This was to be a one-of-a-kind structure for shared decision-making in key strategic areas, but as Guujaaw said later, "The reconciliation agreement was to be an anomaly, but since the Tsilhqot'in agreement, the Crown thinks it looks pretty good." In 2014 the BC Supreme Court, in a unanimous ruling, broke the long stalemate on the title question in British Columbia by recognizing the Tsilhqot'in Nation's rights to their traditional lands. Everything was now up for grabs.

When asked what he considered to be the greatest achievements of the Haida Nation since the Gwaii Haanas decision and the reconciliation agreement, Guujaaw responded, "We've got lots of influence now, but we're still fighting DFO [federal Department of Fisheries and Oceans], Big Oil is back ... people are inspired to fight pipelines but all in the context of failing marine and terrestrial ecosystems ... the effects are reaching every part of the globe ... Fukushima, plastic, oil, sky ... Yet I would never say that the battles were for naught, as by now all of the good cedar would be gone, pretty much all of the natural world would be altered forever. The fights to keep the life-support systems going are still worth the fight. I still enjoy the fight and I'm still in."

The sweeping changes on Haida Gwaii were unprecedented in Canadian history and they continue to carve out a new, more equitable and mutually respectful relationship between First Peoples and the nation of immigrants that followed. Canada is the second-largest nation on earth in land mass with the lowest population density for area, blessed with abundant natural resources and a history of resolving conflicts through dialogue and negotiations rather than grabbing the gun like her sister nation to the south. There's probably no country in the world in a better position to recognize the land rights of its aboriginal inhabitants and right historical injustices than Canada.

While a tsunami of change was sweeping over Haida Gwaii, I was being kept abreast of it from afar. Guujaaw, a clever statesman, likes to bounce ideas and initiatives off people he trusts before implementing them; I guess I was one of those people. While I was spending half of each year living in Asia, working on Indigenous rights issues with the Penan, Mentawai and Moken, the Haida Gwaii grapevine continued to keep me informed of the Islands' affairs, and I religiously returned there every summer to visit my adopted family and friends.

I had stubbed my toe on Thailand in the course of my travels and, like many others, fell in love with the happy-go-lucky and nonjudgmental nature of these largely Buddhist people. An opportunity presented itself to build a small house for myself as part of a family-run beach bungalow project in Krabi province, long before this stunning seascape region was on the tourism radar. Dawn of Happiness Beach Resort was named after the first Thai kingdom of Sukhothai. It was far from a resort; just a collection of twelve bamboo-walled and thatched-roof bungalows set on an isolated beach, but it had an understated elegance and a family feel to it that attracted high-end tourists who could afford better. Here I had a home base for my Asian travels for more than a decade, and during that time the kingdom inspired me to write several more books: *Reefs to Rainforests, Mangroves to Mountains: A Guide to South Thailand's Natural Wonders*; *Waterfalls & Gibbon Calls: Exploring Khao Sok National Park*; and *Krabi: Caught in the Spell*.

As far as the bungalow business went, I summed up my experience in the Krabi book with the observation, "I learned that almost any foreigner can end up with a small fortune in Thailand, especially if they start out with a large one."

As a business, Dawn of Happiness could never really support itself, so I began offering our guests ecotours in the surrounding area to help make ends meet. An international schoolteacher from the Philippines who came on one of these trips liked my rap well enough to go back to the Manila head office of the East Asia Regional Council of Overseas Schools (EARCOS), telling Dr. Richard Krajczar, the executive director, that I should be a keynote speaker at their next conference in Shanghai. I knew nothing about international schools at the time and was surprised to find myself sharing the keynote podium with two illustrious speakers: Robert Hass, the US poet laureate in 1995–97, and Dr. Jane Goodall, the chimpanzee researcher with the National Geographic Society. Conference delegates must surely have wondered, who the hell is Thom Henley?

When I had the opportunity to meet Robert Hass prior to his delivering of the opening keynote, I could see that he was a kindred spirit and true nature lover. I was scheduled to deliver the morning keynote on the second day, while Jane Goodall, who had not yet arrived, was to do the closing keynote on day three.

In all the lectures I gave in the years following the Penan world tour, I never missed an opportunity to bring their plight to public attention. I also spoke about Rediscovery and my Haida Gwaii experiences. The headmasters and administrators from the top schools in Asia seemed like a good audience to possibly effect change. Years earlier, David Suzuki had told me that if you want to get your audience's attention, "shock them"—and I took him up on that advice in Shanghai.

In closing my slide lecture, I told the distinguished audience of international school administrators that Pol Pot had been described by every one of his teachers as "a lovely child." He had received all of his formal education at an international school in Paris before returning to Cambodia to enact the greatest genocide since the Holocaust—the systematic extermination of three million people. And yet there is no proof that Pol Pot killed anyone. The Killing

Fields are filled with the bones of victims with skulls smashed in by farming hoes to save money on bullets. It was all done by schoolchildren doing what they were told to do: obey those in authority.

In closing my Shanghai slide lecture, I showed pictures I had taken a year earlier of a map of Cambodia made out of human skulls, with images of twelve innocent-looking boys and twelve cherub-faced girls bordering both sides, displayed at the end of the corridor of a high school that is now the Tuol Sleng Genocide Museum. My Khmer guide, a woman who was the sole survivor in her family following the evacuation and execution of Phnom Penh's educated "elite," had taken me on a tour through classrooms where torture equipment still sat atop blood-stained floors, and black-and-white photos of thousands of victims lined the walls, each with a serial number. Like the Nazis, the Khmer Rouge kept detailed photographic records of the more than twenty thousand men, women and children they tortured at this school prior to their executions. It was the end of the tour and I was too shell-shocked to look at the map of Cambodia made of human skulls. Instead, my eyes were drawn to the eyes of the children bordering the map; they were as sweet and innocent as any child's eyes one might ever gaze into. "They don't have numbers on their photos," I said to my guide. "Were they the last to be executed?"

She looked at me in disbelief and replied, "They were the torturers. They were the executioners."

I was struck numb, as was my audience in Shanghai when I told this story to the assembled school headmasters and showed slides of these same Khmer children. I closed my comments with the words, "If children are such putty in our hands that we can take them to these depths of horror, imagine the potential in the other direction." I closed the slide show with reflective music and close-ups of children's faces—Penan, Haida, Khmer. There was not a dry eye in the house after my talk, I was told later, so the lighting crew kept the house lights off to give the assembly a moment of privacy. God forbid headmasters ever be seen to show emotion. Far from applause at the end of my talk, there was a deathly silence and I felt certain that I had probably delivered my first and last keynote at an international school conference.

As the lights slowly rose an older woman walked up onstage, burrowed her head in my shoulder and started whimpering. My God, I thought, this is becoming a total disaster.

"Pat me on the head," the grey-haired lady whispered in my ear.

"What?" I asked in disbelief.

"Pat me on the head," she repeated. I did as I was instructed until the room was fully illuminated again.

Going to the microphone, the woman said, "That is how a female chimp greets a male she admires." The audience rose to a standing ovation as I beheld a much older Jane Goodall than the young images of her I was used to seeing in *National Geographic* magazine.

Memorable as our first meeting was, it was what followed that became significant. Because EARCOS was running back-to-back administrator and teacher conferences in Shanghai and all three speakers had been booked for both conferences, Jane Goodall, Robert Hass and I had plenty of time to meet over private dinners. At one of these dinners we posed a question to ourselves as fellow conservationists. "What would be the fastest way to bring about meaningful change in protecting the planet?" Target Asia, we all agreed, for not only does Asia hold the greatest number of people with the greatest economic clout, but it also has the greatest biodiversity. Indonesia alone supports 24 per cent of all species on earth. Next question: "What do we target in Asia?" Answer: international schools. Because there is so little social mobility in Asia, students privileged enough to afford the university tuitions for these elite elementary, middle and high schools are being prepared for positions of decision-making and power their parents ensure they are going to step into.

We now had a mission. "I'll bring my Roots & Shoots program to Asia," Jane Goodall announced. She had initiated this environmental-awareness school program in Africa, and it later spread to Europe and the Americas; now it would be available worldwide.

Robert Hass was the next to come forward: "I'll bring my River of Words program." Robert had spoken of this program he'd initiated in the United States during his keynote. Students are challenged through poetry and art to get a better understanding of the watershed they live in. We all live in one, but very few people can trace theirs from the headwaters to the sea.

It was now my turn, and an idea that had been formulating in my mind for some time went public. "I'm going to tweak the Rediscovery program I started in Canada to offer international students a study of eight ecosystems in eight days; it will be called Reefs to Rainforests." And thus, In Touch with Nature Education began, not as a business but as a mission. Since the turn of the twenty-first century the program has hosted thousands of students from some of the best schools in Asia, Africa, the Middle East and Europe. Our initial eight-day offering, Reefs to Rainforests in Thailand, soon expanded to forty-five outdoor education adventures in twenty-two countries: Bangladesh, Bhutan, Cambodia, Canada, Djibouti, Ethiopia, Guyana, Indonesia, Laos, Madagascar, Malaysia, the Maldives, Myanmar, Nepal, Papua New Guinea, the Philippines, South Africa, Sri Lanka, Suriname, Thailand, Uganda and Vietnam. We not only offer these learning adventures to students but to senior citizens (Boomers and Beyond) as well as to teachers and their families during Christmas holidays.

And so it was on the morning of December 26, 2004, that a group from one of our family sessions was sitting together at a beach resort on the Andaman Sea for our final breakfast after a wonderful week-long Christmas trip. It was a glorious, clear day in paradise with a light breeze, gently swaying palm trees and no hint at all that something was about to go terribly wrong. If the tide was receding much too fast and too far out that morning at 8:45, none of us took notice. The night before, after putting the cap on our Christmas party, Kran, one of my Thai staff, received an emergency call from his mother; she needed to go to the hospital for abdominal surgery and she asked for her son to be at her side. He was planning to catch a bus that night, but it was a two-day trip by bus.

"Let me get on the phone and try to find you a flight," I told Kran as we all headed to bed.

Over breakfast the next morning, I was reviewing the group's flight tickets out of Phuket when I suddenly realized that Kran's flight was scheduled thirty minutes earlier than the others'. "We need to leave right now," I told the group, "or Kran will miss his flight and not be with his mother for her surgery." Reluctantly, everyone stopped eating and boarded the waiting minivans. Twenty minutes later, while we were safely inland, the first global disaster of the twenty-first century struck the Andaman Sea and Indian Ocean coasts, killing a quarter of a million people from over fifty countries. The resort we had just left was now being hit by a series of tsunami waves reaching as high as the coconut fronds; the surviving staff had climbed coconut trees and were phoning my staff on mobile phones to see if we were still alive. Along the road north to Phuket, we saw tourists in shock, and when we stopped to refuel at a gas station crammed with cars, Thais asked us in broken English, "Where you go?"

"Phuket airport," we answered.

"Phuket finished, airport finished, bridge to island finished," they told us with alarm. "Ocean eat everything!" Although it was hard to get our heads around it, it was clear something disastrous had happened on the Andaman coast, so I had our minivan driver cross the Thai/Malay Peninsula to Surat Thani airport on the Gulf of Thailand side. There, I managed to get all my guests on flights, buses and trains to Bangkok to connect with their international flights home. Not until I turned on the news that evening did I realize the magnitude of the disaster we had so narrowly escaped.

By the time I returned to Krabi, the corpses were already coming in from Phi Phi Island and surrounding beaches and piling up in makeshift boxes along the town's main road. It does not take long in the humid tropics for human bodies to decompose, and photos of horribly grotesque corpses were being posted on long bulletin boards for the thousands of tourists and local Thais trying to locate and identify their missing loved ones. It was worse than a nightmare watching people trying to compare their most cherished wallet-sized photos of friends and family to the images of people decomposed beyond recognition posted on the boards. Adding to the horror, the smell of decay from thousands of corpses was overpowering and nauseating. Still, I wanted to see if I recognized anyone. Was that the young boy who had walked his water buffalo down the beach each morning at sunrise in front of my bungalow? The kind Muslim woman who'd made roti on the side of the road? Our gardener and dear Thai friend for the past ten years? It wasn't long before I couldn't take the stench anymore and drove out of Krabi town to clear my head. A rainstorm came on so violently that I had to pull off the road as poor visibility made it unsafe for me to drive. I don't know how long I sat there with the windshield wipers thudding away on high speed before I came to the realization that it was not raining at all and never had been. I was sobbing. For the next few years, I suffered from post-traumatic stress disorder, but I would protest with classic denial any time friends would point this out to me.

As friends and family contacted me to see whether I was alive, they also wanted to know how they could help. It may have been the tsunami's proximity to Christmas, the season of giving, or the fact that more people from more countries had been killed than in any previous global disaster that resulted in the greatest outpouring of generosity the world has ever known. Once the Haida got news that I was, in Guujaaw's words, "still kicking," they wanted to know how they could help. A maritime people themselves, with ancient legends of tsunamis destroying entire villages and wiping out generations of people, the Haida could easily empathize with coastal peoples in the aftermath of a tsunami, even an event that occurred on the other side of the planet.

In the days immediately following the Indian Ocean tsunami, the world organized relief efforts in some distinctly silly ways. International Red Cross, based in London, sent two planeloads of thick wool blankets to Aceh, Indonesia, the worst affected area. Never mind that the temperature was over 30° Celsius in North Sumatra at the time—it was winter in England. Germany's response was far more appropriate. Knowing it could do nothing to bring back the lives already lost, it rushed in water purification systems to prevent an outbreak of cholera from all the contaminated wells, a disease that could easily have claimed more lives than the tsunami.

The Haida Nation wanted to see its donations used most effectively to reach people being bypassed by world relief efforts, and it didn't take me long to think of who might be falling through the cracks—Indigenous peoples, the most marginalized during the best of times. Something about Haida Gwaii being the most isolated and tsunami-prone body of land in Canada made me want to make a trip to Thailand's most isolated isles—the Surin Islands. I knew that this small cluster of islands on the Thai border with Myanmar was home to two hundred Indigenous Moken "sea gypsies" and the islands were right in the path of the tsunami, so it seemed an appropriate place to focus relief efforts from one Indigenous maritime nation to another.

My hunch was correct. Nothing was left of the two Moken villages on Koh Surin but the eerie pilings of former houses snapped from their foundations by the force of the waves. The Moken had

Following the South Asian tsunami on December 26, 2004, all that remained of a former Moken village were house posts snapped off by the force of the first wave.

lost everything—their homes, boats, fishing spears, nets, food provisions, cookware and clothing—but they still had one another. Miraculously, everyone was accounted for. After weeks of warnings from the spirits of their ancestors and many telltale signs from creatures of the deep sea, the Moken responded to the rapidly receding waters on the morning of December 26 with simple, time-honoured wisdom. All the women, children and elderly of the two villages fled to high ground while the men, who were all employed operating long-tail boats for the national park at the time the tsunami struck, rescued countless tourists and Thais.

Almost none of the Moken can read or write, but all of them survived, as did all of the Indigenous Andaman Islanders; not so the literate world. Graduates from the world's best universities, doctors, lawyers, professors, business people and aerospace engineers enjoying their Christmas holiday in luxury resorts all along the coasts of Thailand, Sri Lanka, the Maldives and East Africa were utterly clueless. Fascinated by grounded boats and flopping fish suddenly stranded by the rapidly receding tide, they walked out into the tidal zone and the deadly approaching waves.

The modern world, with its obsession with technology, reported in the press that South Asia had no tsunami early warning system, hence the staggering loss of life. But if the massive death toll was a failure of technology, or lack of it, why did illiterate societies survive with such success? The painful truth in the discrepancy of survival rates has nothing to do with technology. Rather, it represents the most massive failure of modern education in human history. Oral-tradition societies like the Moken and Andaman Islanders knew exactly what to do in the situation because stories of previous tsunamis had been passed down orally from generation to generation. The hundreds of thousands of people who died in this colossal tragedy were literate peoples with no storytellers and no collective memory.

The late Canadian poet and songwriter Leonard Cohen once penned the words, "There's a crack in everything; that's how the light gets in." It took a pretty major crack—a fifteen-hundred-kilometre rift in the Indian Ocean floor that split with the speed of a bullet on December 26, 2004—to let some light in on the value of traditional wisdom, at least as far as the Koh Surin Moken were concerned. They became instant celebrities in Thailand once word got out of their 100-percent survival rate. Thai people now wanted to see and touch a Moken for good luck, as if they were a talisman. A somewhat different scene was playing itself out on India's Andaman Islands, where Indigenous peoples still live in the forests as neolithic societies. The Indian Air Force sent helicopters out to these remote isles to see whether any survivors were in need of rescue after the tsunami slammed into the Andaman Islands. Again, everyone here had survived, but far from welcoming their "rescuers," the tribesmen fired poisoned arrows at the helicopters to drive them back.

Koh Surin National Marine Park was officially closed when I arrived by boat; the national park facilities had been totally destroyed. There, camping amid the piles of cement rubble, broken glass and tangled roofs of the former park headquarters, were two hundred Moken refugees who had been evacuated to a Buddhist temple in nearby Kuraburi soon after their two villages were destroyed. The Thai government and relief agencies wanted to permanently resettle the Moken far inland where they would be "safe" from future tsunamis, but nothing would destroy the souls of sea nomads faster than removing them from the sea. Fortunately, the Supreme Patriarch of Buddhism in Thailand proclaimed that the Moken must be allowed to pursue their own path, and that path led them very quickly back to Koh Surin where I encountered them that day.

The few park officials overseeing the site during the park closure were not at all happy seeing the Moken return. "These people are dirty and lazy," they told me. "They will be hanging out on this beach forever, looking for handouts from tourists." There was nothing new in this sentiment; it was the same ethnocentrism recorded in every account from the time early explorers and settlers here first encountered the Indigenous Moken. But the park official could not have been more wrong. Without anyone even being aware of it, Moken men had rebuilt thirty-two traditional homes at the head of a bay where one of their former villages stood. Quite serendipitously, I had arrived on the day they were moving in.

Jok Klathalay, the son of the village headman, invited me aboard an already overcrowded long-tail boat he'd borrowed from the national park so I could join the entire Moken community as they moved to their new homes. Remarkably, all the women and children knew which house would be theirs as soon as we landed; they ran up the beach singing and laughing with joy. Long before anyone else in Indonesia, Thailand, Sri Lanka, India and East Africa could cope with the shock of the tsunami and the massive loss of life and property, much less start the painful process of rebuilding, the Moken were already comfortably back home. It was the most incredible example of resilience and self-determination I have ever witnessed.

Looking down the long row of neat, palm-thatched houses set on high pilings, I realized there was certainly no need for relief funds to rebuild the village so I asked the village headman, Selamat, how the funds sent to me by the Haida Nation could best be used. Besides their new homes, the Moken had nothing but the clothes on their backs and a few sleeping mats and cooking pots donated by the temple when they were sent as refugees to Kuraburi. "What more do you want?" I tried to ask through a Thai translator friend, but the question was met with blank stares. The Moken have no words in their language for *want* or *worry*—rather a paradigm shift on modern values, when you think about it. The islands and the sea provide them with everything they ever need, so there is no want. There's no concept of worry either, as the Moken believe the spirits of the land, the sea and their ancestors always watch over and protect them. Modern society, by contrast, spends a great deal of time wanting more and worrying how to get it and pay for it.

The question was rephrased: "Is there something that might prove useful for you right now?" The reply was collective and instantaneous: "A drum!" With a drum they could celebrate their survival. The Koh Surin Moken had already come up with a new song and dance to thank the ghosts of their ancestors and the spirits of the sea for sparing their lives. Only an animistic people, deeply connected to the spirit world, would see a drum as the highest priority following a disaster of global proportions, and only an Indigenous maritime people like the Haida would understand how a drum would be a top-priority use of their donation money. Once the drum arrived, an impromptu celebration began with dancing, singing and great rejoicing late into the night. Over the next several weeks I was able to use the donation funds to secure such utilitarian items as fishing nets, food provisions and the first boat that would be truly their own, which they proudly named *Andaman Moken*. But none of these items brought the Moken the joy of that drum.

Geo Klathalay, a Moken living on Koh Surin, displays food he has foraged from the sea by free-diving. Like an apex predator, no underwater food source escapes this young man's attention.

It is not often that tragedy and serendipity emerge from a single event, but were it not for this global disaster, I might not have had the happy accident of getting to know the Moken with the level of intimacy that I did. Very little has ever been written about these shy and reclusive peoples because they have historically avoided contact as much as possible with the outside world. Living semi-nomadically aboard floating houseboats called *kabangs* for much of the year, the Moken of the Surin Islands and Myanmar's Mergui Archipelago used to go ashore only during the monsoon season when storms forced them to seek shelter in small coves. Even then they always built their one-room thatched dwellings on stilts at the edge of their beloved sea so that waves passing under their huts would lull them to sleep. At high tide, children would fish for squid with small lines and bait through the floorboards and jump from the doorway into the ocean

A Moken boy learns to spear-fish at a tender age. Though the Moken are superb hunters, only one out of every ten throws is successful in impaling a fish. The 90-percent survival rate for fish hunted this way has long been part of Moken conservation.

for a quick dip. The word *Moken* literally means "immersed in the water." Traditionally, Moken people had no family names. The Queen Mother of Thailand gave the same family name, Klathalay, to all the Koh Surin Moken; it translates as "Courage of the Sea," and few names have been more appropriately bestowed. No one knows for sure how many Thai and foreign tourists Moken men pulled from the ravaging tsunami waves on December 26, 2004, but it was many, and all of this was done without knowing first if their own wives and children were safe.

At one time large flotillas of Moken kabangs could be spotted in the wilderness waters of the Andaman coast, but the Moken's survival instinct was to flee in all directions like a school of fish under attack at the first sign on the horizon of a boat that was not of their own. Over countless centuries this survival strategy served the sea nomads well in fleeing from pirates, slave traders, colonial missionaries wanting to convert them and government officials conscripting them for Burma's military and forced labour camps. Today, the kabangs have all but disappeared as the Thai and Myanmar governments are now seriously determined to settle these peoples.

There is something about the nature of nomadic peoples that settled societies find very unsettling. Is it their freedom of movement we resent, the fact that nomads are so unencumbered? Do we feel threatened that people like the Moken refuse to buy into our consumer values for wealth, happiness and prestige; that they challenge our minds with no words in their language for *want* or *worry* when modern societies seem so preoccupied with both? Everywhere I have travelled in the world I have seen the same agenda again and again, even at the United Nations level—attempts to make over hunter-gatherer societies in our own agrarian image.

I had shown Selamat, the Moken village headman, two of the books I had written on Indigenous peoples in Southeast Asia: *Penan: Voice for the Borneo Rainforest* and *Living Legend of the Mentawai*. The thought of capturing images and stories of a living culture in the pages of a book captivated him, and he made me promise to one day make a book about the Moken. Selamat had already lost five of his six children, the worst fate to befall any parent, but he assigned his last living son, Jok, to be my informant for the book.

Over the years Jok and his nephew Geo became my good friends and such capable informants on all aspects of Moken life that I made them both co-authors on the cover of the book that was published in 2013: *Courage of the Sea: Last Stand of the Moken*. It might have marked the first time two completely illiterate people became the co-authors of a book. Unfortunately, Jok Klathalay never got to see the book he helped create. He died suddenly in 2012 from what the

Jok Klathalay (right) and his nephew, Geo Klathalay, are both illiterate but such amazing informants of Moken ways that I made them both co-authors of my book *Courage of the Sea: Last Stand of the Moken.*

villagers regarded as black magic, but his spirit was very much alive guiding me through three sleepless nights as I wrote the text for the book.

They say change is the only thing that can be predicted with certainty in life. Indigenous elders have told me, "If you really want to make the Great Spirit laugh, tell of your plans." The tsunami that had serendipitously brought Jok and me together on the shores of Koh Surin was becoming more distant, but my narrow escape from that calamity was still vivid in my mind years later when I led a tour group of senior citizens to Nepal and Bhutan in April 2015. Just two hours after they all boarded a flight home from Kathmandu International Airport, a 7.8-magnitude earthquake devastated the country, destroying over 40 per cent of all homes and claiming the lives of over nine thousand people. Sacred One Standing Still and Moving—the Haida name for the earthquake spirit—was definitely moving.

Like Haida Gwaii, which is moving northward at a rate of about thirty centimetres a year on its own plate from its original location near Baja, Mexico, the entire subcontinent of India is being driven

For three nights after Jok Klathalay died I could not sleep, but found myself compelled to write the entire text for the Moken book—as a ghostwriter, if ever there was one.

slowly but surely underneath Nepal and Tibet at an average speed of 4.5 centimetres per year. In the decades since the 1934 Bihar earthquake that killed ninety-three hundred people in Nepal, the land mass of India has been pushed about four metres into Nepal. But on Saturday morning, April 25, 2015, an area between 2,590 to 5,180 square kilometres over a zone spanning the cities of Pokhara and Kathmandu slid a staggering ten metres in a matter of seconds. It brought about the second-worst natural disaster in Nepal's history.

As word reached us on the flight home of what was transpiring on the ground below, a deep sadness overcame everyone who had been on the Nepal journey with me, and the Mentawai name bestowed on me decades earlier—Utut Kunan, meaning Forever and Always Lucky—never resonated more strongly. As Guujaaw said following my second narrow escape from global calamity, "You always seem to be one step ahead of the crocodile, Huck."

CHAPTER XIV

Full Circle

Serendipity is a wonderfully expressive word, coined by English writer Horace Walpole in his 1754 Persian fairy tale "The Three Princes of Serendip." Walpole based his new word on the old name for Sri Lanka—Serendib—to describe the three princes in his book who were repeatedly making discoveries, through accidents and sagacity, of things they were not in quest of. That sounded like my story—a series of happy accidents and unintentional outcomes that kept bringing me back to Haida Gwaii no matter how far away I roamed.

In the summer of 2013 my involvement on Haida Gwaii came full circle in more ways than one. Parks Canada was celebrating twenty years of the Gwaii Haanas Agreement, the cornerstone of a groundbreaking co-operative management relationship between the Haida Nation and the government of Canada. So successful is this relationship that *National Geographic Traveler* magazine has called Gwaii Haanas the best-managed national park in North America and Indigenous peoples and foreign nations sent delegates to Haida Gwaii to see how they had achieved it. The Archipelago Management Board, composed of an equal number of Haida and government of Canada representatives, was now renowned throughout the world as a model for cultural and natural resource governance.

The federal government knew there was much to celebrate when it commissioned the carving of a forty-two-foot monumental pole to mark the twentieth anniversary of the Gwaii Haanas Agreement. They conveniently overlooked a campaign that had really begun nearly forty years earlier when Guujaaw and I drew the line to save Gwaii Haanas, but Parks Canada had not supported it at the time.

It seemed more than appropriate that Guujaaw's second son, Jaalen Edenshaw, would be chosen from accomplished Haida carvers by a six-person selection committee to carve the Legacy Pole. Proposals had to be put before the committee with no names attached so they would be evaluated by storyline and design alone. I had watched Jaalen grow up from the day of his birth in 1980 and was always amazed at his vivid storybook imagination, bequeathed to him by Jenny Nelson, his elementary schoolteacher and mom. Guujaaw instilled in his second son a profound sense of Haida identity combined with the carving skills and courage needed to release mythological creatures from deep within the wood. Jaalen's older brother Gwaai, himself a master carver in gold and silver jewelry, had already collaborated with his brother on the *Two Brothers* pole raised in Jasper National Park, Alberta, before joining Jaalen on this endeavour. Together with Tyler York, a friend from Skidegate, the young men now undertook the slow, chip-by-chip process of creating a monumental masterpiece from a five-hundred-year-old cedar tree.

The pole design was selected for its "land, sea, people" theme, inspired by the connections between the Haida Nation and all those who take care of Gwaii Haanas from mountaintop to sea floor. Parks Canada claims that Gwaii Haanas is the only park in the world offering total protection from the highest summits of the land mass to the abyssal depths of the sea, though the claim is not entirely true as the area is still open to commercial fishing. The pole was to officially tell the story of how Canada and the Haida Nation came together through a historic agreement to protect Gwaii Haanas, but Jaalen had grown up with the South Moresby struggle and was not about to exclude that history from the design. To commemorate all those who had participated in protests and arrests at Athlii Gwaii (Lyell Island), he put gumboots on the three Haida Watchmen figures near the top of the pole—real gumboots—to remind everyone of the sacrifices those arrested had made. It was a whimsical touch that only Jaalen could have come up with, but it will be a lasting legacy to his humour and creativity.

Jaalen also carved "Sacred One Standing Still and Moving" onto the pole—the Haida supernatural being responsible for earthquakes. This figure honours the 7.7-magnitude earthquake in October 2012 that cut off the flow of geothermal waters to Hotspring Island. It seemed ironic that the only island in Gwaii Haanas that Parks Canada ever fought to protect because of its hot springs' recreational value had the tap turned off by Sacred One Standing Still and Moving.

Mary Swanson, my Haida mother through adoption, was asked to bless the pole as it was carried from the carving studio to the *Gwaii Haanas II* boat that would tow it to Windy Bay. This was increasingly becoming a family affair and I needed to be there.

No longer kids, Guujaaw's sons and Legacy Pole carvers, Jaalen (left) and Gwaai (right), pose with Justin Trudeau at the completion of the pole raising at Windy Bay.

While Parks Canada had never mentioned anyone's involvement prior to the Haida logging blockade in connection with saving Gwaii Haanas, the Haida Nation had not forgotten and I was formally invited to the pole raising and the feast that followed a few days later in Skidegate Village. As soon as I heard that the pole raising was to be in Windy Bay and that Uncle Percy Williams would be present, I commissioned a friend, Rod Brown in Terrace, to carve a yellow cedar eagle to present as a gift to the revered elder. It had been forty years since I'd found the real eagle carcass on the Windy Bay beach that I presented to Percy Williams at Vertical Point, so a carved eagle depicting features of Gwaii Haanas etched and wood-burned into the feathers—towering cedars, salmon, black bears, starfish and seabirds—seemed quite appropriate.

It was a huge undertaking moving four hundred guests to the remote Gwaii Haanas wilderness on August 15, 2013 to raise the Legacy Pole at Hlk'yah GaawGa (Windy Bay). A fleet of ships was departing from Queen Charlotte City dock at first light and I had

The South Moresby campaign's principal players gather together at Windy Bay in 1988 to celebrate the signing of the South Moresby Agreement—an early victory in the long process to protect Gwaii Haanas.

I am pictured here with (from left to right) John Broadhead, Ann Haig-Brown (the wife of Roderick Haig-Brown) and former House Speaker John Fraser at the Windy Bay celebration in 1988.

reservations to sail aboard the largest of them. The ship was filled with so many Haida friends and other Islanders who had been instrumental in saving Gwaii Haanas that I felt I was aboard a family reunion cruise. With boats arriving from all directions, Windy Bay looked like a yacht club by the time we arrived to a salute of ships' whistles. As I disembarked on the clean gravel beach, Guujaaw was there to greet me in the same location we'd held the celebratory feast to mark the signing of the South Moresby Agreement in 1988. It was great to see Jaalen and Gwaai again, both putting finishing touches on a pole, in typical Haida fashion, just hours before it would be raised.

A Haida pole raising is a celebratory affair charged with anticipation and the sexual energy one might expect from raising a giant phallus. I can recall the nonstop teasing from the Raven clan women at a pole raising in Old Massett when a Staastas Eagle clan chief struggled for hours to raise a massive cedar pole beside his new longhouse. "Hey, Chief," they taunted mercilessly. "Leave it to us—we know how to raise a Staastas pole." Under Haida customary law it is taboo to marry within one's clan; "an eagle must the raven wed," so the humour was lost on no one. An eagle carving, a separate carved piece, had to be mounted to the top of the pole once it was off the ground a good distance so as not to damage the wings. As the pole-raising official announced to the two teams of rope pullers (one Eagle clan and one Raven clan), "Okay, stop pulling, it's time to mount the eagle," a huge cheer went up from the Raven clan pullers. Hours later the pole was still hanging by ropes halfway to its fully upright position when a Raven woman brought down the house by shouting, "Come on, Chief, it's been five hours. When are we going to see your erection?"

While I talked with Guujaaw at the much more official Windy Bay pole raising, where this type of humour would have shocked the government officials in attendance, a young man approached and stood directly in front of us. We carried on talking until the stranger reached out his hand to us. "Justin," he said.

"Yeah, I know," Guujaaw replied casually as he carried on his conversation with me.

"No, Justin Trudeau," the man replied. I had not recognized the federal leader of the Liberal Party, but Guujaaw had. He usually made a point of treating people in power like anyone else.

"Do you remember being a little guy at Huck's cabin in 1976?" Guujaaw asked the future prime minister of Canada. It had been thirty-seven years since Pierre and Margaret Trudeau had visited my cabin on Lepas Bay with Justin and his brothers Sacha and Michel. Aged four at the time, Justin could hardly be expected to remember the event.

"No, I think I must have been too young," the statesman replied. "Although I do recall my father saying he had a very special place in his heart for these islands." Nearly four decades earlier, Pierre Trudeau had sent my parents and I personal letters after his visit, including a photo of himself and Justin walking on the beach in front of my cabin.

Before the historic raising of the Gwaii Haanas Legacy Pole, the first new totem pole in the southern islands in 130 years, I decided to take a hike up Windy Bay Creek where I'd had such a profound

The once and future kings, Pierre Elliott Trudeau walks five-year-old Justin Trudeau along the beach in front of my hippie hut in 1976. CANADIAN PRESS PHOTO

experience forty years earlier. This was the day that Windy Bay had the largest number of visitors it would probably ever have, and yet I found the same magical solitude here as on my first trip. The bear and deer trail into the woods was now lined with white clamshells to keep visitors from wandering from the path, but other than that simple park "improvement," it was still a moss-smothered forest, completely enchanting with shafts of light and showers of hemlock needles raining to the ground with every fresh sea breeze that stirred the canopy. Taking time to sit in that cathedral-like setting and calm my mind, I had the most profound sense of coming full circle in my life. By the time I broke the meditation and returned to the beach, the high drama of a Haida pole raising was well under way.

Donnie Edenshaw, who had first came out to Rediscovery on Lepas Bay in baby diapers and was now a powerhouse Haida man and singer, was rushing onto the beach from the forest, adorned in hemlock branches and screaming like a *goghit*—a wild man of the woods. Guujaaw was symbolically trying to tame him with a deer-hoof rattle as they danced around the pole in a tense dramatization. Donnie's full-page photo had appeared in the July 1987 issue of *National Geographic* magazine along with my own photo and a story on Rediscovery in a feature article called "Homeland of the Haida."

Now songs came from out at sea as the Swan Bay and Haida Gwaii Rediscovery crews paddled Bill Reid's fibreglass replica of *Lootaas* (called *Looplex*) and another canoe toward the beach. Haida chiefs in full regalia went down to the shoreline to welcome the Rediscovery youth and grant them permission to come ashore. All of this was taking time, and none of it was on the Parks Canada schedule of events. Ernie Gladstone, the MC for the event, told me that he was between a rock and a hard place trying to not interrupt cultural protocol but still keep to schedule so four hundred people would not become stormbound at Windy Bay should a southeaster blow up. This was, after all, Windy Bay, and the name shows on nautical charts for good reason.

The real test of wills came when Diane Brown, daughter of Ada Yovanovich, who had been one of the elders arrested on Lyell Island, was told there would not be sufficient time to bless the pole; it had to be raised—now! It was clear that the federal government, in spite of twenty years of working closely with the Haida, was still on a sharp learning curve. Protocol is everything at a Haida function; weather doesn't matter. For a Haida to skimp on ceremony for fear of an approaching storm might actually bring on that storm. Four hundred people stranded in Gwaii Haanas for an extra day or two, or a week? So what? Time to start clam digging, jigging for rockfish from the headlands, gathering seaweed and picking wild nettles. The pole was going to be blessed. After Diane had wafted eagle down all around the pole, she brought out her grandchildren to do it, one by one, all over again. It may have been the longest pole blessing in Haida history, but it needed to be. An elder was teaching an important lesson about time and priority.

When it finally was time for the pole to be raised, I was shocked to see Rolly Williams taking charge. Rolly was a friend and had been a junior guide on Haida Gwaii Rediscovery when I was program director on the west coast from 1978 to 1985. He was both fearless and reckless, and I'd had to fire him once after he walked out on a tree overhanging a thirty-foot cliff face. He wanted to clear some branches with a chainsaw so the kids in camp could get a better swing from a rope, but he was endangering his life and those below him. Now he was in charge of safely raising a forty-two-foot cedar log weighing 214,000 pounds over a crowd of approximately four hundred. I bit my knuckles out of sheer nervousness, but Rolly performed the task more calmly and easily than any pole raising I had ever witnessed. With just a few soft-spoken commands, he had the Legacy Pole standing upright to the cheers of the hundreds on the beach and a nearly equal number of people witnessing the pole raising via a livestream feed on the big screen at the Haida Heritage Centre back in Skidegate. He was definitely the right man for the job.

My only regret at the pole raising was that Uncle Percy Williams was feeling too weak that day to make the trip to Windy Bay. I asked Ernie Gladstone if I could have a minute to present the carved eagle gift to Guujaaw so he could present it to his uncle. "Sorry, Huck, there's no time," Ernie replied. "We've got to get everyone on boats and get out of here before the weather comes up; you can present it at the feast in Skidegate, okay?" I was fine with that, but I had to remind Ernie of his promise two days later as over a thousand people crammed into the Skidegate hall for the commemorative feast on August 17.

If ever there was an event on Haida Gwaii that brought together the full renaissance of Haida culture, this was it. As the hereditary chiefs from both Masset and Skidegate were announced entering the hall, everyone rose in respect. Sharing the master of ceremonies role this night were former Rediscovery youth who had not only found their big-house voices, they were speaking in fluent Haida. I had the honour of sitting beside my adopted Haida mother, Mary Swanson, who had devoted her past forty years to teaching Haida language in the schools. At age ninety and receiving blood transfusions twice a week to stay alive, she was still teaching. Every missionary and

Coming full circle with Rediscovery, I share a moment with former program director Marnie York (left) and Rolly Williams (centre)—a former Rediscovery participant and staff member now in charge of the pole raising at Windy Bay in 2013.

It took hundreds of pullers to raise the Legacy Pole at Windy Bay, among them Justin Trudeau, the future prime minister of Canada.

Guujaaw beats his bear design drum at the first Windy Bay celebration following the preservation of South Moresby in 1988.

residential schoolteacher who had ever slapped a Haida child in the face for speaking their own language would be rolling over in their graves if they witnessed this night. The Haida Nation had not only survived a century of state-sanctioned ethnocide, they seemed stronger despite it.

The federal government had set out a strict schedule of speakers to adhere to, but the Haida found their own voice on this night. Buddy Richardson boomed from the entranceway, "We stand for our rights; Lyell Island will not be logged," as all seventy-two Haida who had been

A Haida spirit dancer blesses and cleanses the feast hall for the opening of the Gwaii Haanas Agreement's twentieth-anniversary celebration in 2013.

arrested on Lyell Island in 1985 solemnly paraded into the hall and a thousand cheering people rose to their feet in tribute. There followed spectacular masked dance performances telling the stories of Foam Woman, and of the first spruce tree that colonized Haida Gwaii after the retreat of the ice sheet. This was not a show staged for spectators so much as the unveiling of a cultural legacy and oral history three times older than the oldest books.

It was an incredible night, but I was getting pressed for time as I had promised to drive my Haida mother onto the ferry to the mainland departing at 10:00 p.m. She was heading to a big potlatch in Alaska so I could not linger too long at this event. I asked Ernie Gladstone when I could present the eagle carving to Percy Williams. "He's on the list of speakers," Ernie said. "Do you want to present before or after him?" After seemed more respectful. When Chief Percy Williams rose to speak he had the room's complete attention; he was, after all, the eldest chief present. "Where is Huckleberry, Thom Henley?" he asked, looking around the room as he opened his talk. I stood briefly to be acknowledged and then he went on to tell the story of our first meeting at Vertical Point in the summer of 1973. Ernie Gladstone, who was sticking his neck out allowing me to speak, flashed me a quick thumbs-up from behind the speaker's podium. He now had the excuse he needed to break from the strict speaker schedule and call on me to make the presentation.

As soon as Chief Percy sat down I carried the eagle carving to the podium veiled under a red cloth. I thanked the assembly for the opportunity to make the presentation and told the story of seren-dipitously encountering Uncle Percy in 1973 when I presented him with the eagle carcass I'd found in Windy Bay. I went on to recount how Guujaaw and I had drawn the line that is now the park reserve and how countless people had dedicated over a decade of their lives to creating the global stage the Haida Nation stepped onto at Lyell Island. "Many people here in this room should be acknowledged for their lasting contributions to the event we're celebrating tonight," I said. "People like John Broadhead, Richard Krieger, Jack Litrell, Jeff Gibbs and many others." I went on to talk about how these people had championed the South Moresby cause long before Parks Canada showed any interest. "But it's different today," I concluded. "The relationship between the Haida Nation and Parks Canada is so close it's almost as if the agency has been adopted. But anyone adopted into the Haida Nation, as I have been privileged to be, knows that along with the honour comes responsibility. So if Parks Canada really wants to see Gwaii Haanas protected in perpetuity from mountaintop to sea floor, it now has a responsibility to return to Ottawa and tell this government to stop the needless and reckless expansion of oil ports and tanker traffic in these waters."

The crowd went wild with applause. After I presented Percy with the carving, the MLA for the Islands rushed up to me to say, "Thank you so much. I've been waiting for days for someone to raise that issue." Haida Gwaii residents were all but unanimously opposed to the Conservative government's plans to expand oil

Foam Woman, one of the earliest supernatural beings that appeared when Haida Gwaii "emerged from concealment," is portrayed at the 2013 celebration through a dramatic mask carved by Jim Hart.

terminals in the North Pacific so I knew I was preaching to the converted, but I wanted to challenge Parks Canada to show some backbone for once. As fate would have it, the next speaker was the director of national parks for all of Canada. "I'm not sure who the previous speaker was," he began his talk, searching the speaker list in vain for my name, "but I want everyone here to know I heard his words and will take this message back to Ottawa." Whether he did or not is uncertain. Harper's Conservative government approved the pipeline plans shortly thereafter, but it was replaced by Justin

A masked dancer representing the first spruce tree on Haida Gwaii performs a story older than the Bible at the Gwaii Haanas legacy celebration.

Trudeau's Liberal government in 2015, which pledged to stop the pipeline.

Mark Dowie, an investigative historian, recently put the Haida situation in global perspective: "By creatively and patiently using the courts, human blockades, public testimony, and the media—all the while building strategic alliances with environmentalists and neighbouring tribes—the Haida won the support of enough Canadian citizens, government officials and Supreme Court justices to come within reach of a goal that thousands of Indigenous communities around the world have struggled for generations to win ... the Haida are only one Supreme Court decision away from obtaining aboriginal title."

As I was leaving the feast hall to rush Mary Swanson and her daughter Goldie to the ferry terminal, several former Rediscovery participants I had worked with in their youth stopped me in the hallway for hugs. "You never told us that story before, Huck, about you and Uncle Percy and drawing the line with Guujaaw," they said. "We thought everything started at the Lyell Island blockade. You need to write a new book."

Riding on the ferry to Prince Rupert that night I had the same melancholy feeling I'd had when I first left the Islands. Haida Gwaii had become home for me in a spiritual sense even if I no longer physically resided there. Why is it, I wondered, that governments are so reluctant to acknowledge citizen actions responsible for saving areas from destruction? I had watched Vicky Husband almost single-handedly save the Khutzeymateen, the world's first grizzly bear sanctuary, and I'd seen the pivotal role Haisla leader Gerald Amos played in saving the Kitlope, the world's largest intact temperate rainforest watershed. Peter McAllister had championed protection for the Great Bear Rainforest along the mid-coast, Colleen McCrory had led the campaign to protect the Valhalla Wilderness area in BC's Interior and Paul George had saved countless areas of British Columbia through the organization he co-founded with photographer Richard Krieger— the Western Canada Wilderness Committee. But nowhere in the history of these protected areas were those who initiated them ever acknowledged. The deliberate slights suggest more than governments

Packed to the bleachers, the Skidegate Community Hall hosts the anniversary celebration of the historic Gwaii Haanas Agreement.

While Parks Canada was celebrating twenty years of the Gwaii Haanas Agreement in 2013, I marked the occasion by presenting a carved yellow cedar eagle to Chief Gidansda (Percy Williams) in recognition of the eagle carcass that started it all forty years earlier, in 1973. JEFFREY GIBBS PHOTO

wanting to take credit for enlightened policies; it is as if they don't want to encourage citizens to follow these leads.

As the *Queen of the North* ferry made the slow passage across Hecate Strait that night, my mind was preoccupied with thoughts of what our efforts would mean in the end. The world's population had tripled since I was born, and humans had impacted the earth more in that short span of time than in the last two hundred thousand years since the emergence of *Homo sapiens*. Over half the world's wealth has filtered its way into the hands of a mere 2 per cent of the world population, and for many personal greed now far surpasses personal needs.

"Everything you do will be meaningless, but you must do it," Mohandas K. Gandhi once said. On a cosmological scale there is no denying this statement. I have had the good fortune to experience sixty-eight revolutions around the sun so far, but that is insignificant compared to the 4.6 billion orbits since earth was formed, as has been widely determined by scientists. In universal time we, and our actions, are meaningless; but not in human time. When I see fellow conservationists holding signs like "Save the Earth," I like to remind them that the earth is not in need of saving and humans are certainly not capable of saving it. Our challenge is to stop mucking it up so it does not shed us off as a species before our time. On average, species survive three to five million years before going extinct, so humanity's best days should be ahead of us. Our greatest challenge, socially and environmentally, will be having our behaviour catch up with our numbers.

Whenever a religious zealot corners me, I cut short the proselytizing with the question, "What do you think is the most often violated of the Ten Commandments?"

"'Thou shalt not commit adultery,'" is the usual response.

"Not even close," I counter. "What about 'Thou shalt not covet thy neighbour's goods'?" That's all modern society does—covet. We have a global economic system based on coveting. The teaching is a sound one, as is the Buddhist lesson that desire causes pain; when we lose desire for more than meets our needs, we lose the pain associated with not having it.

I was still awake by the time the ferry was pulling into Prince Rupert Harbour at first light. I had arranged a stateroom on board for my Haida mother and sister, but I chose to sit out on the deck myself for the fresh air and possibility of stargazing. The energy of the feast house takes a long time to dissipate, and my thoughts were still very much with what I had witnessed hours earlier. If there's hope for humanity, I thought, I have just seen it. It lies in young people grounded in the best values of their culture, respecting one another and the earth and not having a shred of doubt in their minds that a future lies in this.

Bill Reid, in his opening chapter to *Islands at the Edge*, wrote, "When, or if, we should ever decide that subduing is not the only, or even the most desirable way, of making our way through the world, these shining islands may be the signposts that point the way to a renewed, harmonious relationship with this, the only world we're ever going to have."

That's my hope too.

Acknowledgements

I am deeply indebted and grateful to a number of people who have been instrumental in the realization of this book. Elois Yakley encouraged me every step of the way and carefully reviewed the text, along with Dr. Bristol Foster, Richard Krieger and John Broadhead. I wish to thank Gregg Sheehy for his contribution to the chapter "All Aboard!" and all the other photo contributors, most notably Richard Krieger, Jeffrey Gibbs and Mike Randall at Langara Lodge.

None of this would have been possible without the love, support and encouragement of friends and family, through adoption or bloodline, who are too numerous to mention. None have figured more prominently in this book than Guujaaw—Chief Gidansda, my teacher and lifelong friend. Haw'aa.

Note: To view more images please go to the following websites:
Rediscovery International Foundation www.rediscovery.org
Soaring Spirits Camp www.soaringspiritscamp.com
In Touch With Nature Education www.nature-ed.com

Index